S0-BXH-558

THE POLITICAL ECOLOGY
OF THE MODERN PEASANT

The Political Ecology of the Modern Peasant

◻ CALCULATION AND COMMUNITY

Leslie Anderson

HD
1531
. N5
A53
1994
West

THE JOHNS HOPKINS UNIVERSITY PRESS

Baltimore and London

© 1994 The Johns Hopkins University Press
All rights reserved
Printed in the United States of America on acid-free paper

The Johns Hopkins University Press
2715 North Charles Street
Baltimore, Maryland 21218-4319
The Johns Hopkins Press Ltd., London

Library of Congress Cataloging-in-Publication Data

Anderson, Leslie E.
   The political ecology of the modern peasant : calculation and community / Leslie E. Anderson.
     p.   cm.
   Includes bibliographical references and index.
   ISBN 0-8018-4708-7 (alk. paper)
   1. Peasantry—Nicaragua—Political activity. 2. Peasantry—Costa Rica—Political activity.
I. Title.
HD 1531.N5A53   1994
305.5'663'097295—dc20   93-5388

A catalog record of this book is available from the British Library.

for Larry

CONTENTS

ACKNOWLEDGMENTS

The acknowledgments for this book were surprisingly difficult to write. Anything I can say here falls far short of recognizing the encouragement and assistance I have received from many quarters during the research and writing of this book. Needless to say, without the support and faith in me shown by numerous institutions and individuals it would never have been accomplished.

During the academic year 1985–86 the research was launched and intitial writing completed with the support of a generous Fulbright Grant from the International Council on Educational Exchange. The Rackham School of Graduate Studies at the University of Michigan generously funded three separate research visits to Nicaragua in 1985, 1986, and 1987. The Council on Creative Research and Writing and the Department of Political Science, both at the University of Colorado, provided funding for further research in 1989 and 1990.

I benefited from generous fellowship support during the writing of this book. The Kellogg Institute at the University of Notre Dame provided gloriously protected space and time into which I could retreat and write in peace. At the same time, my colleagues at Kellogg were always ready to listen, comment, and engage whenever I chose to emerge from my shell. Among those who were most helpful at Kellogg I include Guillermo O'Donnell, Samuel Valenzuela, Father Ernest Bartell, Scott Mainwaring, Leigh Ann Payne, Lynn Wozniak, Jaime Mesera, José Maria Ghio, and Albert LeMay. I was also fortunate to receive a Research Fellowship from the Center for International Studies at Cornell University. Additional support from a Junior Faculty Development Award and a Dean's Fellowship, both from the University of Colorado, helped me take full advantage of the Cornell opportunity. While I was at Cornell, Norman Uphoff, Mary Katzenstein, Milton Esman, Phyllis Corey, and Ginny Hicks were extremely helpful.

In the field I received priceless support and assistance from many people. Among those to whom I owe the greatest debt of gratitude are the peasants of the six villages in this study. They enthusiastically applauded my work in all six locations. They helped locate places to live and work, worried over my health and eating habits, helped repair my motorcycle, and rescued me from tropical rainstorms and raging rivers. They tolerated and even smiled at my mistakes in etiquette, cultural savoir faire, and the language. In Nicaragua they supported my seemingly endless search for food and gasoline. Throughout it all they deeply appreciated the chance to tell their story and to be heard. Without their help my work would never have even begun.

In Costa Rica I received substantial help from the Solano family, particularly from Victor Solano, Daisy Flora Valverde, Audrey and Yamileth Delgado, and Liliana Solano. Other supporters were Marielos Monge, Arturo Jiménez, Freddy Murillo, Guido Vargas, Carlos Campos, Rafael Murillo, Juan José Herrera, Grace and Elsa Calderón, and the officials of UPANacional and UPAGRA. In Nicaragua invaluable advice came from Marvin Ortega and Laura Enríquez, who helped me carefully select research sites where I might be safe from Contra attack. Other Nicaraguan supporters include Cirilo Otero, Magadalena Torres, Carlos and Velia Zamorro, Juan José López, José Ruiz, Denis and Coco López, José Donaldo and Marela García, and officials from UNAG in Masaya and La Concepción.

Several academic audiences listened to parts of the argument and improved upon it substantially. They include attenders at brown bag seminars at the Kellogg Institute as well as talks at the University of Minnesota, Cornell University, and the University of Colorado. My position on the Scott and Popkin theories was scrutinized, questioned, and refined by students in my graduate seminar on Peasant Politics and Society at the University of Colorado. The argument and theory presented here received encouragement, challenge, and constructive criticism from the participants in a conference on "the dimensions of peasant power" held at the University of Colorado in April 1992. The participants in that conference who were most helpful were Forrest Colburn, Barbara Engel, William Kelly, Ronald Herring, James Scott, and Teodor Shanin.

A number of dedicated people read this entire manuscript at one stage or another or devoted substantial time to discussing it with me. These include Daniel Levine, James Scott, Gary Hawes, John Watanabe, Mark Peterson, Teodor Shanin, E. P. Thompson, Eric Wolf, Melanie Manion, T. H. Anderson, Erwina Godfrey, and Larry Dodd. Others offered challenging criticisms or raised probing questions while also having the good sense not to suffer through the entire manuscript. These include John McIver, Cal Jillson, David Maple, Laura Stoker, and Gordon Adams. During the fall of 1989 Martha Gibson offered conscientious assistance in the search for appropriate statistical methods for use with ethnographic data. Holly Arrow provided expert editorial input, as well as some challenging questions, through several versions of the manuscript. Toward the final stages of the writing and manuscript production I received excellent copyediting service from Christine Desai and Erwina Godfrey as well as supportive input from Henry Tom of the Johns

Hopkins University Press. The photographic artwork for this volume was produced by Amaranth Laboratories of Boulder, Colorado.

A special kind of support came my way from my father and mother, Thornton H. and Elizabeth P. Anderson, and from my brother, Ross Anderson, as well as from Meredith and Christopher Dodd. Throughout the writing and analysis, my most selfless and steadfast supporter, including during extended research and fellowship absences, as well as my most demanding and challenging critic, has been Larry Dodd. It is to him that I affectionately dedicate this book.

INTRODUCTION

Poor and seemingly powerless, apparently unorganized and unimportant, peasants living far from modern societies have long been the object of study for many scholars, policy makers, and activists. In previous generations of scholarship, the study of the peasantry was primarily the preserve of anthropologists. Over the past two decades, however, political scientists and others have joined them in their effort to understand peasants. In political science, the large number of peasant rebellions and revolutions, particularly in Vietnam, Algeria, Cuba, and Nicaragua, have generated many questions and a search for explanations of these surprising political explosions from an apparently quiet and submissive people.

Yet this interest in peasant revolution has led to some imbalance in scholarly and theoretical approaches to peasant studies. There is a plethora of literature offering different explanations for violent political action among the peasantry. Insofar as scholars have perceived peasants as political actors at all, they have seen them as participants in revolt or revolution. Less widely acknowledged and studied are the nonrevolutionary types of peasant political action, including nonviolent collective behavior. As a result, our image of the peasantry is that of normally submissive, quiescent people who suddenly rebel or revolt.

By nature, any image that portrays only two extremes is incomplete. Its simplification leaves much of the story untold. What happens among the peasantry between quiescence and rebellion? Is there a middle ground in between these two choices, and if so, what kinds of political action fall within it? Is nonviolent collective action, such as demonstrations or land invasions, part of that middle ground? What motivates peasants to remain quiescent, to rebel, or to choose collective nonviolent political action? These questions have not been addressed by previous studies of the peasantry. Theories of peasant rebellion, for instance, do not address collective nonviolent action among the peasantry. Yet, in the real world, peasants normally do not move swiftly from quiescence to rebellion. They usually move incrementally, first trying that, now trying this, depending on whom they are addressing with such action and what they are trying to accomplish.

If we step back and ask generally about peasant politics instead of specifically about peasant revolution, the reasons behind peasant political actions become clearer. First, we begin to see that different types of peasant political action are connected to each other and are part of an overall picture. Second, we start to ask questions about why peasants choose one tactic over another and how they decide to change tactics. How do peasant goals affect choices of tactics? How does the nature of the audience determine political strategies? How do peasants speak to local, regional, or state authorities? How do they address a tolerant, receptive audience as opposed to a repressive one? Finally, we come to realize how *uncommon* peasant revolution really is and to grasp the reasons for its infrequency. We begin to understand that from the peasant perspective, nonviolent behavior is always preferable if it is effective, and it often is. We also comprehend why sometimes peasants do rebel.

Broad and inclusive questions, such as these, about the general nature of peasant political action lead us to ask even more basic questions about the nature of peasant society. How do peasants see themselves and their communities, and how does that vision determine their political choices? Peasant politics is increasingly moving beyond the village to address wider issues and distant authorities. How is that expansion grounded in peasant views of their world and society? How do peasants see themselves in interaction with the world beyond the village and how does that vision affect political action and choices of political tactics? How is peasant politics affected by the nature of peasant society? How can we better understand the one and, therefore, the other?

This book is a broad and inclusive study of the nature of peasant politics and society. It offers a description of peasant society that is also an explanation of peasant politics. It is a study of peasant society that focuses both on the individual and village community and on the world beyond the village—the agrarian environment and national society. The book takes a comprehensive approach to peasant politics by seeking to explain not only the extremes of quiescence and rebellion but also the activist middle ground in between and it shows how peasant society leads to particular political motives and therefore influences the choice of political tactics.

This study of peasant politics and society helps answer yet another question about the peasantry: the question of peasant survivability. How is it that peasants have survived despite all expectations and against all odds? Although many scholars and most policymakers have long foretold the disappearance of the peasantry, peasants have survived, unconvinced, if not unaffected, by predictions of their imminent demise. How have peasants devised a system that allows for adaptation and survival despite all expectations to the contrary? If peasants are so persistent and, all things considered, successful, is there anything the modern world can learn from them? Are there skills and understandings that the peasantry retain that might also serve and protect the modern world or modern actors such as ourselves?

The locus for this exploration of peasant society and politics is the Central American nations of Costa Rica and Nicaragua during the 1970s and 1980s. My approach was to investigate the experience of peasants by spending three to four months in each of six villages, immersing myself in the history and daily life of the community and conducting extensive interviews. Although these interviews explored the political and social histories of each village, they focused primarily on three areas: the types of political action in which villagers had engaged; the motivations for their actions; and the nature of the society out of which these actions grew. The interviews revealed a spectrum of political tactics that peasants may undertake and suggested a relative hierarchy of different kinds of action in each village. They also uncovered a type of society and a particular world view that explain peasant politics and the choices of political action. The political perspective that results from this world view is part of the peasant's political ecology.

Central America is a particularly appropriate place for this study, for it offers an extraordinary opportunity to study peasant politics of several kinds. Recent history of the region includes peasant involvement in politics at many different levels. Nicaragua in particular offers an opportunity to study quiescence and rebellion. Between 1960 and 1979, Nicaragua underwent a social revolution in which peasants played an essential role. Yet peasant participation in the revolution was neither nationwide nor simultaneous. The country thus offers opportunities to study quiescence and the motivation to avoid revolutionary participation as well as the motivation to engage in revolution. The peasant experience in Costa Rica helps fill in the middle ground. In Costa Rica, unlike in the rest of Central America, the peasantry has not chosen violence as a form of political action. Nonetheless, in recent years the Costa Rican peasantry has been among the most activist in Latin America. Costa Rica thus offers an opportunity to study nonviolent collective action in a national context where it has flourished.

In seeking to understand peasant politics and society, this book joins two debates relevant to the social sciences, one theoretical, one methodological. In the first, scholars of the peasantry have described the nature of peasant society and the motivation of peasant politics as being either individualist, private and self-centered, or communitarian—shaped and restrained by community preferences, norms, and traditions. In the second debate, scholars have disputed the best and most appropriate methods for uncovering political opinions and motives. One side argues for breadth, survey research, and statistical forms of analysis. The other side argues for depth and detailed ethnographic knowledge. This book enters each debate by drawing on both sides rather than by choosing one or the other. The resulting theory of peasant political ecology underscores the strengths of each of the above theoretical positions.

1 ◻ THE PEASANT
POLITICAL ECOLOGY
Politics and Community

An old man, partially blind in one eye, sat crouched over his coffee cup; his jaw set in anger, he glared at me across his kitchen table: "They are always stealing my tomatoes!" he growled. "I get so sick of it, I never even get to eat my own tomatoes. And they steal my sheep too! Cut the fence and let them out. Afterwards there is always one missing. But no one ever knows anything, and I can never find out who did it. If I ever catch the thief, I'm going to give him the beating of his life!" These were common complaints by Pedro in the Nicaraguan village of Pedregal, Boaco. When I lived there and interviewed him, these thefts formed an important part of his concerns about village life. He made the same complaints every time I passed his house or saw him in the street, and he gave the impression that he was suffering substantial loss.

Although most villagers lived with large families, Pedro lived with only his wife and an adult daughter in a cement-walled house at one end of the village. Once the house had been affluent compared to many of the other village homes, but when I was there it was run-down and badly in need of repair. Pedro was getting old: his strength and eyesight had begun to fail, and he was no longer strong enough to properly maintain the house alone. He had no one to help him.

Pedro struck a pathetic figure whenever I saw him in the village street. His pace was slow, and he walked with a limp. His back was hunched over by age, hard work, and poverty. Yet it was always difficult to feel sympathetic with Pedro because of his harsh and bitter attitude toward the world and the hardness in his eyes. I sensed that if I got into trouble and needed help, it would be better not to ask Pedro for aid.

I visited Pedro's tomato patch with him several times. He had indeed lost many tomatoes. On another occasion he showed me where his barbed wire fence had been cut. His neighbors confirmed that he had lost both sheep and tomatoes many times, but theirs was not an empathetic, concerned confirmation. No one said, "It's really too bad, the poor old man." Instead they spoke of Pedro's financial losses with a nod of satisfaction and a faint, barely audible note of glee in their voices.

According to the neighbors and other villagers, Pedro could have avoided these losses, and he was substantially responsible for his own plight. Pedro had always systematically refused to participate in the ecological support system in Pedregal village. A social system of interdependence and mutual support, where individuals depend on the community and the community depends on everyone's participation to survive, Pedregal's political ecology protects and sustains both individual and village life. The system has allowed the village to adapt and survive dictatorship and repression, revolution and political controversy, all the while protecting life and responding to the interdependent needs of villagers, the community, and the world around the village. However, those who do not support the system receive little support from it; most villagers understand their own dependence on and vulnerability to the community better than Pedro does. They prefer to support the system, and in turn, it supports them. They live with some margin of safety around them and are more likely to survive tragedy.

Pedro, on the other hand, struggled to survive outside that system. Increasingly incapacitated, bitter, and resentful, he needs his neighbors even if he doesn't realize it. His self-destructive anger endangered him and his family. He was vulnerable to poverty and disaster as all peasants are, and now he was even more vulnerable than most because of his increasing age and growing infirmity. Pedro held on from one day to the next, barring tragedy. I wondered what he would do if he could no longer round up his stray sheep or repair his fences for himself. How would he manage if a hailstorm caved in the sagging roof on his front porch? What would he do if he needed immediate medical assistance? The village is twenty miles from the nearest hospital, and he doesn't have access to modern transportation.

Villagers who participate in the community emergency medical support network help each other when someone falls ill or needs urgent medical care. The network is an excellent example of the function of Pedregal's interdependent ecological system, the purpose of which is to protect and sustain peasant life. Consider the story of Maria's little boy Panchito, who was bitten by a poisonous snake. Panchito's father had been away for some time. Maria said he was working in Managua, but no one knew exactly where he was or when he would return. With six children to care for, Maria made do by washing clothes, selling homemade items at the market on Saturdays, and raising a few pigs and chickens. Her husband had built the family a house before he left, and she had a brother in Pedregal, who stopped by and did heavy work for her from time to time.

Yet Maria was not prepared to deal with the emergency caused by Panchito's encounter with the black viper. The boy was playing alone near the abandoned outhouses when she heard him scream. When she got to him the snake was gone, but Maria immediately recognized the telltale bite marks. She screamed the news to her nearest neighbor, Concepción, who ran to get her husband, Marcelo. Marcelo ran for Juan, who owned the quickest and most sure-footed mule in the village. Juan was at Maria's house within minutes. He gathered the boy into his arms and turned his mule toward the steep, rocky trail that led eight miles down the mountainside to the nearest town below.

As Juan hurried down the mountain, Maria's neighbors also came to her assistance. Several women arrived to take charge of Maria's five other children. Carlos arrived to lend her his own mule, and Eduardo came on another animal to escort her down the mountain. Only minutes behind Juan, Eduardo and Maria started down the mountainside. In the hours after Maria left to follow her son and Juan down the mountain trail, Lilita and others took up a collection among the villagers. The sum they gathered was sufficient to cover the cost of the doctor's visit, medicines, and even partially compensate Juan for the use of his mule. Maria stayed in town overnight, confident that her other children and her household were in good hands back in Pedregal. Panchito did not die but grew up quite proud of his encounter with the snake. When his father next returned to the village, the boy told him every minute detail and finished by showing off the scars on his leg. Alone, financially strapped, responsible for five other small children, without transportation, and eight miles from the nearest doctor, Maria would have been helpless to save her boy without the village medical support system.

Peasant villagers are always vulnerable to the hardships of rural poverty, as Maria and her family were. They live in a world of scarcity and danger. As farmers, they are as vulnerable to the ravages of natural disaster as they are to accidents such as Panchito's. R. H. Tawney described the peasant as standing up to his neck in water such that even the smallest wave will drown him. Living life on the edge of disaster makes peasants constantly aware of their own vulnerability and of the extent to which they depend on community support for survival. This reality makes individual and community interests blend and become one and the same. The individual depends on the community for protection from disaster, but the community support system depends equally on individual input in order to survive. Pedregal's medical support system is dependent on numerous small contributions made by individual villagers, and without these inputs it would fail. Villagers know that they themselves may need the medical support system someday, and they know that without their support the system would die. So they contribute, both for Panchito and Maria but also for their own individual well-being and security. Theirs is a participant perspective. They do not control the community, but neither does it control them. Rather they are participants in an interactive system.

The extent of the participation ethos is illustrated by Juan's membership in the medical support network. Juan is single and consequently has no family who might come to need medical assistance someday. I asked him why he didn't leave the work to those with families who were more likely to depend on the support system. I even reminded him how much money he had lost by taking a day away from his farm to help save Panchito's life. "One never knows," he told me, "I could break a leg and need help getting down the mountain. I couldn't ride. Look at Jorge, laid up after a hernia operation. His neighbors have done all his planting for him. When Marta went into a bad labor it took six men and a stretcher to get her down the mountain. I must be at least as heavy as she is. It's true that I may use the system less often than other families, but we have to keep it going because it's good for everyone and because someday I might need it too."

Juan did not view Panchito's accident from the calculating perspective of a traditional rational actor. If he had, he would have focused only on short-term gains for himself, and he would have stayed home farming on the day of the accident. In fact, in the interview, I presented reasoning based on such calculations of individual, short-term benefit; Juan rejected that reasoning. Such behavior characterized Pedro, but Juan calculated differently. Juan saw his welfare as intertwined with Panchito's and Maria's. What was good for them might also be good for him some day. Thus Juan is not a hero or a saintly altruist who places the welfare of others ahead of his own well-being. Nor was he merely serving self-interest. In the end, then, Juan's action was both self-interested and community-oriented; it helped both Panchito and Juan.

In fact, even in good health, Juan was dependent on the support and goodwill of his neighbors. Pedro, who was always losing his tomatoes, did not have that support and paid a heavy financial price in repeated small losses. The financial contribution Pedro might have made to help Panchito and others is actually much smaller than the financial loss he sustained each year in lost tomatoes and sheep. Juan had figured out that it was wise and foresightful to contribute to the community system, and ultimately, it was impossible to separate Juan's self-interested motives from his communitarian concerns. Indeed, to try to do so is to impose an unusual and self-defeating understanding on Juan's world that he would find incomprehensible. Juan, like most of his neighbors, did not make a rigid distinction between individual and group interest, and he was confused when I kept asking him to do so.

Pedro, on the other hand, did distinguish between individual and community interest. He had followed what political scientists call a traditional rational-actor model in his relations with other villagers. "I don't help anyone around here. They [his neighbors] are just thieves, all of them. All they want to do is take and take, as much as they can. I don't need any of them. Getting together with them you just get more poor." Pedro defined his own well-being as individual. He saw his own interests as confined to direct gain and immediate profit. He owned more land than some of his neighbors, and for him, it made sense to seek to preserve that relative affluence by sharing nothing with others. His understanding of rationality was immediate and short-sighted. In the peasant context, it was irrational.

It was Juan's belief in *long-term* self-interest that was rational in the peasant world of Pedregal. It was not that Juan didn't make calculations of self-interest. He was aware of the short-term financial loss he sustained by spending a day taking Panchito to the doctor instead of farming, but for him, it was far more rational to invest in the community, and to receive its protection when he needed it than it was to focus on immediate profits and discount future risk. Moreover, by investing in the community, Juan, unlike Pedro, didn't incur immediate financial losses to disgruntled neighbors who saw him as selfish and therefore fair game. The effect of Juan's action thus moved outward through the village and then back again toward himself.

The Peasant Political Ecology

This community approach to individual and group well-being is, however, far more than a medical alert system capable of saving a little boy's life. The fact that peasants can organize to help each other in time of need also means that they can organize to deal with threats that are much larger and more dangerous than, for example, Panchito's snake. The understanding of interdependence and need for mutual support demonstrated by Juan and others has significant political consequences when turned toward the outside world. It provides strength among the powerless; it is a protective shield for those who would otherwise be defenseless; and it can be a dangerous weapon, when turned toward political purpose.

This understanding of interdependence and need for mutual support is at the heart of a theory that I developed during the eighteen months that I spent studying politics and political action in peasant villages in Costa Rica and Nicaragua.[1] The theory is described in the phrase *political ecology*; the peasant's political ecology is this ecological understanding and an ecological perspective or world view which influences peasant actions. Such terms are of course not part of the peasants' conscious vocabulary. Though peasants don't think in conscious terms of maintaining a political ecology, they do think in terms of interdependence, mutually supportive interaction, and need, and they work to maintain and protect these.[2]

The peasant political ecology embraces virtually all elements of peasant life—self, community and community institutions (e.g., Pedregal's medical support system), the natural environment, and the nation. The peasants' understanding of interdependence causes them to see these elements in interaction with each other and with the national society beyond the village. I found this political ecology and its political results present in similar and recognizable form in village after village even when the political action taken varied greatly in form and context. The peasants' political ecology caused them to consider political action vis-à-vis the external world; helped them determine whether or not political action was necessary; and assisted them in choosing specific political tactics. The political ecology theory I present here explains peasant political action along a wide spectrum, from quiescence to rebellion and including collective nonviolent tactics in between these two.

I came to describe the peasant perspective on the world as an ecological one because the peasants perceived the world as interdependent.[3] They saw themselves, each other, their communities, their surrounding natural world, and their wider society as part of an interacting, interdependent whole. By describing the peasant perspective on interdependence as ecological, I broaden the term to include the social and political interactions in which peasants are involved as well as an awareness of the natural environment. Yet the new usage of the word retains the basic conceptual power of environmental ecology, which argues that a complex interdependence, interaction, and balance exist among such components of the natural world as soil, air, and water. In nature, energy flows back and forth among these elements. A chemical introduced into the system at one point will diffuse and reappear in all the elements in the system. Thus events in one sphere will eventually indirectly affect other elements in the system and the condition of other spheres. I came to learn that the peasant world operates in a similar way: individual and community interests overlap, and action moves outward to affect others and then returns to touch the original actor. Juan, Panchito, and the others understand this.

Just as environmental ecology refers to interaction and interdependence among soil, air, and water, the peasants' political ecology also refers to interactive interdependence among spheres—the individual, the community, the natural world, and the national society. Accordingly, activities by one individual affect the wider community and vice versa, in positive or negative ways. In such an ecological relationship, the survival of the peasant depends on an awareness of and attentiveness to interdependence with the broader social and agrarian environment. In such an interdependent system, events affecting one component eventually indirectly influence many other elements in the same system. Nothing occurs in a vacuum. Every action or choice is felt at many points throughout the system. Energy and the results of actions flow back and forth constantly.[4]

This new theory of peasant political action stands in contrast to previous theories of peasant political action. Previous theories have focused primarily on rebellion, and some have been quite useful in understanding certain aspects of peasant revolution. Yet none has been able to fully explain the combination of individual and group interests that are evident in the community action surrounding Panchito's accident and that also exist in peasant politics. None has offered a theory of peasant quiescence and collective nonviolence as well as of rebellion.

However, in the development of the theory of political ecology offered in this book two previous schools of theory have been particularly useful, because, taken together, they focus on both the individual and group interests involved in political action. These two schools of theory are best represented by Samuel Popkin's *The Rational Peasant: The Political Economy of Rebellion in Southeast Asia* and James Scott's *The Moral Economy of the Peasant: Subsistence and Rebellion in Southeast Asia*. These two theoretical paradigms have dominated the study of peasant politics and particularly of peasant rebellion. They are also known respectively as the political economy or rational actor paradigm and the moral economy paradigm. In this book I have labeled the two explanations the individualist and communitarian schools of thought because of their respective focus on individual and community concerns in the theories they offer. Thus the individualist school presents peasants as individuals whose primary concern in political action is the benefit of self and the maximation of individual gain. The communitarian school, by contrast, sees peasant political actors as primarily members of a community who are concerned with the preservation of long-standing community traditions. Although each of these explanations is partly right, each is incomplete. The individualist theory places too much emphasis on individual self-interest and uses a limited and unrealistic definition of "rational." The communitarian school, by contrast, places too little emphasis on individual interests and stresses group concerns too much. This is also unrealistic and implies that peasants are altruists who place their own individual interests below the interests of the community.[5]

Elements in the Political-Ecological Mentality

The theory of political ecology is a blend of these two theories but also moves beyond them. Unlike them, it explores the presence of both individual and group interests. Also unlike them, it addresses quiescence and collective nonviolence as well as peasant rebellion. Finally, the theory of political ecology incorporates crucial elements of the peasant world other than the individual and the village. Let us now explore the elements of the peasant mentality that result from their ecological view of the world.

The most basic component of the peasant world is the individual, who survives in interaction with other elements. Just as the quality of the soil affects the quality of the water and in turn is affected by the quality of the air and rainfall, so the peasant influences the character of the surrounding community and natural environment and in turn is affected by them. The second critical component is the village, which interacts both with the individual and with the natural and national world. Again, just as the water helps determine the nature of rain, so the village influences the quality of the natural environment, and in conjunction with other communities, impacts the wider society. The third element in the peasant world is the natural environment, which influences peasant life and in turn is affected by peasant behavior. The final element in that world is the national society; like the air in nature, the national society influences all aspects of individual, community, and natural life, and in turn, is influenced by each of these. In this complex system of interdependent elements peasants develop a political-ecological mentality with which they evaluate politics and choose whether or not to take certain kinds of political action.

The purpose of this book is to explore the peasant political ecology and resultant mentality in a variety of different contexts and to understand how and why this perspective leads peasants to different kinds of political action in different places and times. In the section that follows, we will consider the four elements of the peasant world—the individual, the community, the environment, and the national society—and examine how each, in interaction with the others, shapes the peasants' political ecology. By understanding their own interdependence peasants are influenced politically in two ways. First, they see the need for collective action. Second, they see the appropriateness, indeed the inescapability, of political goals that serve both the individual and the group.

The Individual: The Responsible, Rational Peasant

Although obviously motivated by self-interest, the peasant is not just an individual calculator of short-term maximized interest. He or she is also aware of the long-term foreseeable consequences of decisions. For example, faced with Panchito's accident, Juan calculated the financial costs of a day spent away from his farm and balanced these costs against the possibility that he would need medical help in the future. The communitarian school of theory sees peasants as social beings captured and constrained by unchanging community traditions and norms, as people doomed always to harken backward. But this is not so; the peasant is a conscious, efficacious actor capable of assessing and reassessing community norms and traditions. Individual peasants understand that such norms have an impact on their survival and consider how norms might be altered to assure survival in a changing world. For example, Pedregal's medical system has changed with the modern world. Once it might have resorted only to herbal and natural remedies; now it has modernized to bring access to scientific medicine.

The essence of the political ecology theory is that the individual peasant is a complex, responsible political actor, who assesses and acts in several different dimensions rather than solely within an individualistic or communitarian one.[6] Furthermore, the dimensions along which the peasant acts mesh and overlap to create a whole perspective that is more than the sum of its parts. The individual has both immediate interests and foreseeable interests, both an individual self and a community self. The rational actor gives attention to both and understands the way in which they reinforce and protect each other.[7] The individual is politically more powerful when acting as part of a group, and interdependent, responsible rationality is political power.

The Community: Interdependence and Egalitarianism

An interdependent view of the individual within the community prevails in peasant society because of the nature of peasant life. The peasant lives at the edge of existence and is always peering over the brink. Survival is never guaranteed either by the state or by economic cushioning and is always at stake, always threatened. The support of community often provides the only barrier between life and death in case of catastrophe. To ensure the survival of both individual and community, the community must be structured to provide *group* life insurance that includes each individual.[8]

A group insurance system that includes each individual addresses the insecurity of each poverty-stricken life and offers each peasant an incentive to join in and protect community, yet such a system can only survive within a normative order that prescribes relative human equality. Notions of egalitarianism and of a group system that protects individual life are common in popular culture where survival is precarious. Poverty causes the belief system that gives rise to and sustains a political ecology. In his study of injustice and revolt, Barrington Moore writes, "Equalitarian ideas and practices are likely to flourish in situations where supply is precarious and any given individual is liable to face an unpredictable shortage."[9] In the context of insecurity in the rural world, equality acts as a kind of group life insurance. The belief in egalitarianism offers peasants a normative standard against which to compare the wider social and political world. When that normative expectation is compromised, peasants know that their own survival is or will be threatened. Egalitarian ideas help keep peasants alert and aware of what is happening around them.

At the same time, ideals are tempered by pragmatism. Absolute equality is difficult, if not impossible, to achieve. Yet rural communities have frequently been able to develop a relative equity among members that provides the insurance needed in the face of insecurity. Thus community norms must respect basic human needs and not permit a minority to become wealthy if the majority suffer dire want. Relative egalitarianism recognizes the legitimacy of some differences and does not demand absolute equality. E. P. Thompson has argued that egalitarian rural norms constitute a "moral economy of the poor"[10] that predated the modern market economy and demanded a respect for consumption needs over individual profit.[11] Egalitarianism and respect for minimal subsistence needs would preclude severe subordination, including subordination to individual profit or the desire for individual wealth at the expense of the many. The popular culture described here includes elements of resistance to subordination and of relative egalitarianism.[12]

Egalitarianism and resistance to subordination are crucial in maintaining community and the social insurance that community provides. Community insurance requires that individuals be interdependent, that is, dependent on one another. That interdependence would be destroyed if individuals did not maintain the community and, with it, group insurance. The loss of community would threaten each individual within that community as well as the village as a whole. Thus voluntary actions that result in harm to others violate community norms, threaten group and therefore individual survival, and are defined as wrong, no matter how well vindicated by the laws of government or of market economics.[13] Community norms take precedence over state laws and market economics because the latter may override individual or community needs.[14]

Peasants resist policies, for example, of land concentration or high levels of taxation that violate the norms of their political ecology, first because such policies allow one human being to injure others with impunity, and second because they fail to respect the rule of human need.[15] Such policies do not recognize interdependence or the rights and responsibilities of all. Moore has called popular opposition to the concentration of unused wealth "the taboo of the dog in the manger." "The essence of the taboo is the belief that personal and private retention *without use* of resources that are in short supply and needed by others is somehow immoral and a violation of the morally superior rights of the community."[16]

In the peasant system, the preservation of interdependence and therefore of community demands relative equity of economic position. An individual who attains wealth will need the support of others less and will be less inclined to offer support to others. The achievement of independence by first one and then another peasant will slowly erode interdependence and mutual need, and ultimately it will threaten everyone. Thus a peasant who has some relative affluence, such as Juan with his sure-footed mule in Pedregal, is a protected community member because he recognizes his own dependence on the village and therefore contributes to it. He does not see himself as self-sufficient by virtue of his greater economic comfort, and indeed, he is not. Pedro, on the other hand, also has relative affluence in the form of sheep and tomatoes, but does not recognize his dependence on the community. Thinking himself self-sufficient, he does not contribute to the system and is vulnerable to it.

Norms that favor community and mutual need are especially prevalent in a small village because they are more easily made and enforced on a microscale where everyone knows everyone else. Small community size permits actors to see more clearly the full effects of their actions—to see the ripple all the way to the edge of the pond. Seeing the effect of their actions and of their dependence on the community encourages individuals to apply to their own behavior the standards used by the community in general. Community citizens are constantly aware of how their behavior appears to others and of what their neighbors might think. Relative egalitarianism helps to pragmatize ideals of equality, and resistance to subordination provides a rule of thumb for when political action becomes legitimate.

Reciprocity and Political Ecology

The peasants' political ecology is much more than the system of reciprocity within villages that has been described elsewhere.[17] Reciprocity is an exchange relationship between two persons of unequal means: a landed villager and a landless laborer.[18] Yet it does not fully capture the multifaceted, crisscross of supportive relationships among individuals and groups. The multidimensional understanding of interdependence that includes all these elements is more accurately described as ecological interdependence because it, like the natural

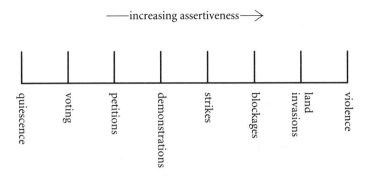

Figure 1.1. Spectrum of Political Activity

environment, contains multiple patterns of interaction. Ecological interdependence is a more complex and extensive set of relationships in which participants do not necessarily return benefits or support directly to the person from whom they have received aid. Rather, they return support to a general community system and trust that system to support the person who directly aided them whenever the need arises. Moreover, peasants may contribute directly to one individual but may also proffer aid to a community system in general, such as collections in Pedregal's medical support system.

Reciprocity does not describe a belief in mutuality between the peasantry and society nor does it include the outward-looking nature of the village. It refers only to individual relations within a village, whereas ecological interdependence captures the extent to which peasants also look beyond the village for support. Their awareness of such interdependence alerts peasants to their place in the wider society. Ecological interdependence and the expectations it carries with it help define what peasants can legitimately expect from the outside world. These expectations help them decide when political action is needed and what kinds of demands can be made. (See Figure 1.1.)

The theory of political ecology has much more explanatory power than a theory of moral economy because the former explicitly recognizes the role of both individual and group interests in the peasant world. Peasants are self-interested actors, even though they define rationality broadly. They are not only community actors, and they are not only altruistic. They are traditional only when tradition pays off, and they are willing to change and adapt their norms and traditions if such change will preserve the community and the individual. They cannot afford to neglect calculations of self-interest. Rather, they see the protection of self and of self-interest as part and parcel of the community system, and the protection of one is also the protection of the other. Thus there is no incompatibility between individual and community interest, individual and group action. To hurt the one is to hurt the other when both are rolled into a bundle and are one and the same.

The Hostile, Fragile Environment

As farmers and people who live with and on nature, peasants are always aware of the role of the environment within their lives. The products of the natural world feed, clothe, and house them; enrich, support, and teach them; and sometimes threaten them. It is impossible to survive as a peasant without acknowledging one's daily interaction with the natural environment. That interaction includes both an understanding of the dangers nature poses for people and for crops and a sense of the danger human carelessness can pose for the natural environment. Thus nature is part of the interactive, interdependent, or ecological, system of the peasant world and composes another element in the political ecology.

Peasants watch the natural world for dangers and prepare contingency plans that may help shield them from natural disasters. If a village stands on the slopes of an active volcano, peasants may respond by dividing landownership at the base and the top of the mountain, so that no person owns only the safest land and the danger is spread out. By being aware of their own vulnerability to natural disasters, peasants can use community interdependence to minimize environmental danger. Threats of natural disaster also encourage peasants to include society when they think about interdependence with nature. If a natural disaster strikes an entire community equally (hail, a hurricane) and intravillage support is inadequate, peasants may look outward to the state and society for support, pointing out the interdependence between the village and society. In requesting disaster aid, they will emphasize society's dependence on them for food. Yet peasants also know that in the interdependent relationship with nature, danger flows both ways. People, including peasants, can harm the ecosystem if they do not take care to protect it. Knowing that they depend on nature for subsistence and survival, peasants watch their natural environment and protect it insofar as they can.[19]

This understanding of how vulnerable the environment is helps frame the issues around which peasants act politically. They may become environmental activists, making demands that directly protect the environment. Alternatively they may request better economic circumstances for themselves, enabling them to deplete natural resources more slowly and protect the environment indirectly.[20] It is important to note that I am *not* arguing that peasants are perfect environmental ecologists in all ways and at all times. No one is such an unflawed environmentalist. I am simply saying that peasants have a keen *awareness* of the natural world around them, and that this awareness forms one part of their ecological perspective in which the individual, the community, and the wider society are all equally important elements. Peasant environmental awareness grows out of the proximity of peasant life to nature, but it does not necessarily mean that peasants always act in a protective way toward their environment. Frequently, however, their environmental consciousness leads them to incorporate environmental concerns in their political demands and to do so more often than most other actors in political movements.[21] Sometimes, peasants are trapped into a situation where their own well-being and that of the environment are partly or directly at odds.[22] If possible, they will use their political clout to avoid or modify such a zero-sum situation. Even where they are powerless to modify an environmentally destructive system, their political perspective still retains an environmental awareness.[23]

National Society: Peasant Change and Adaptation

The willingness to change and adapt is one of the most obvious sources of peasant power and ability to survive in today's world. The belief system of the peasant community subscribes to rationality, responsibility, and relative egalitarianism, all with an eye to maintaining interdependence and survival. Within that belief system, there is room for tradition as well as for change and adaptation. Between tradition and change, the choice is always for facilitating survival, both that of the group and that of the individual. Where tradition best protects survival, traditional claims, such as on landlord reciprocity, will prevail. Where change best protects survival, new norms, such as an appeal to national and international agencies, will become the order of the day.

The peasants' political ecology is thus adaptable and pragmatic. Peasants will use all available tools in the struggle for survival, now touting tradition, now moving beyond it, and making new demands in accordance with a changing society. Such flexibility and adaptability explain how peasants in one village may enforce the norms of a traditional moral economy whereas elsewhere villagers take a struggle for environmental preservation to the international stage.[24] In each case, the struggle is for survival. In each instance, the peasants perceive an interdependent world. Whether through traditional norms or new demands and tactics, the ecological perspective helps peasants see how they can maximize their chances for survival. This approach helps explain modern peasants in a contemporary world.

Change and adaptation result from peasants seeing themselves and their communities in interdependence with a society that is always modernizing. Interdependence between village and society creates obligations and rights or opportunities just as does the interdependence between individual and village. As interdependent members of a modernizing society, peasants have an obligation to change and adapt, to move with that society if they expect to survive. Such modernization may, for example, include trying new crops or new farming techniques. Also, as interdependent members of modern society, peasants feel that they have the right to expect support from society, including supportive agricultural policies and even aid in times of crisis.

Many contemporary movements, including the examples in this book, contain rhetoric and action that addresses peasant obligations and rights as they adapt to the modern world. Movements may underscore the peasant contribution to society and demand more land, better fertilizers, or improved transport, all to enhance production. Other movements may emphasize the need for the contribution to flow in the opposite direction—from society to the peasant. Such actions may demand higher prices, better price supports, or even crop-failure insurance and disaster compensation. Thus the political ecology includes not only the local region but also the national society. Peasants see themselves as contributing to and supporting society. They expect society to also support them.

Political Ecology and Political Action

Peasant understanding of ecological interdependence empowers them to protect themselves and promote their own interests in ways that would be impossible if they only acted individually and were unaware of the protective strength found in community. As farmers and citizens of underdeveloped, modernizing countries, peasants are exposed to numerous threats and dangers, both to themselves and to their communities, throughout their lives. Their crops and livelihood may be destroyed by hail, a hurricane, an erupting volcano, or disease and pests. Peasants may be exposed to economic policies that drain away their meager profits through high taxes or that destroy their profits entirely through low prices or overproduction. They may be victims of a social reality that condones land concentration and crowds larger and larger numbers of them onto a steadily dwindling land base. Or they may be exposed to political dangers, such as a nonsupportive ministry of agriculture, oppression of peasant organizations, state repression and terror, and even revolution.

Individually, peasants are powerless before a flood or a land-grabbing neighbor, just as alone Maria would have been powerless to help Panchito when he was bitten by the snake. As part of a group, the opportunities for self-preservation are much greater, just as they were for Maria. Among themselves, peasants may distribute the effects of natural or social disaster so that disaster weighs less heavily on each person. They may unite in the face of discriminatory economic and social policies, creating organizations that demand better prices or that reduce landlessness. They may even support social revolution by sending new converts to join a revolutionary cause (feeding, clothing, and arming guerrillas) or providing a social camouflage into which those fleeing repression can melt and be protected. Any community that can organize so effectively to provide medical support can also turn that capacity toward political purpose with equally effective results.

The ecological perspective and understanding of interdependence and the need for mutual support thus has very real effects as the united village looks outward. Community cohesion becomes political cohesion all the more easily because peasants see the wider political world as part of the interdependent system. Just as peasants define their relationship with their environment as mutually supportive and protective, they expect their place in society to be interactive and interdependent. They and their society each have certain rights, responsibilities, and obligations vis-à-vis each other.

Recognizing the political effects of the peasant understanding of ecological interdependence is the first step toward comprehending the persistence of peasantry in the modern world. Although historians have long predicted the disappearance of this class, the majority of the world's population is still peasants. Peasants persist because of their ability to cohere socially and politically. They survive because of their capacity to translate ecological interdependence into political power. The peasant world view influences peasant decisions about whether to take action and about what kind of action to take. An understanding of the origin and components of the political ecology and its accompanying ecological mentality enables one to interpret peasant political action more precisely than does any unidimensional approach and to explain peasant choices of political tactics. Peasants transfer the ecological perspective derived from community to the wider world.

Although the peasant's ecological perspective begins with the village and may remain concentrated there, the ecological world view can also extend to the wider society. To the extent that peasants perceive the village as dependent on and contributing to national society, they devise actions that respond to perceived disequilibrium in the wider social system that threatens their own survival and that of their community. A decision to act may come through village discussion, trial and error, or through a general process of learning; the ultimate goal is to respond as effectively as possible to perceived external threats. The threat may be to peasants individually, to their communities, to their way of life, or to the peasant class as a whole. They respond with tactics carefully chosen to maximize their own chances of success. If they see the wider society as contributing something to their own survival, they will act to reform the system but not to destroy it. If they see the system as primarily dangerous to them, they will withdraw if possible or join efforts at destroying the system if withdrawal is impossible.

Peasants change the way they act depending on the circumstances; an adaptable political ecology permits this flexibility. When the community and the system of interdependence are not threatened by immediate individual-interest maximization, the peasant may behave very much like a traditional rational actor. In another instance, it may be socially rational to adhere to traditional norms, overriding short-term personal interests. If, however, community is threatened both by unlimited short-term individual-interest maximization and by blind adherence to traditional norms, the peasant is capable of recognizing both threats and acting to preserve community. Such action is both individualistic and communitarian. A complex and holistic understanding of self in the context of community leads the individual to see that community norms may have to change as the external world changes, in order to facilitate individual and group survival. Because nonviolent collective action is reformist activism, the incremental modifications that result from it are the best way for communities to facilitate survival and participation in a changing world. The ecological perception of self within community thus encourages collective action and individual participation out of personal self-interest. If the individual pursues only short-term self-interest, acting as a free rider in the rational-actor sense, the limited rationality of this action will undermine community and endanger the individual. At the same time, if the individual adheres blindly to tradition and fails to update community norms, community will also be undermined, endangering the individual.

This ecological perspective gives peasants a responsibility to act in ways that benefit both community and individual. Peasants must balance short-term consequences with long-term interests and keep middle-range foreseeable consequences clearly in mind. At times in that process they may fail to assess the balance accurately and make mistakes. Some peasants may act irresponsibly or with limited rationality. Nonetheless, the overall perspective is one of self within community. The political calculus of the peasant is more complicated, more rational, and more thorough than previously understood.

The main reason why some peasants act politically and others do not lies in how well the individual understands ecological interdependence of the world. Within a given village that understanding will vary, just as Pedro and Juan understood their own relationship to their village very differently. Awareness of ecological interdependence primarily develops within the village itself, but it may also come from travel beyond the village and experience with the loneliness and vulnerability of life without the community. It may come from religion or education which provides a similar understanding or it may derive from an experience of poverty in which a community could not or would not offer protection.

Seen as a product of an ecological mentality, peasant political action is not just a response to the violation of immediate interests. Nor is it simply a protective response to the transgression of traditional norms. Both of these views imply that peasants move dramatically from quiescence to revolution, without any possibility of participatory nonviolent political action and its consequent readjustments. Peasant political action is not merely a reaction to the modern world but a means of participating in it and keeping up with it. It is a systematic attempt to readjust the community and community life so that they will continue to protect and enhance the individual. In this sense, peasant political action is both moral and economic, both communitarian and individualistic. It supports community norms and is economically rational because it promotes survival.

To create an adaptive, resilient community, peasants must be capable of many forms of political action, including quiescence that holds to the status quo or rebellion that attempts to destroy all. They must be able to choose the appropriate action, the one most likely to sustain their world, and to move from one tactic to another in pursuing their goals. They must be able to participate in a variety of ways and to change their mode of political participation as circumstances and their goals demand. In one case, they must be able to sustain and enforce relationships of a moral economy. At another point in time, their survival may dictate as little contact as possible with the wider society. In yet a third instance, they may have to master national politics and speak directly to the state. In still another scenario, they may enter a world stage and join an international cause. This deliberate readjustment explains why the peasantry has survived into the modern world. A flexible range of political action gives the peasant community a resilience that Eric Wolf failed to recognize, and it explains why the village has not necessarily crumbled under capitalism, as he anticipated it would.[25] Nonviolent collective action enables the community to grow and change instead of stagnate and disappear.

In some cases, of course, these strategies fail and peasants are unable to protect community and survive as peasant villagers. However, peasants' frequent success is attested to by the large number of modern rural dwellers who call themselves such today. The case study material in the chapters that follow helps clarify how peasants use political action to preserve themselves and their communities. Community survival can be pursued via collective action along a spectrum of political activity that includes quiescence and revolution. Voluntary quiescence results from the perception that there is no need for change, no immediate threat. This inaction preserves community in its appropriate current position. At the opposite extreme, revolution responds to a total crisis by destroying all and attempting to re-create everything. Nonviolent collective action recognizes smaller problems before they become revolutionary crises and responds to them by initiating incremental change. The gradual readjustment that results allows re-creation of community again and again and the readjustment of norms to fit and participate in the modern world.

This book draws upon the multiple concerns of peasants to create a model of human social interdependence and a theory of political action. It explores the power of both individual economic concerns and of communitarian concerns in numerous instances of political action. This investigation is both quantitative and qualitative. Political actors are allowed to state their reasons for political action so that the extent of each kind of consideration is evident. In addition, statistical techniques show precisely how significant each consideration is in each case of political action.

This detailed understanding of political motivation and the careful comparison of the relative importance of different considerations in specific cases required extensive fieldwork and thoughtful listening to the context of and reasons for political action. It necessitated data collection methods that are sensitive to the depth of the human experience being uncovered. Such methods cannot confine themselves to brief, preprogrammed encounters with subjects because these would never uncover beliefs, values, and moral concerns. Data collection for this study, therefore, combined social science techniques with the ethnographic practices of anthropology in a way that is both unusual and more conducive of understanding than is either technique alone. Data analysis moves back and forth between a qualitative approach and quantitative statistical techniques. In-depth knowledge of each community informed the statistical techniques chosen for the tests made. Statistical results obtained were then reality-checked against my detailed knowledge of the villages to be certain that results "made sense" in view of what I already knew about the respondents and their story. All of this constitutes a departure from traditional methods used in studying the peasantry. I have combined surveys and anthropological techniques of gathering data with qualitative and quantitative data analysis. The results illustrate ways in which social science, including peasant studies, can benefit from combined methodologies and a broad range of analytical techniques. For the interested reader, the Appendix discusses in detail the methodology involved.

The case study data indicate the presence of both individualistic and communitarian concerns and confirm the importance of a multidimensional ecological perspective. In a broad view of political action of many kinds, across various contexts, and within two very different countries, neither individualistic nor communitarian explanations always prevail. In fact, the data show strong support for both the economic concerns of individuals and for moral communitarian considerations in a way that demonstrates the blending of individual and community interests in an interdependent manner.

The Nicaraguan cases explore peasant choices of quiescence and rebellion and the movement between the two. The Costa Rican cases offer examples of political action that was neither voluntary quiescence nor violence. All of the Costa Rican villagers chose to participate through different kinds of nonviolent collective action. These respondents make it clear that both individual economic concerns and moral considerations of community were of relatively equal importance for their choices. For them, choices among different political tactics were governed by economic goals as well as by the moral vision they held of social justice. The way in which individual and community concerns and economic and moral motivations come together indicates the need for a theory that explains the interconnection between them. An ecological view of the individual within society and of self-interest within community interest provides this explanation. The data thus support a multidimensional and holistic theory of political action that combines both individual and communitarian concerns and provides an ecological perspective on peasant political action.

2 ∎ THE BROADER CONTEXT
Contrasting Political Traditions

The comparative context of this study allows it to develop the political ecology theory within two different political systems. The study of political action in Costa Rica and prerevolutionary Nicaragua contrasts action within a democracy with that under a dictatorship. Yet the selection of two Central American nations holds constant broad variables such as culture, ethnicity, religion, geography, and geopolitical position.[1] Both are dependent, agricultural countries with economies that rely on the export of a few agricultural commodities. The theory of political ecology offered here explains political motivation according to individual variables that appear in any national context. It does not attempt to explain the final outcome and success of specific types of peasant political action, for that would require an analysis of national context and international setting quite beyond the scope of this book. Yet a full understanding even of individual political motivation and action requires some knowledge of the surrounding political system. The actual manifestation of the ecological perspective and political actions that result from it are powerfully influenced by context. Political history and the nature of the current regime help determine modes of thinking, possible options, and political choices. Regional variation in the behavior of a given regime also helps shape local expectations and decisions. This chapter explores and constrasts national and regional historical, governmental, social and economic characteristics within and between Costa Rica and Nicaragua.

Setting the Stage: State Influence on Individual Perspectives

The nature of the state or the character of the national government shapes the peasant perspective and influences peasant political attitudes and choices. A country's political traditions mold the nature of political discourse. Costa Rica and Nicaragua have different traditions of relationships among elites and between elite and popular classes. Costa Rica is a relatively pluralist society, with a tradition of dialogue among elites. The elites show some tolerance for

Map 1

dissent and a measured willingness to hear the demands of society's poorer classes, including the peasants. Nicaragua, by contrast, has a history of conflict and tension in which differences have been resolved by force and other extralegal means. From 1933 to 1979 the Somoza regime took these traditions to extremes of repression and intolerance which extended even to the elite class.

The state helps determine what peasants define as proper governmental behavior and plays an important role in creating social history. If the state has historically taken part in developing the country or has periodically acted for societal benefit, then the population will expect, even demand, that it continue this pattern. If the state has always distanced itself from the process of social development, then the population will have much lower expectations, with peasants anticipating little or no positive contribution from the state. They may even prefer that the state remain uninvolved.

The state directly influences peasant behavior. It partially determines the portfolio of political tactics from which peasants may choose, regardless of the local economic structure. A democratic regime specifies certain kinds of polit-

NICARAGUA

COSTA RICA

Caribbean Sea

El Hogar and La Lucha

San Luis

Alajuela

Puerto Limón

San José

Pacific Ocean

PANAMA

N

Map 2

ical action as tolerable and others as illegal, and peasants will choose the form of action most likely to succeed. The democratic stage set by the state also restricts how the government may react to peasant action. Democracy restrains the behavior of each side and limits the manner in which the law can be enforced. Those who break the law may not be prosecuted, or may be punished only mildly. When the state does punish lawbreakers, castigation is limited by certain constraints, such as respect for human rights. Thus political action is safer and more predictable in a democracy but restricted in prespecified ways. The price for deviation from legal channels can be at least partially foretold. On the other hand, political action under a dictatorship which seeks to prohibit popular political input and to severely restrict the space for political action is qualitatively different. Because the state is unrestrained by law, its actions are capricious and arbitrary. The price for inappropriate or unlawful political action is high, because laws are designed to benefit the dictator at the expense of the population and offenders cannot count on any protection from the law or respect for their rights as human beings.

In either a dictatorship or a democracy, the state plays a direct role in determining subsequent action after peasants take the political initiative. Once peasants have opted for organized action, they have entered the political arena, for their acts have a political effect. The acts themselves may be intentionally aimed to either attract or escape state attention. The state may respond to all or part of peasant demands or it may ignore their actions entirely. It may repress the peasants or threaten repression if actions do not cease. The state response will help determine the peasants' subsequent course of action.

Beyond the broad national differences between regimes, there exist regional differences in regime or governmental policies. Regime character varies somewhat among geographical regions. In the province of Alajuela within Costa Rica's Central Valley, the land is fertile, and Alajuela has enjoyed a fortunate economic and social history. Peasants grow profitable export crops, and consequently the state maintains a supportive political attitude toward Alajuela and provides good public services there. The peasants of San Luis in Alajuela have had a positive political experience. The other two Costa Rican villages are in Limón, the nation's poorest and most neglected province. Limón peasants grow staple crops that command low domestic prices. They are economically weaker than peasants in the Central Valley yet must struggle to compete with large agro-export interests, particularly the banana industry. The political experience of the peasantry in this province is more tense and confrontational than in Alajuela. Limón's political history is conflictual, and its residents have been more neglected by the central government than residents of other provinces. Higher poverty levels and the difficulty of attracting government attention contribute to the peasants' choice of more assertive forms of political action there.

Nicaragua also offers regional contrast. In Boaco, where Pedregal is located, economic and political circumstances provide a strange combination of misfortune and good luck. It is difficult to grow any crops in the rocky soil, so poverty is endemic and progress unlikely. Yet a determined peasantry supports itself on staple crops and manages to ward off catastrophic poverty in the process. Between 1933 and 1979 poor land quality actually proved to be a blessing in disguise. The rocky soil discouraged agro-export businesses and attracted very little attention from the Somoza regime. Peasant farming was allowed to function largely according to peasant preferences and was not subject to the elite land concentration and peasant landlessness prevalent elsewhere in Nicaragua. The region received neither positive nor negative input from the state, and peasants came to expect benign neglect. The other two Nicaraguan villages studied are in the Pacific department of Masaya. Fate has played tricks in Masaya, for fertile land brought political misfortune to the local peasantry. Because the soil is ideal for staples, it is also profitable for agro-export industry, particularly cotton. The Somoza regime played a heavy role in Masaya, and local experience illustrates the nature of the dictatorship.

Agrarian policies of the Somoza state were destructive of the peasantry. State influence took the form of extreme economic exploitation, brutal repression, or both. Masaya is the only region where we find peasants pushed below the subsistence level. We would expect political action in such circumstances, yet the opportunity for political participation was almost entirely closed under Somoza.

Working from an ecological perspective, the peasants in this study expected interdependence and mutual support between themselves and their social and natural environment. Precisely where the lines are drawn around that environment and what specific forms interdependence takes, however, are shaped by context, political history, and regional and national atmosphere. Thus, most peasants in Pedregal included their village and the closest town within their expectations of interdependence but did not expect interdependent interaction with the state. These expectations were met and Pedregal villagers remained quiescent during the revolution. Villagers from Pikin Guerrero also expected relevant boundaries of interdependence to stop at the local town. Their expectations, however, were not met, and they suffered repression. The repression forced them to include the state in their ecological expectations. Having done so, they saw no option but to join the revolution. The Nicaraguan state thus shaped peasant expectations and their political actions in the face of those expectations. In contrast to Somoza's dictatorship, the Costa Rican state has assumed greater responsibility toward its peasantry and has become more involved. Consequently, the Costa Rican peasants in all three villages included the state in their ecological expectations. The boundaries that they drew around their interdependent environment extended all the way to the national society and government. Their political rhetoric and demands refered to the mutually supportive interdependence between themselves, society, and the state.

Costa Rica: A Tradition of Tolerance

The history and political development of Costa Rica are unique among Spain's Central American colonies. Far from the colonial seat of power in Guatemala City, and distant from the Andean colonial seat in Peru, Costa Rica experienced very limited Spanish influence.[2] From the Spanish perspective, Costa Rica had little to offer, neither gold mines nor a supply of Indian labor. With the chronic labor shortage, large agricultural plantations were not feasible, so the development of farming was more like small-scale private agriculture in the United States than like the elite and foreign-dominated agro-export pattern found elsewhere in Latin America. But small farms did not produce the wealth associated with plantation systems and poverty in the Costa Rican colony became chronic. Despite this poverty and isolation, a few Spaniards came to Costa Rica, settling on the fertile land of the Cartago Valley. Most came as homesteaders intending to put down roots and stay. Samuel Stone has argued that these early Costa Rican settlers were poor Spaniards who sought land—peasants rather than aristocrats.[3]

This history set the stage for an unusual political atmosphere. Far removed from the seats of Spanish political and military power, living among a very small indigenous population, Costa Rican settlers were unable to enforce many of the Spanish crown policies designed to extract wealth from the local population. Even when settlers were able to find Indians, they were often unable to force them to pay tribute.[4] Because Spanish colonists could not rely on force to gain Indian cooperation, the local colonial government was more tolerant and less exploitative than elsewhere in Central America. Given the scarcity of Indian labor in Costa Rica, the Spanish settlers recognized it as an asset to be protected. Laws attempted to provide for Indian access to land. The governors recognized that landless Indians could not survive, much less pay tribute to or feed the city.[5] Over time, the distinction between Spanish settlers and Indians became less relevant. The scarce Indian population declined even further while the number of Spanish settlers grew. The mestizo population eventually became the largest racial group, and the Costa Rican population assumed a relatively homogeneous character. Mitchell Seligson has argued that this ethnic homogeneity explains the less repressive character of rural political relations.[6]

After Costa Rica gained independence from Spain in 1821, the newly independent government reflected the local quality of tolerance as well as a certain national pride, and its policies aimed to benefit the national territory as a whole rather than individual or colonial interests. Leaders emerged who were more concerned with developing the country constructively than with making a fortune. In time they gained a fair amount of control over internal affairs and were able to impose some limits on outside interference. In conflicts after independence, the national government sometimes took the side of wealthy and foreign interests, sometimes stepped in to protect those who labored for those interests, and sometimes stayed outside the conflict altogether or acted as a mediator.[7] The Costa Rican national government never allowed itself to become dominated by foreign interests to the extent found in Nicaragua. Instead, small producers often pressured the government into defending them or accounting for their interests in policy decisions. After several unsuccessful attempts at developing an export crop, Costa Ricans succeeded with coffee, which flourished on the plentiful mountain slopes. Mestizo smallholders sold their coffee to export houses. Although some large coffee farms developed, the political power of their owners was checked by the small and medium farmers who competed with them on the political scene.[8] Although landlessness has grown rapidly in recent decades, the Costa Rican peasantry has never been as powerless or as exploited and marginalized as other Central American peasantries. The historical tradition of political efficacy is very important in the experiences and actions of Costa Rican peasants.

Independent Costa Rica still struggled with population scarcity and labor shortage. Agrarian laborers and peasants had more bargaining power than was usual in Central America. Skillful use of this leverage and a periodically sympathetic national government combined to produce an unusually positive national labor tradition. Like the peasants, laborers were never completely powerless and were periodically supported by the national government, by the Church, or by a growing atmosphere of political tolerance.

By the late nineteenth century, Costa Rica began to attract foreign attention despite its drawbacks. Responding to Costa Rica's desire for a railroad, Minor Keith and his British Railroad Company proposed to build a railroad through the jungle to Port Limón for exporting coffee. Keith underestimated the cost of opening the jungle in a country of scarce labor, however, and ended up importing workers from China, Italy, and finally Jamaica. Then he found himself embroiled in labor disputes, especially with Italians who had been exposed to socialist ideas in their home country. As early as 1889, the railroad company confronted labor strikes,[9] and as a foreigner, Keith had few national allies. The Costa Rican government was as likely to remain outside labor conflicts or to support the workers by passing labor protection laws as to support Keith.[10] In an attempt to recoup extensive losses, Keith planted bananas on the cleared land along the railroad tracks, introducing the banana industry to Costa Rica.[11]

In the new banana industry working conditions were harsh, and workers died of tropical diseases, snake and insect bites, and from occupational accidents.[12] These conditions were likely to evoke resistance in the context of a dissident labor tradition. In 1934, the United Fruit Company faced the largest and longest strike in Costa Rica's history. Organized by the Communist party and led by author Carlos Luis Fallas, the strike paralyzed the company for two weeks. The government remained stubbornly outside of the conflict, and the strikers won salary increases, better working conditions, shorter hours, and improved medical treatment for job-related injuries. The United Fruit Company also agreed to recognize the new union.[13] The strike was a real and symbolic victory for the Costa Rican popular classes. It followed and strengthened a national tradition in which the poor exercised political and economic power, and it represented a further step in the development of a democratic political tradition. The state's unwillingness to take sides reinforced labor confidence and sent a message that strikes were an acceptable political tactic in Costa Rica. The success of the strike proved the utility of the tactic and nonviolent strikes became a part of the portfolio of political action.

While the United Fruit Company was vying with its workers for concessions and control in the late nineteenth and early twentieth centuries, its monopoly over transport was generating opposition from small and medium-sized Costa Rican banana farmers, who felt exploited and wanted to escape from company control. The smaller farmers successfully pressured the government into imposing a tax on exports and sought government action against monopolistic domestic transport practices. The passage of this early bill established a trend toward governmental independence from foreign control that would continue over the next seventy years. It also blended with the political tradition of tolerance and compromise which refused to allow a few narrow interests to dominate the economy. From 1909 on, the Costa Rican government gradually gained some control over the United Fruit Company and was able to extract taxes from it. As part of the ongoing effort to decrease the power of the United Fruit Company, in 1929 the government began constructing a highway from San José to Limón. The railroad ceased to be the only method of transport through the Atlantic province.[14]

During this period of tension, competition, and compromise, the Costa Rican peasants established another tradition, which became particularly strong in Limón province. As the banana companies and the railroad spread across the region, strips of fertile land along the tracks were cleared and left unused. Even before 1900, landless peasants from other parts of Costa Rica and ex-banana workers began working the land as subsistence farms. By 1907 this had become a common practice. These peasants won the name *precaristas* and their form of subsistence cropping on company land, *precarismo*.[15] For many years precarismo continued undisturbed on company land. The peasants believed that they had a right to the otherwise unused land because they needed it for subsistence, and the banana company did not need it at all. This accorded with peasant beliefs that land is a basic right connected to survival. This conviction, still present today among Limón peasants, has helped determine their political outlook and expectations of interdependence. It has also shaped the actions they have taken in response to those expectations. In 1913, tension over this land arose when the United Fruit Company imposed a rental charge of two colones per hectare per year.[16] However, because the company already owned thousands of hectares of land and millions of dollars in assets, this policy violated the peasant understanding of land use that recognizes need as grounds for uninhibited use and advocates a relatively equal distribution of wealth. The peasants appealed to the national government for support. Their appeal reflected their understanding that the government was not always a champion of large economic interests and indicated that they believed in written communication with the state as another potentially useful tool within the portfolio of political action. Although the company won this round and imposed land rent, its victory did not imply a change in popular beliefs. Precarismo and the precaristas still clash with public and private authorities in Costa Rica and have become an integral part of the country's political tradition. This tradition plays an important role in the two Limón communities we visit in Chapter 5.

Tradition Formalized: Social Democracy

Costa Rican history shows the gradual development of political traditions of tolerance, limited mutual understanding among opponents, and self-restraint in times of conflict. During the first fifty years of this century, these political tendencies were formalized as the political pluralism Costa Rica enjoys today. The state is not immune to the pressures of powerful economic interests, yet it has retained a degree of autonomy unique in Central America.[17] In keeping with the tradition of nationalistic concern for general prosperity, these fifty years also engendered a pattern of social legislation. The state formally recognized workers' rights and established a labor code.

Governmental social awareness and its periodic support for the popular cause helped shape peasant expectations and perceptions of the state role. Costa Rica's poorer classes had learned that they might sometimes obtain an audience with the state. They realized that the state felt some obligation toward them, and they knew they had at least some chance of convincing it to honor that obligation in a conflict. If they could convince the state of their own economic need, the state might tolerate, if not support, their actions. At least they could rely on the state not to destroy them. They had also learned which political tactics had sometimes proven successful in the past. Because the boundaries defining acceptable political action had solidified, the peasants knew approximately what action they could undertake and more or less how the state would react.

Despite a violent conflict among political parties in 1948, the tradition of democracy and social welfare continued. The victors in that conflict, José Figueres and the National Liberation party, continued the social reforms started by their predecessors. The traditions of democracy and reform were strong enough to survive civil war and were essentially supported by both sides. Some of the most important steps that set Costa Rica apart from her Central American neighbors were taken after 1948 under Figueres's direction. The Figueres government established a social security system (in Costa Rica the equivalent of a national health plan); developed production and export cooperatives; and set up the National Agricultural Council (Consejo Agropecuario Nacional), which addresses agricultural problems, the National Production Council (Consejo Nacional de Producción, CNP), which holds prices on basic foodstuffs at reasonable levels, and the Land and Colonization Institute (Instituto de Tierras y Colonización, ITCO). Some of these institutions, particularly the CNP and ITCO, have not functioned as successfully as intended. Nevertheless, the original purpose was commendable. These reforms improved the condition of the poor, including the peasantry, and helped make the difficulties they encountered easier in Costa Rica than elsewhere in Central America.

Although the pattern of regular elections and social legislation continued despite the civil war of 1948, Oscar Arias has argued that 1948 marked a change in the character of the Costa Rican state. Prior to 1948, the wealthy, oligarchical class had been quite powerful, but with the ascension of Figueres and the National Liberation party, the government moved into the hands of a growing middle class.[18] Mitchell Seligson has argued that, despite its "bourgeois and anticommunist" nature, the 1948 revolution strongly encouraged the United Fruit Company to submit to further reforms.[19] The Liberation party has not won every election since 1948, however, and the middle class is not as firmly in control as either the government or Arias would have us believe. Powerful conservative elements still exist within the Costa Rican ruling class. Nevertheless, the ideology and political priorities of the Liberation party have had a greater impact upon the political scene since 1948 than have those of any other political party. Although politicians in Costa Rica come almost exclusively from among the wealthy, the state still has something of a middle-class character. The National Liberation party attempts to strike a balance and reflect middle-class values rather than those of either the wealthy oligarchy or the lower classes.[20]

The state is thus neither an unthinking tool of the wealthy nor an unswerving champion of the lower classes, including the peasants. When middle-class and peasant interests clash, for example over basic food prices, the state is not likely to support the peasantry. The operation of the CNP exemplifies state bias toward the middle class at the expense of the peasants. When freezing basic food prices means an inadequate return to peasant producers, the CNP would rather squeeze the peasants further than raise prices for the middle class. Chapter 5 illustrates the extent to which the CNP has injured peasant producers in Limón province. Peasant political action in El Hogar and La Lucha originated as a form of defense against the CNP. Statistics of upward social mobility provide further evidence of the state's bias toward the middle class. Such movement is available to the middle classes, but it is much more difficult for the lower class.[21]

Within the Liberation party, the loyalties of some members go upward and the sympathies of others go downward. In trying to walk a line between the wealthy and the poor, the party sometimes takes on a schizophrenic appearance. Because the Liberation party has had such a powerful impact on the modern Costa Rican state, the government itself also periodically appears Janus-faced. This is particularly true when the Liberation party is not in power, but the institutions it established continue to function. The peasants are fully aware of this contradiction within the state. As political actors, they attempt to address those elements of the government that are more likely to be sympathetic. Sometimes they succeed, and sometimes they are forced to confront the more conservative side of the state.

Despite difficult economic circumstances, so far the peasants have managed to find some space within which to operate. When one course of action has been closed off, they have usually invented an alternative response to events. In the Central Valley, many small and medium landholders have kept their land and continue to participate in the national export economy. The struggle over land in Limón is still volatile and unresolved. The peasantry face formidable odds against powerful banana companies and elite private landowners. Some actors are allied to the conservative elements of the state. Yet in the past, some of the peasants have managed to obtain subsistence land through the use of precarismo.[22] This tactic continues to offer the peasants a potential alternative to landlessness.

History, the political tradition, the contradictory nature of the state, and the values held by some members of the government have worked to provide the peasantry with alternatives. These alternatives are crucial to the political action studied in this book. Costa Rica's rural majority is vulnerable to economic crisis, natural disasters, and changes in government policy. The state has already shown that it has priorities other than the peasantry. Yet for the present, the political and social traditions of Costa Rica afford the peasants a degree of protection.

Alajuela

As the previous section suggests, political and social experiences have not been identical in all provinces of Costa Rica. The state defines the general parameters for political action by both itself and the peasants, yet regional variance in the behavior of the state specifies the outside limits of those parameters. The behavior of the state within a given province reflects the nature and strength of the large financial interests invested in that province. It may also reflect one or another of the competing priorities within the state. Alajuela and Limón exemplify these variations.

Costa Rica is divided into seven provinces. The province of Alajuela, north of San José, reaches from the Central Valley to the Nicaraguan border. The first Costa Rican village in this study, San Luis (Chapter 4), is in southern Alajuela. The political and developmental history of this province has spared these villagers the most extreme economic hardship, and their political attitudes are testimony to their relatively favored position. Alajuela exemplifies a pattern of rural development based on smallholdings, although this has recently changed. There are a few large plantations, but most landholdings are medium or small farms. In recent years, population growth has outstripped land availability and created landlessness. About 30 to 40 percent of the provincial population has no land, but neither large plantations nor landlessness predominates. As demographic pressure on the land has increased, some of the landless have migrated to less populated provinces. Peasant families who own more land than they can work may hire one or two permanent laborers. The landless make ends meet with employment on medium and large farms in the area and by relying heavily on the harvest when labor is still somewhat scarce. Many of the landless are unemployed for a small part of the year.[23]

From colonial times, the Central Valley has been the nation's demographic and cultural center. It has historically received more public investment than have other regions. Schools, health facilities, and roads are better than elsewhere in Costa Rica. The relative equity of land tenure, the availability of employment for the landless, and the exit option combine with the superior level of public services in Alajuela to produce a rural life style enviable by Central American standards. The social reforms enacted prior to and after 1948 and, more recently, the activity of the local peasant union, UPANacional, have provided some protection for rural life in the province. Many of the landless prefer the comfortable life style of the Central Valley to landownership in a more remote area of Costa Rica. They recognize that they are fortunate, even by Costa Rican standards.

Limón

Two of the Costa Rican villages studied in this book, El Hogar and La Lucha (Chapter 5), are located in Limón. These communities have been affected by the troubled and poverty-stricken history of this province. Limón has produced great wealth but benefited little from return investment, particularly in its experience with the banana industry. Just as it has long been on an unequal footing with the rest of Costa Rica, there is more inequality in Limón than in many other provinces of the country. Despite the large number of peasants living in Limón, land ownership is more concentrated than in many other parts of Costa Rica, and large expanses of land belong to the banana companies or elites from the capital city of San José. The local peasantry, who believe in the basic right to land, see land concentration as grievous, especially as many of the large plantations are used for cattle or left lying fallow and unfarmed. This contrasts sharply with the situation in Alajuela, where all land is used and landlessness stems at least in part from surplus population. From the perspective of the rural poor, poverty is unacceptable when it is avoidable, and the poor perceive unused land tracts as an unnecessary cause of peasant poverty in Limón. Limón also suffers from underinvestment in public services. Educational and medical services are notoriously poor; highways are inadequate; and more homes lack electricity or running water here than in most other parts of Costa Rica.

Limón peasants grow rice, corn, and beans and sell them at artificially low prices on the domestic market. Living standards are much poorer in Limón than in Alajuela. Higher levels of landlessness leave a greater percentage of the population unable to support itself, and even landed peasants, whose income is much lower than in Alajuela, often cannot afford to hire extra workers. Although poverty in Limón cannot compare with that in Nicaragua or elsewhere in Central America, the Limón peasants are very poor by Costa Rican standards.

Despite this poverty, Limón is no longer isolated from the rest of the country, as it was in the nineteenth century when Minor Keith arrived. Two highways, as well as the railroad Keith laid, connect Limón with San José and other major cities. The superhighway, finished in 1987, cuts by two-thirds the time of the trip from San José to northern Limón province. Telephone lines reach many parts of the province, as do radio and television waves. A bus trip to the capital city takes between one and three hours. Limón residents travel back and forth frequently.

Thorough integration into the national scene allows Limón residents to know what life and politics are like beyond the local area. They are well aware of how their living standard compares with that in the Central Valley and they follow political events both within and beyond the province. They are familiar with rural history in Limón and have absorbed stories of the precarista struggle and the 1934 strike. The peasants know basically how the state behaved toward the strike and with the precaristas. Thus the Limón peasants have some familiarity with democratic political traditions in Costa Rica and know more or less what kinds of political action hold some possibility of success. They know that public opinion places some restraints on the behavior of the democratic state. As Costa Rican citizens they have also grown to expect something from the state. They know from national history and campaign rhetoric that the government feels some obligation to all citizens and will invest some of its resources in social development. This awareness of the social democratic tradition helps determine peasant attitudes toward the government and possible political action.

Nicaragua: Repression and Resistance

In contrast to the colonial and developmental history of Costa Rica, Nicaragua's development more closely resembles the pattern found in the northern part of Central America. Closer to the colonial seat of power in Guatemala City, Nicaragua was fully integrated into colonial Central America. It benefited from colonial trade and became a wealthy colony, but it also experienced the full impact of Spanish political and military strength. Being accessible from Guatemala City, Nicaragua offered great wealth in the form of mines and Indians, who provided labor and a taxable population base. Most of what the mines and plantations produced, however, was exported back to Spain. This extraction pattern sowed the seeds of a particular political tradition. It also deprived Nicaragua of a colonizing elite who would consider the land a home and work for its constructive development. Instead, Nicaragua represented a source of wealth for use elsewhere. We have seen something of this pattern in Limón, Costa Rica, but the practice was more widespread in Nicaragua and much more extreme. Prior to the arrival of the Spaniards, the Nicaraguan Indians practiced subsistence agriculture in small, self-sufficient groups. They resisted Spanish colonization, and the Spaniards sometimes became violent in an effort to subjugate the Indians. Unlike Costa Rican settlers, in Nicaragua the Spanish could resort to military strength to coerce cooperation, labor, tribute, and tax payments. At the same time coercion inspired organized Indian resistance.

The Spanish settlers of Nicaragua thus introduced a political tradition in the new colony that emphasized self-interest and greed. Nicaragua was a source of wealth rather than a homeland to be nurtured and developed. The political tradition also included coercion. The first Spanish governor of Nicaragua, Pedro Arias Davila, who took office in 1527, quickly acquired a reputation for repression.[24] Repression evoked resistance, and resistance evoked repression rather than compromise. Differences of opinion were silenced rather than tolerated. The Spanish demonstrated no understanding of the needs or plight of the Indians, viewing them instead as a source of wealth. If Spanish demands placed an intolerable burden on the indigenous population, this was of little interest to the colonizers. Indian labor was plentiful, so if many died, others could replace them.

In response to the Spanish settlers, the Indian inhabitants of Nicaragua developed their own political tradition. It was one of resistance, armed or otherwise, to the Spanish form of rule. Many avoided Spanish demands by the non-violent tactics of evasion and flight, but others were willing to confront the colonizers' force. The history of colonization records numerous confrontations between the Spanish and the Indians. The colonizers confronted Indian uprisings in 1617, 1647, 1651, and 1654.[25] The Indian communities on the east coast were particularly rebellious, generating major uprisings in Subtiava in 1681 and in León in 1725.[26] Records from the early 1800s show continued Indian resistance to the Spanish colonizers. In December of 1811 the Indians of León petitioned the colonial authorities to decrease the tributes and to abolish slavery. These same Indians rebelled later that same month when the petition was ignored. Uprisings also took place in Masaya in December 1811 and January 1812, and in Granada in 1811 and again in 1812. The Indians of Rivas rebelled in 1811 against slavery, forced labor, and colonial tributes.[27] Although Costa Rica had never established slavery, Nicaraguan elites stubbornly continued the practice despite widespread, violent opposition. Violent resistance was hardly a daily event, but it occurred frequently enough to become part of the political tradition. The subordinated classes attempted to broaden the range of available political tactics, but the petition utilized in León proved ineffective and was closely followed by violence. Elsewhere in colonial Nicaragua, there are more records of rebellion than of petitions. The historical record does not reveal whether slaves and forced laborers frequently attempted to negotiate for improvements, but we can surmise from the number of rebellions that conditions failed to improve.

The wealthy, dominant position of the Spanish and the exploited, subordinate position of the Indians established sharp class lines between the rulers and the ruled. Nicaragua never acquired Costa Rica's ethnic homogeneity, and the obvious racial differences made repression, resistance, and intolerance easier for the rulers to justify. Compromise seemed unnecessary and irrelevant for the group that held most of the legal, political, and military power. After achieving independence in 1838, Nicaragua retained many Spanish political traditions: the use of government for self-interest and personal wealth, a proclivity toward violence, and exploitation of the cultivating classes. The Nicaraguan elite divided into two rival factions: the Conservative and Liberal parties. Both groups were intolerant, especially of each other, and unwilling to compromise. Just as the Spanish had ignored Indian needs, the elite factions were equally unsympathetic toward the Indians and toward each other. Each party strove to gain and hold power and viewed state power as a tool for self-aggrandizement rather than as an office to be used for national development. Once in power, the incumbent party would remain until forced out, and neither side hesitated to search abroad for reinforcements or support. Transfers of power usually happened through military force. Typically, the incoming party staged an "election" to legitimize its move into office. Election results, however, were decided beforehand, and usually only the wealthiest strata of the population could vote at all. Whereas Costa Rica slowly but surely developed an independent state with a national agenda, politics in Nicaragua resembled a free-for-all in which aggressive military maneuvers were the most promising path to power.

The result was a weak and divided state, pulled in opposite directions as it changed hands between the parties and unable to remain independent from narrow economic interests. Instead of defending the nation from manipulation by foreign interests, internal actors often invited support from abroad, establishing a pattern of frequent foreign intervention in Nicaragua. The United States became extensively involved in Nicaragua's internal affairs. First, United States citizens such as William Walker and later the United States government intervened.[28] The precedent of foreign intervention became so firmly established that the Nicaraguan state was unable to protect the nation from outside—particularly U.S.—involvement and manipulation even when it wanted to.

The United States continued to intervene politically and militarily in Nicaragua until 1933. An armed confrontation between the Liberals and Conservatives brought another dictator, José Maria Moncada, to power, supported by the U.S. Marines. One independent general in the Moncada army, Augusto César Sandino, saw the war as a struggle for national liberation rather than as a quarrel between political parties. He refused to accept a peace treaty as long as the U.S. Marines remained in Nicaragua. He and his peasant army launched a guerrilla war against the Marines, which eventually succeeded in 1933.

Sandino's adventure was the first instance of a widespread peasant movement in Nicaragua. Unlike other national leaders, Sandino had been raised in peasant surroundings in northern Nicaragua and was aware of the peasants' plight. He was the first national leader to focus on the needs of the peasantry and to enact local measures to alleviate their problems. In the mountainous areas he controlled, Sandino attempted to carry out his political program by returning land to the peasants in the form of cooperatives. Sandino's popularity and the size of his peasant following are testimony to the discontent the

peasants felt with the status quo and their gratitude for his constructive attention. His program of cooperatives responded to their yearning for land. Unfortunately, Sandino's hour of triumph was short-lived.

Tradition Strengthened: Dictatorship and Repression

As the United States withdrew in 1933, it established the National Guard under
the direction of Anastasio Somoza García. The establishment of the Guard
meant that the United States had a strong military force favorable to its interests in Nicaragua without having to maintain a military presence in the country. The United States left an unstable government, however, because military
strength still determined political power in Nicaragua, and the president, Juan
Sacasa, did not control the National Guard. Within months after the Marines
departed, Somoza García had maneuvered his way into the presidency, using
the Guard to discourage any opposition. Somoza perceived Sandino as a
threat and, after signing a disarmament pact with him, had him assassinated.
Thus began the dictatorship of the Somoza dynasty, which included Somoza
García and his two sons, Luis Somoza Debayle and Anastasio Somoza Debayle. The Sandino affair was an important learning experience for the nation's peasantry. Sandino's limited reform illustrated that something could be
gained through organized violence, and his assassination demonstrated that
elite promises such as the disarmament pact were unreliable.

From 1933 to 1979, the Somozas proved to be faithful followers of political
custom, except that they were more ruthless, more extreme, and more greedy
than their predecessors. Somoza García refused to share or relinquish power
and was intolerant of dissenting opinions. Like earlier presidents, he used far-
cical elections to legitimize his regime and state power to enhance the family
fortune. By 1945, Somoza García was estimated to be worth between ten and
sixty million dollars.[29] Each of the three Somozas managed national legislation and the financial system to obtain an increasingly monopolistic hold on
the industrial and financial operations of the country. Anastasio Somoza Debayle is famous for his comment, "Nicaragua is my farm."[30] Although resentment grew even among Nicaragua's urban middle class, the Somoza family's
exclusive control over the military discouraged resistance. When the dictatorship was overthrown in 1979, U.S. sources estimated Anastasio Somoza Debayle to be worth $900 million.[31]

During Anastasio Somoza Debayle's reign, Nicaraguan agro-industry expanded profitably. Controlled by a few landowning elites, it revolved around
coffee, cotton, and cattle. Wealth permitted elites to expand across much of
the richest farmland, crushing the peasant population in the process. This
wealthy sector, broadly termed "Somocistas" by the peasantry because of its
apparent alliance with the Somoza family, sought to steadily increase the
farmland at its disposal for export cropping. The Nicaraguan peasantry became increasingly landless and poverty-stricken, but the expansion of agrarian industry continued. By the time Somoza Debayle's political and economic

system had solidified, the nation's peasants had learned a great deal about politics in Nicaragua. They had learned that the state was an enemy and a tool of the wealthy; state military power consistently supported the upper classes against the peasantry; the wealthy viewed the peasants only as a productive tool and had no interest in their survival needs.

A realistic understanding of how the state and the elites viewed them did not result in acquiescence by members of the peasant class. Instead, peasants periodically appealed to government authorities for redress of grievances— evidence that they felt the state *should* feel some responsibility for them even if it did not. Their experience with petitions illustrated the low utility of this political tactic. But petitions were a nonconfrontational, low-risk form of political action that at least expressed grievances and were less likely to be repressed than other tactics. The case studies show that the peasants did not forget this possible, albeit limited, tactic. In contrast to petitions, organized violence had periodically proven useful. The peasant classes had used this tactic throughout Nicaraguan history. Moreover, as a form of political action, it was used constantly by the elites and the state itself. Nevertheless, although the Nicaraguan tradition of violence was widespread and long-standing, it remained risky and unattractive to peasants, because it could not guarantee success and frequently elicited heightened levels of repression, making the situation even worse.

The political portfolio available to peasant actors reflected the political stage the state had set up until that time. It was a very small stage in Nicaragua: most forms of popular political action were forbidden. Within the political atmosphere established by the regime, peasants sought to survive and to defend their interests. Their options were few: flight had become a less and less viable alternative, as it could no longer guarantee survival; submission was another temporary and unsatisfactory strategy that might gain a little space or time; petitions and protest were illegal and unproductive, although they might periodically be worth a try; and voting was meaningless. Yet survival was becoming increasingly difficult. The need for defensive political action was growing steadily. If the peasants were to survive as a class, eventually something would have to be done.

Resistance Organizes

By the 1950s, the Somoza regime had created opposition among the upper and middle classes as well as among the peasantry. Large parts of the traditional Liberal or Conservative parties were excluded from politics and wealth and resented the Somoza family's tight control of the national economy. Open opposition to the dictatorship began as early as 1956, and members of the elite classes participated in it. In September, a young poet, Rigoberto López Pérez, assassinated the first of the three Somoza dictators, Somoza García, whereupon his son, Luis Somoza Debayle, became president of Nicaragua.[32] In 1961, three university students, Carlos Fonseca, Tomas Borge, and Silvio Mayorga, founded the Sandinista National Liberation Front (Frente Sandinista de Liberacion Nacional: FSLN). The FSLN was strongly influenced by the Sandino tradition of nationalism, anti-imperialism, and the use of a peasant army for guerrilla warfare. It established its original stronghold in the northeastern mountains of Nicaragua, where Sandino and his "Crazy Little Army"[33] had made their stand against the U.S. Marines. Far from Managua and any urban center, the nascent FSLN was forced to rely on the local peasantry for support and sustenance. The task of winning the peasantry was not an easy one, given the suspicion which had developed among them over years of poverty and oppression. However, the local memory of Sandino's struggle was still alive in 1961, and the FSLN was able to build a peasant base in northeastern Nicaragua.

Elsewhere in the country, peasant and middle class opposition to the dictatorship grew, independent of the FSLN. Luis Somoza Debayle was still in power before the elections of 1967. His younger brother, Anastasio, director of the National Guard, announced his intention to run for the presidency. Although the Liberal party did not officially embrace Anastasio Somoza, the younger Somoza claimed to belong to it. Thus some of the hopes of the rural population lay with the Conservative party. The departments of Boaco and Masaya were Conservative strongholds. For the elections, the Conservatives supported Fernando Agüero. Ultimately, however, Agüero struck a deal with Anastasio Somoza. Anastasio Somoza took over the presidency from his brother, who died a few months later. The experience diminished peasant loyalty to the Conservative party and dispelled peasant illusions that the regime could be removed by traditional or democratic means.[34] This third and last Somoza ruled Nicaragua from 1967 until he was overthrown in 1979.

The blow to the Conservatives in January 1967 was followed by a major FSLN confrontation with the National Guard in the mountainous area of Pancasán, east of the northern city of Matagalpa. By the end of 1967, the Conservatives had lost credibility as an alternative to the dictatorship, whereas the FSLN had gained visibility and strength as a nontraditional source of opposition.

Between 1967 and 1979, Anastasio Somoza and other agrarian elites acquired ever greater quantities of land. They used numerous methods for depriving the peasants of their land, and the peasant condition deteriorated still further. Sometimes the National Guard physically expelled peasants from village land. Another method was to squeeze them economically until they needed to borrow money to survive. Under pressure from the Somocistas, banks became increasingly reluctant to lend to peasant farmers, who were then forced to borrow from the Somocistas themselves. Such loans carried interest rates of between 50 and 300 percent and required the use of the peasant's family land as collateral. Usually peasants were unable to repay such loans and lost their land to the lenders. Slowly, over several generations, the wealthy elites gained control of most of Nicaragua's farmland, and the Nicaraguan peasantry became a landless class.

The monopoly of landownership and the increasing scarcity of rental land were part of an agrarian arrangement that served two purposes. First, it gave the export sector larger expanses of land for lucrative crops. Second, it deprived the peasantry of its livelihood and economic autonomy, forcing it to turn toward agrarian labor to stay alive. The elites wanted more land for more profit and needed a large labor supply during the three-month harvest season. Peasants migrated long distances to the coffee and cotton plantations. The three months of plantation labor eventually became the only source of income for most of the peasantry, but it did not support a family for the calendar year. The arrangement left the peasants unemployed for at least seven months each year.[35]

The rural experience of Nicaragua's peasantry contrasts sharply with that of Costa Rican peasants. Whereas the latter might lose an appeal to the state for support, such an appeal was far more likely to be taken seriously. The Nicaraguan peasants, on the other hand, correctly perceived that the state was part of the agro-export machinery that was destroying them.

Masaya

The experience of the Masaya region exemplifies the Nicaraguan national pattern of land concentration in the hands of elites, peasant impoverishment, and repression described above. The villages of Quebrada Honda and Pikin Guerrero (Chapters 6 and 7) show how this pattern affects people's lives, as the extreme suffering in both communities drove people into revolution. One of sixteen departments, Masaya is geographically central and agriculturally fertile for both cash and staple crops. These attributes proved disastrous for the local peasantry, however, as the value of this land attracted elites who grew cotton. Land concentration was worse in Masaya than in many other parts of the country. The experience of its peasantry was, if anything, even more harsh than the typical national pattern. The central location of the department involved the peasantry more closely in the national economic system, both in borrowing from money lenders and in patterns of labor migration. Centrality also afforded them a thorough understanding of the causes of their situation. They understood how their own poverty and suffering related to the wealth of their neighbors and could easily compare their living standard with that outside the village.

The scarcity of land and work in Masaya drove the peasants into a migratory pattern during the harvest season. Life on the plantations during these months was a miserable and radicalizing experience. As the revolutionary movement gained momentum, Masaya became a center of sympathy for the cause. The presence of a revolutionary center in the city of Masaya also brought increased opportunities and risks. The political sympathies of the city attracted the ire of the National Guard, who repressed the city and surrounding rural areas with increasing vigor. Repression often increased village sympathy for the FSLN, but increased revolutionary involvement brought on further repression and so on in an upward spiral of revolutionary activism and repression.[36]

Boaco

Pedregal (Chapter 3), in the central province of Boaco, provides a sharp contrast to the villages of Masaya. Its story is one of political attitudes and actions shaped by a context of tranquillity. Eighty kilometers east of Managua, Boaco is isolated from it and was of little importance for the agro-export economy. Eastern Nicaragua contains only 10 percent of the total national population and, prior to 1979, was only minimally integrated into the political and economic life of the country. Political and economic insignificance and relative isolation from the mainstream of national life derive in large part from the poor soil in Boaco. Vegetation and rainfall are sparse and, although peasants could scratch a meager living from the soil, the land in this region was most profitably used for ranching. The soil was useless for agro-export crops such as coffee and cotton and was not even as profitable for cattle ranching as the southern department of Rivas.

In Masaya, centrality and fertile land only brought calamity to the peasant population. By a similarly strange logic, isolation and poor soil proved to be blessings in disguise for Boaco. The Somocista elites had little interest in Boaco, so peasant villages were mostly left to use their own land resources as best they could. Many controlled their own land and were able to eke a living from it. Land and an adequate subsistence economy made usurious loans and migration in search of wage labor unnecessary. A further advantage to the region was its sparse habitation. Demographic pressure was as mild in Boaco as it was heavy in Masaya, and peasants who had been forced off their land in other parts of Nicaragua were unlikely to go to Boaco. The land barely supported the current population, and peasant common sense kept it from being pushed beyond its capacity.

Detachment from the agrarian elites also entailed separation from the political traditions of the state and the country. These villagers had little knowledge, positive or negative, of the regime. They were not exposed to state repression and avarice and had no experience of violence as a political tactic. They received nothing and expected nothing from the government. As long as the regime left them in peace, as it had always done, they saw no reason to pressure or attack the government. Just as the region was isolated from state actions under the Somozas, it was also relatively untouched by the revolution. The eastern region around Boaco was militarily, politically, and ideologically the weakest FSLN front.[37] Guerrilla presence was low, and the population was uninterested in and even unsympathetic toward the revolutionary struggle. These two factors reinforced each other, since minimal involvement by the

FSLN kept large segments of the local populace ignorant about the struggle. Low guerrilla presence in the area also restricted revolutionary opportunity for the few local sympathizers.

The Boaco region developed a political subculture that countered the national norm. Although poverty was endemic, the counterculture limited its destructiveness. In contrast with the political atmosphere elsewhere, tension was low and conflict absent. Elite attitudes toward the rural population were less ruthless than in other parts of the country. In stark contrast with the atmosphere elsewhere, local government demonstrated some understanding of peasant needs, providing a few services to the population, including the peasants. The Boaco hospital treated indigent villagers for free or for very low fees, a practice unknown in the rest of the country. The pacific atmosphere touched even the local National Guard units, who behaved less violently toward the population than elsewhere. Though still an unfriendly police force, the Guard was not as unrestrained and repressive as it had become in other parts of Nicaragua. Local tranquillity affected, and benefited from, the Guard's moderate behavior. Just as revolutionary activism and Guard repression had reinforced each other in Masaya, so isolated calm and a more subdued police corps sustained each other in Boaco. Some mutual decency and respect for human life were still evident in Boaco even after they had entirely disappeared between peasants and Guards from the rest of Nicaragua.

3 ▫ ECOLOGICAL HARMONY AND QUIESCENCE
Pedregal, Boaco, Nicaragua

The primary goal of peasants everywhere is survival. Yet the requirements of survival differ dramatically from one community to the next. These distinct settings demand different strategies from peasants in different places even as they all engage in the common struggle for survival. In prerevolutionary Nicaragua political activism and political violence had become norms in many areas of the country. Despite such a setting, most villagers in this first case deliberately chose quiescence as the strategy most likely to ensure survival in a dangerous world. This was true even when some forms of political activism in Pedregal were relatively safe from repression, and a minority of villagers actually became activists. Why did most of these villagers choose quiescence? How did their sense of interdependence with their world cause them to remain withdrawn into political inaction, even as social revolution raged throughout their country?

Neither individual calculations of maximized self-interest nor fear of repression explains the choice of quiescence by most villagers in Pedregal. That decision was a reflection of the ecological perspective at work in the village. These peasants perceived their interdependence with society. That perception helped them understand that their interaction with the outside world was limited and would increase with political activism. They also saw that the wider society was self-destructing, and they estimated that life in Pedregal was relatively tranquil compared with life in the rest of Nicaragua. They surmised that if they could *limit* their interaction with the outside world they would also restrict their interdependence with it and thus improve their individual and collective chances for survival. Their sense of justice was fulfilled by the extent of ecological interdependence in the village. They did not want life in the community to change.

By explaining these peasants' choice of quiescence with the theory of political ecology, we can incorporate both the peasants' determination to survive and their understanding of interdependence. We can also see the full extent of flexibility that an ecological perspective allows peasant actors. Where action is unnecessary or unwise, no action is taken. The political ecology perspective is a more comprehensive and multidimensional explanation for quiescence than any unidimensional approach. The rational actor model, for example, explains individual quiescence as being a result of free-ridership—personal calculations that the rewards of action can be gotten without political participation. Rational consideration of political action precludes it when incentives are inadequate or the risks too great. A moral economy approach, on the other hand, argues that quiescence results only when there are no threats to subsistence or when repression makes action suicidal. Each of these explanations has some relevance to the story of political quiescence in Pedregal, but neither is sufficient to fully understand individual and community decisions not to participate in the Nicaraguan revolution. In particular, the villagers didn't decide to be free-riders, and fear of political repression was not critical in the political choices.

Any comprehensive theory of peasant political action must be able to explain quiescence as well as action. Pedregal, as a nonparticipant in the national revolution, offers an ideal opportunity to study quiescence and a chance to understand this political strategy as a function of the ecological perspective. In this chapter I will examine the political story of this village between 1970 and the Sandinista victory in 1979. What economic, political, and social factors could account for quiescence at the heart of a social revolution? What political attitudes might such villagers display? Did villagers substitute other kinds of political activity for involvement in the revolution? These were the questions that drew me to Pedregal when most researchers primarily studied the revolution.

It is logical to begin the study of peasant politics with Pedregal for two reasons. First, it lies at the left of the political action spectrum and exemplifies quiescence. Second, unique among the villages in this study, it illustrates the peasant ecological community described so far only in general terms. Pedregal is an interdependent community constructed according to peasant preferences. The experience of the village also illustrates the political implications of a situation in which the members of an ecological community are more or less satisfied with their life styles. The political ecology of Pedregal made voluntary quiescence the most logical choice of political action for most villagers, but when the political ecology of a minority of villagers was subtly altered—their perceptions of the boundary of community extended—their political ecology resulted in nonviolent political action.

Community Context

Pedregal is located in the hills of the isolated department of Boaco, ninety miles east of Managua on the eastern side of Lake Nicaragua. The land in and around Pedregal is rocky and dry. Wealthy Nicaraguans who could choose to own land anywhere would never purchase land in the region. Yet peasants who moved to the area after losing their land elsewhere have learned to survive despite the poor soil quality. Given a sufficiently large land plot, families could subsist on staple crops. The most common staple was a coarse, large-grain wheat that was ground into flour for thick tortillas and which also served as livestock feed. The sparse vegetation made the area suitable for grazing stock, and most families owned a few sheep or cattle as well as pigs and chickens. Villagers also raised beans and a few dairy cows.

Isolation, independence, and ecological harmony rather than national integration characterized the village experience and helped determine political choices and attitudes under the Somoza regime. The trail into Pedregal was itself a political factor in the peasant experience and epitomized village isolation from mainstream politics and society in Nicaragua. The village lay eight rough, rocky kilometers (4.8 miles) up into the hills from the main paved highway to the interior city of Rama, which is situated deep in the jungle of eastern Nicaragua. Travelers heading to the Atlantic coast along that highway picked up the Escondido River where the highway ends in Rama and traveled by water to the Atlantic Ocean. The approach to Pedregal was nothing but a narrow mule trail studded with huge boulders. In the dry season the trail was barely passable by four-wheel-drive jeep or on foot, horse, or mule. By foot the trek took two hours. The trail passed through streams or rivers eight times. There are no bridges, and during the rainy season, the trail, which at some points joins the riverbed, becomes an impassable torrent of mud and water. At the height of a tropical rainstorm, swift waters could rise to chest level on a man, making pedestrian travel dangerous and jeep travel impossible. A surefooted horse or mule could still manage the trip early in the rainy season, but at the height of the rains no one traveled into or out of Pedregal. Even in the village center travel was difficult, as parts of the community nestled against steep mountainsides or rested on a cliff high above the village entrance.

The low provision of public services in Pedregal further illustrated the village's isolation from the national center of social and economic life. In the 1970s, Pedregal had no electricity or running water. Most villagers hauled water from streams. The nearest public telephone required a six hour, round-trip, walk into Teustepe. No public transport reached Pedregal, although one could flag down a bus on reaching the main highway. Until the schoolhouse was built after 1979, classes were held in private homes. Limited schooling, grades one through four, was sometimes available, although poverty and the need to work seriously limited attendance even when classes were held. People over age fifty explained, "I didn't go to school because there wasn't one." Some medical care was available during the Somoza era at little or no cost in the small town of Teustepe, eight kilometers distant, or the city of Boaco, twenty-seven kilometers from the village. Even radio usage was sporadic because both radios and the batteries to operate them used up scarce currency.

In 1986 the village of Pedregal was home to over one hundred peasant fam-

Table 3.1. Pedregal: Surplus/Deficit of Community Land Ownership (in manzanas)

Land needed to support average peasant family	33.1
Average village land ownership	41.6
Average surplus	8.5

ilies. I interviewed thirty household heads, twenty-two men and eight women. The land owned by village families supported all the villagers. Landed peasants (47 percent) lived off their own land; the landless worked for them as agrarian laborers and tilled land lent to them by the village landed. The village operated at a subsistence level with respect to basic grains, vegetables, and milk. Each family grew enough on private or borrowed land for its own consumption and supplemented the income from farming with wages.

Different aspects of Pedregal's isolated community context reinforced each other. Geographical seclusion reinforced the need for subsistence agriculture and limited the influence of more individualistic, market-oriented patterns prevalent elsewhere in Nicaragua. Location also encouraged particular production patterns. Trips to the market were feasible only every four to six weeks during the dry season so villagers had to be quite self-sufficient and able to make or grow most of what they needed. Limited wage-employment opportunities encouraged the community system to support all villagers on resources locally available.

The land in and around Pedregal is of such poor quality that, historically, it had attracted little or no attention. Over time, deforestation and erosion had rendered the soil even less productive. Subsistence plots needed to be much larger here than in other parts of Nicaragua. Between 1970 and 1979, the average land plot among respondents was 41.6 manzanas.[1] Respondents estimated that an average of 33.1 manzanas was necessary to support a family.[2] (See Table 3.1) Community mutuality assured that surplus land would be used by the landless.

Questions about the quality of life in the thirty years prior to 1979 revealed the protected nature of village existence. In describing life in past decades one respondent answered, "We lived more or less well . . . We were never hungry." Others said, "We never went hungry because the land yielded everything"; "Some years were bad, without rain, but generally life was not bad." Although some explained that twenty or thirty years ago they and their families had been poor, many respondents recalled that soil fertility had been higher in past decades. To the extent that a decrease in living standards occurred between approximately 1940 and 1979, peasants thought that the change was primarily due to deterioration in the land itself, and the decrease was not perceived to be sufficiently severe to threaten subsistence. "Life was better then [ten to fifteen years ago]; it was easier to produce. Fifteen years ago it rained more. Now it rains less. They say it's because of a lack of trees."

Answers to questions about the experience of hunger and childhood diseases as well as socioeconomic indicators support the peasants' testimony that poverty was endemic but not desperate. Meager family and village resources precluded any luxury but did not jeopardize life itself. As children, most respondents had worked hard and had little, but survival was never in doubt. Although 53 percent of respondents recalled having gone hungry at some point in their lives, most still stressed that food shortages had been infrequent and due to natural causes rather than to a lack of land or work. "There were shortages during the summer [the Nicaraguan dry season] for lack of rain, but we never went hungry." In some respects life even improved between 1930 and 1979, despite the decline in the soil quality. Whereas 70 percent of respondents had lost siblings to childhood diseases, only 40 percent had lost children. Among all respondents, 17 percent had owned a television (battery-powered) and 77 percent a radio prior to 1979. Only one village resident had ever owned an automobile.

The low level of education in the village indicates the extent to which the central government neglected Pedregal. In prerevolutionary times, thirteen respondents, or 43 percent, had never attended school at all. Even those who had completed the education available in the village had only four years of primary education. Illiteracy was highest among older villagers. Among all respondents, the average level of education was only 1.8 years.

In contrast to most Nicaraguan peasants, however, villagers in Pedregal usually had access to affordable medical care, thanks to the exceptional political atmosphere of the entire Boaco region and the support of other villagers. Fifty-seven percent of respondents had visited a hospital in Boaco prior to 1979, and 53 percent had visited a private physician. The cost of medical care varied somewhat with the ability to pay, as reflected in the following responses:

When you got sick you went to the hospital. We always had that.

When you had any money you went to the hospital and when you didn't have any money, you went to the hospital anyway to see if they would give you [medicine] for free.

When you got sick you went to a doctor in Teustepe or Boaco, where they gave you the medicine for free, or at least sometimes it was free.

Only three respondents had felt they could not visit a physician or hospital and relied solely upon herbal medicines and home remedies within the village.

Ecological Interdependence

The peasants' ecological perspective in Pedregal shaped their perceptions of events around them and determined their decisions about political action. Those decisions reveal an awareness of the need for interdependence and an assumption that the protective ecological system would perform smoothly. The political story in Pedregal shows how this awareness and assumption manifested themselves and how they shaped political action. In Pedregal, peasant expectations about the ecological system were largely fulfilled. This was true even in the late 1970s, when repression and revolution raged elsewhere in Nicaragua, because the isolation of Pedregal preserved the integrity of the peasants' ecological system, which operated according to peasant expectations of interdependence and mutual support. Community members and even individuals from the region sustained interdependence and supportive mutuality in a way that satisfied the peasant sense of systemic, ecological coherence. For most villagers, this satisfaction eliminated any motivation for protest or participation in the revolution. We can see interdependence at work in the villagers' use of land, their medical support system, and their understanding of the natural environment. The peasants also had an effective method of responding to individuals who threatened their ecological system.

There were a few exceptions to this general rule of satisfaction and quiescence. A handful of villagers engaged in protest action against the Somoza regime. The individual experience of these villagers led them to perceive a violation in the proper functioning of the ecological system. Yet even here, their choice of action reflected their perception of the need for interdependence and their desire to preserve it.

Land Management Patterns

Prior to 1979, poverty in Pedregal had always been endemic. Each year subsistence needs remained within income only by the slimmest of margins. The peasants lived constantly aware of the proximity of catastrophe: any individual crisis (a parent's broken leg; the death of a horse, mule, or the only dairy cow; a child's expensive illness) could easily push a peasant family below the subsistence minimum and threaten survival. Fortunes could shift as suddenly as the winds of the rainy season. The thin measure of economic security was ever vulnerable to the whims of chance.

This precarious existence was unprotected by immediate extra-village assistance, even in a department that was not openly hostile to the peasantry. Government authority almost never made an appearance in Pedregal and, given the nature of the regime, was better absent. Medical aid lay hours distant, and the sick could only get help by going to it. The group insurance of a mutually supportive ecological system offered the only available protection against disaster. Villagers made the supportive system as robust and inclusive as possible because they knew that their own survival might eventually depend on the community.

Village relations thus benefited from a healthy reciprocity system which functioned in Pedregal in the same way that it functioned among the peasants in Southeast Asia that James Scott studied. However, the basis for its functioning was neither the sum of individual calculations, as he implies in *Weapons of the Weak*,[3] nor solely the result of enforced, long standing moral norms, as he asserts in *The Moral Economy of the Peasant*.[4] The community system in Pedregal depended on both of these and much more. It relied on a commitment to an ecological system that included individuals, the village as a whole, and the natural system that surrounded and sustained the community.

The most important evidence of reciprocity and mutual sustenance between community and individual was found in peasant land management practices. Although all land was privately owned and more than 50 percent of villagers were landless, landlessness did not cause disproportionate poverty. Most members of the community followed an unspoken rule that village land, which was legally the private property of individuals, existed for the benefit of all and was supposed to support all villagers. This rule was so basic that respondents saw no need even to discuss it and initially neglected to describe unwritten agreements for land and labor exchange. Landed peasants described their own operations without mentioning that some of their own acreage was farmed by landless villagers. When specifically asked about such arrangements, a typical response might be, "Oh, yes, José uses [some number of] hectares on the other side of that mountain." The interchange of land and labor was so commonplace that landless villagers also neglected to mention that the land they worked was not legally theirs. Only in response to probing questions did these peasants acknowledge that the land they tilled officially belonged to another villager. Yet they were careful to emphasize that the loaned land was their *only* way of making a living and that the landed, therefore, held an *obligation* to provide their landless neighbors with land to farm. When asked about unemployment in the village before 1979, one man responded frankly, "There was no unemployment. Those with land always gave work or land to those without land."

As a result of this system, all landless respondents had access to land free-of-charge. Most were able to scratch subsistence from plots they borrowed. Therefore, although land supported its owners, community norms also recognized that most family land plots were more than enough to support a family. They could and should be shared among landless families.

Landed families who lent out portions of their land or shared food benefited directly from their own participation in community mutuality and had individual incentives to follow community norms. There were thus individual rational reasons as well as community reasons for land sharing. In return for land use, the landless worked on the farms of their landed benefactors. Sometimes they earned a small wage, but often the labor served as payment for the land they used. Landed members of the village usually raised cattle in addition to subsistence farming. It was important to these part-time ranchers to have village labor available because the length and condition of the trail made it impossible to import labor. Those in the cattle business sometimes had to spend time away from home while buying or selling livestock. When these rancher-peasants were away from home they could rely on one or two landless villagers to work their farms. The landless recipients of land loans felt some obligation and responsibility toward those who provided them with this most necessary resource. They were willing to provide such labor as was needed on the ranch, although they spent less time on such labor than in working the borrowed land. One respondent explained his own arrangement this way.

Question: So if you had no land, how did you make a living?

Response: Well, of course, Juan let me use part of his land so I always had plenty [of land] to live on, to support the family.

Question: You mean Juan rented you enough land to live on? However much land you wanted?

Response: No, he let me use whatever I wanted to use for free, whatever I needed, free. He didn't charge me anything.

Question: He let you use it for free? No rent?

Response: Of course. What else was he supposed to do? We have to have land to live on. How else were we supposed to live? Everyone needs land to live on, so he let me use enough land to live on.

This respondent also explained that in return for the land he did a certain amount of work for Juan on Juan's land. He also felt a sense of obligation. If Juan asked him to work on a day he had planned to do otherwise or if Juan needed help with some task, this respondent always felt it was his duty to give Juan a hand.

In the dialogue above, the reader will note my incredulity about the arrangement the respondent is describing. The norms he describes reveal an underlying awareness of interdependence between himself and Juan. This awareness is part of the peasant political ecology. To someone like myself, who belongs to a contemporary urban society, these norms seemed strange and foreign, particularly after extensive fieldwork elsewhere in Nicaragua. Yet my surprise seemed unnatural and ill-informed to this peasant respondent. The underlying interdependent norms that governed his world seemed so natural to him that he saw no need even to discuss them and was astounded at my ignorance. Norms are often such an inherent part of human society that people do not even recognize that they are being governed by such underlying expectations; consequently, they are surprised when others raise questions about these societal norms and do not treat them as inherently natural and universal.

Land management in Pedregal exemplifies ecological interdependence within the village. Although the reciprocal land/labor exchanges that existed between individual landed villagers and one or more of their landless neighbors can be partially explained by individualist and communitarian incentives, a complete understanding of the full interactive system can be achieved only when one understands the political ecology that underlies social interaction. Both landed and landless participants in land/labor exchanges stood to gain individually and economically by such participation. Yet rational calculations of immediate self-interest cannot explain the extensive prevalence of

Reciprocity   The Ecological Community

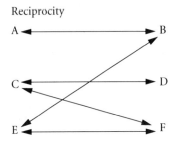 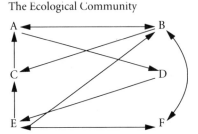

Figure 3.1. Reciprocity versus Ecological Interdependence

Reciprocity describes simple bilateral relationships between two people, i.e., between A and B, B and E, etc. The ecological relationships within a peasant community, like the peasant reality, are more complex, more interdependent. A helps B, but B helps E, who indirectly aids A.

land sharing or the fact that borrowed land was used free of monetary charge. Short-term immediate self-interest within the rational-actor model would have led landed peasants to charge rent, particularly as exorbitant rental rates were the national norm.

Traditional norms of a moral economy that strive to protect the subsistence of all villagers come closer to explaining Pedregal's land-sharing arrangements than do individual incentives. Yet this explanation is also limited. It stresses reciprocity between two individuals rather than a generalized system that describes multiple interdependent ties. Figure 3.1 illustrates the difference between reciprocity and ecological interdependence. Reciprocity describes bilateral relationships between two people: between A and B, between B and E, etc. The ecological relationships within a peasant community, like the peasant reality, are more complex. A helps B but B helps E, who indirectly aids A. Relationships are more interdependent. Each participant does not necessarily receive support directly from the person to whom he or she gave support.

In the quotation above, a landless respondent explains his own access to land not in terms of patronage ties of reciprocity, as the moral economy theory would argue, but in terms of access to a general system to which all villagers belong—an ecological system. Land/labor exchange contributed to building and sustaining community and a group insurance system, both essential components of the ecological system. In Pedregal, however, interdependent support was not limited to land usage.

Medical Support System

Although one or two landless recipients of borrowed land might be adequate to help bring cattle to market or to work a farm during the owner's absence, in some contexts the help of one or two other people was not sufficient. The need for urgent medical care is one such context. The system of community action at times of sudden illness or an accident clearly shows how the village system functioned to preserve life through communal input. The trip from the village to a physician in Teustepe or a hospital in Boaco was long and expensive, especially if the patient was unable to walk. When the family of a sick person lacked the resources to provide transport, it was village custom for the entire community to pool resources, time, and energy to take the sick person to the source of medical care. This form of support was most frequently activated in response to a difficult childbirth, but it also worked for accidents and illnesses, such as Panchito's encounter with the snake described in Chapter 1. Furthermore, if the patient anticipated medical fees and lacked the wherewithal to pay them, villagers often took up a collection to cover at least part of the fees, as they did for Panchito's mother, Maria. Villagers and families who had benefited from such collective action were expected to pull their weight when crisis befell someone else, and usually they were eager to do so because the peasants were acutely aware that their participation in the community system was noticed and remembered by the village at large.

I have called this mutual support in times of illness a medical support system. It is part of the ecological system that sustains, indeed saves, individual life. It is a system in which individuals participate out of an awareness of the way in which their lives are dependent on the maintenance of viable, cooperative community. Individual incentives of the traditional rational-actor sort cannot account for individual participation in the medical support system in Pedregal. A rational-actor model can neither predict nor explain individual participation in the system. The supposedly rational free-rider would pay a heavy individual price for free-ridership. These peasants clearly recognize the foolishness of free-ridership and are more individually rational and foresightful than the free-rider. On the other hand, these peasants do not participate in the medical support system solely out of adherence to traditional norms or out of superior altruism and morality. Although the support system is supported by village norms, individuals also stand to gain a good deal by their participation in it. Accordingly, their support for community and the community itself are stronger and more resilient than support based on a system that relies solely upon norms and tradition, such as the traditional moral economy.

The Natural Ecosystem

Beyond immediate human interaction within the village, the peasants' ecological awareness of interdependence between themselves and their natural environment also influenced action, choices, and attitudes. Like peasants in many places, Pedregal villagers were caught in a bind between their need for immediate survival and their long-term reliance on the natural environment for sustenance. Part of that bind consisted of the fact that their awareness of environmental vulnerability extended beyond their actual power to fully protect the environment. Where they had the power to act in protective ways toward the ecosystem without endangering their immediate survival they tried to protect the environment. Where they lacked such power, they nevertheless remained aware of environmental interdependence. Their concern showed in their interviews.

In the area of soil/population management the peasants were not powerless and took measures to protect the land from overpopulation. Although the villagers could not rely on any official policy of population settlement, they did what they could through word of mouth to avoid unsuitable levels of immigration. Aware of the soil's limited carrying capacity, the peasants had settled sparsely in the region, and they discouraged immigration from outside that might overtax the natural system and endanger the wider community. Outside the local area would-be migrants I interviewed had gotten the message and did not consider moving to the Pedregal area. They knew its soil was inhospitable. Essentially, Pedregal peasants had been instrumental in giving the area a reputation for difficult farming. The success of the peasant's efforts to restrict migration explains the fact that Pedregal's soil still supports its population.[5]

In the area of scientific soil protection the peasants had less power and were less effective in maintaining soil quality. Soil in the area was subject to gradual erosion and deterioration. It was becoming more arid. Villagers understood the processes of deterioration and correctly claimed that erosion was due to deforestation, which had also brought a decline in rainfall. Whereas villagers were aware of the wider ecosystem and were concerned about threats to it, there was little they could do about the problem beyond migration control, which they had already done. Wood was the only local source of fuel for cooking and heat during the rainy season. Farming and cattle, both incompatible with reforestation, were the only methods by which villagers could survive. This situation reflects the bind villagers experienced between the demands of immediate survival and what they knew to be the long-term requirements of ecosystem protection. They were powerless within this broader system to affect extra-village forces that might have helped them to relieve the pressure on the ecosystem. Such outside pressures, for example, forced them to cut trees in order to meet their own fuel needs when they would have preferred access to some other type of fuel. Under ideal circumstances they would have had access to another fuel type, but in a political climate where survival depended upon minimizing outside contact, demanding alternative fuel options would have been unrealistic and dangerous.

The peasants' sense of interdependence between themselves and their natural environment manifested itself first in awareness and concern and second in action where possible. Most interviews that spoke of life in the past compared past and present soil and rainfall conditions in a worried fashion. Many respondents expressed concern without having solutions:

In the past the soil was better. We can still get along, but I wish there was something we could do to stop the soil deterioration.

We need more rain. It used to rain much more here, when my grandfather was farming. I think we need more trees but we also need the wood. The situation is very bad with the soil erosion. I wish they would help us to maintain the soil but Nicaragua is so poor there is no money for anything.

The interviews reflect a situation the villagers found frustrating. With their limited power they did what they could to restrain immigration and protect the soil. In the broader national context, however, they were powerless and could only worry. Their concern is itself evidence of their awareness of ecological interdependence between themselves and nature. Their willingness to take action where they could reveals their commitment to sustaining the ecological system, both natural and social. As natural environmentalists their frustration is akin to that of many environmental groups in developed and wealthy countries today. Their knowledge that current practices may endanger long-term survival increases the sense of precariousness in the village. It might even have increased their commitment to mutual support within the community.

Ecological Equilibrium within the Village

Within their own village, however, the peasants had more control over their own lives and the lives of their neighbors than they did over external factors. Within the village, they could and did construct an interdependent, mutually supportive system that protected individual life and community. Although they had no control over larger external forces that threatened the system, they could sanction village members who refused to support the ecological system or who tried to be independent and refused to support others. The villagers' treatment of Pedregal's "affluent" families illustrates clearly what form these sanctions took.

Within the village, three respondents enjoyed a level of affluence above most of their neighbors. Pedro, Carlos, and Jorge had access to luxuries, such as electricity or an automobile, that were not available to most villagers.[6] Pedro had married a woman of some independent means. Carlos owned more land than many villagers and was a skilled rancher. Jorge had a level of education above the village average and used his education to learn and apply superior agricultural techniques that increased the productivity of his land. All three of these villagers lived in houses that were larger than average and were more solidly built than other village dwellings. Jorge owned a fine horse and had installed a shower of which he was immensely proud. Pedro had both a small television and an ancient phonograph. Carlos had a refrigerator on display on his front porch. Such affluence brought an illusion of independence to which Pedro and Carlos succumbed by defying community norms of mutual support. Jorge, however, continued to partake of village mutuality, contributing generously to the group insurance system.

Villagers' perceptions and treatment of these three individuals exemplify their efforts to protect the village system. The behavior of these three individuals underscores the extent to which they understood that relative affluence did not replace individual dependence upon the community. Jorge lent land and sometimes gave away homemade milk and cheese. During one of my visits to his home, a young boy came to purchase homemade cheese but only had enough money for a small portion. Jorge's wife insisted that the boy take a larger cake of cheese and told him not to worry about the price difference. Jorge received the gratitude, affection, and kind opinion of his neighbors. Although some villagers resented his relative wealth, many acknowledged his kindness and generosity. When he was temporarily disabled and recovering from an operation, his wife had no difficulty in finding villagers who would take over his farming and ranching duties while he recuperated. During my visits to the house there seemed to be a perpetual surplus of young neighbors hanging about, waiting to be asked to take over some small chore for Jorge or his wife.

Pedro and Carlos, on the other hand, tried to be independent of community. They defined rationality in terms of short-term gain to themselves and their families alone, but this definition was uncommon in the village and was not perceived as acceptable. The neighbors considered Pedro and Carlos stingy and arrogant, and these two men paid a high price for that perception among their neighbors. Pedro and Carlos had inspired a great deal of bitterness and resentment. Their poorer neighbors criticized them with relish. Both were frequently the victims of spiteful remarks, malicious gossip, and dirty tricks. Both lived in a state of paranoia and suspicion, cynically certain that they would soon be victimized again. They spoke with harsh bitterness about the dishonesty and laziness of their neighbors who were, they assured me, always ready to exploit an advantage. As mentioned in Chapter 1, Pedro complained vehemently, both during his interview and at every subsequent opportunity, that his sheep were always being stolen. He frequently found that his fences had been mysteriously cut and that the animals had wandered away. Sometimes the sheep were never recovered. He also declared that someone was always pilfering the vegetables from his garden. He was never able to catch the thief and none of his neighbors ever seemed to know anything about the crime. The theory of political ecology explains why the short-term calculations of Pedro and Carlos were not rational at all and in fact elicited a high price, both for the individuals and for the community. By being short-term, self-interested maximizers Pedro and Carlos ignored the negative foreseeable consequences of their behavior. Fortunately both for the individuals and for the village, Pedro and Carlos are atypical in Pedregal, and most villagers reason more like Jorge and Juan. Jorge subscribed to a more rational method of calculation and one that better served both him and the community.

Juan also made the same calculation of foreseeable consequences when he carried Panchito to the doctor. Jorge and Juan acted in ways that did not maximize short-term gain but that yielded more in the foreseeable future and that protected against risk. At the same time, Jorge's and Juan's behavior is not explained by altruism or by community norms alone. Tradition alone cannot explain the extent of their generosity or of their commitment to the ecological system. Each man has real, personal gains to be made by contributing to community. Each can calculate real or potential rewards that have accrued or could accrue to them from community input. In fact, Jorge's entire harvest and annual income the year he was disabled came through community labor. Moreover, each man perceives himself as dependent upon the entire community and not just upon one or two neighbors. Each can easily imagine real financial loss resulting from the loss of community support. Despite their relative affluence, these four villagers are dependent upon the village system. Even in good times and without a personal crisis they need the goodwill of their neighbors.

Village Contact with the Somoza Regime

The community system of Pedregal functioned with an ecological interdependence most peasants found satisfactory. This interdependence extended even beyond Pedregal to some members of service professions in nearby towns. The continued survival of any sense of ecological community was most unusual in Nicaragua under the Somozas, and it resulted from the absence of repressive and exploitive forces predominant elsewhere as well as from regional isolation. The regime's benign neglect of the entire Boaco region also contributed to Pedregal's unusual experience. Neglect was the best the villagers could hope for, inasmuch as regime involvement usually brought grief to the local population. The fact that the region escaped land concentration and the repressive political apparatus that enforced it and epitomized regime rule elsewhere had a crucial impact on the reality of peasant life. A good example of this impact can be seen in Pedregal's money lending practices. In most of Nicaragua, banks were unwilling to lend to peasants, most of whom could not survive on the land and employment that were available. Instead, the peasants turned to private loan shark lawyers, who charged interest rates anywhere from 50 to 300 percent and forced bankrupt peasants to use their land as collateral. When families could not repay the loan and interest they lost their land. This pattern was critical in the gradual process of land concentration prevalent elsewhere in Nicaragua.[7]

Pedregal was different. Peasants were usually able within the community system to make ends meet and did not need to borrow money. Even when they did borrow, their experience was benign:

> There were no lawyers lending money here. I borrowed money from a friend sometimes but normally from the bank.

> They [the banks] had programs of two-year loans and I borrowed money several times after I got land. Without land they wouldn't loan you anything. Each

> time they lent me 2,000 córdobas. Sometimes it was difficult to repay, but I always did. I even have a letter congratulating me on always having made my payments on time.

> Interest was low and it was no problem either to get the loan or to repay it. You just had to show your [land] title, that's all.

Interest rates were between 4 percent and 6 percent. Of those who had borrowed, all but one had been able to repay the loan. No one had lost land as a result of borrowing money.

Another hardship characteristic of Nicaraguan peasant life but absent from Pedregal was the experience of migratory labor. During the harvests large landlords needed plenty of labor, and peasants who had no alternative flocked to take advantage of the miserable wages. The labor experience during migration was cruel and frequently politicizing for migrants. Circumstances in Pedregal had made survival easier and migration unnecessary. Villagers who left did so voluntarily in search of an urban life and were not forced to travel every year.

A third component of the regime's repressive apparatus was the National Guard. Professionally trained and equipped, the Guard acted as the dictator's personal army. In Nicaragua the Guard's purpose was to protect, defend, and enforce regime policies and to prevent or repress resistance. The Guard itself was extremely corrupt. Its tactics toward the general population included theft, false arrest, torture, and indiscriminate murder. In most parts of Nicaragua this paramilitary force inspired fear and hatred among the population. Pedregal was also atypical of the rest of Nicaragua in its experience with the National Guard, in large part due to the isolation of the village.

> The Guard came here to take care of parties. Sometimes they hit someone but they didn't come very frequently. It was really far and difficult for them to get here. They were too lazy to come so far.

> They came here very little, and when they came, it was for some problem with a drunk or a fight.

> Sometimes they came through here looking to see who was making moonshine, and they broke the bottles. If they caught you, they put you in jail for two days and then nothing. That was all.

Tolerance and matter-of-fact acceptance replaced the terror with which the rest of Nicaragua viewed the Guard.

> They never came through here to mistreat us. Some of them were mean, others were not. It depended on what you had done. If I never did anything nothing happened to me. The way you saw them depended on if it was a mean one or a good one. Many people were afraid of them, but some of them were good people.

Villagers were aware of the Guard's reputation elsewhere but were influenced by its behavior in their immediate vicinity.

> I felt afraid when I saw them because I knew they arrested people and were unjust to people and fired if you tried to run away. But they came here only to arrest those who made moonshine.

> I saw them in [local cities]. They had ugly faces and I was afraid of them. But they never arrested me or anyone from my family, and they never killed anyone from my family.

> They came through here, but they didn't do anything. They seemed normal to me.

Many Pedregal respondents had had no contact whatsoever with the Guard. A few had brushed up against the law without being mistreated.

Pedregal in the Revolution: Quiescence and Political Ecology

While revolution raged elsewhere in Nicaragua, Pedregal remained a quiet corner where life was still fairly good and from which the ravages of the struggle were still distant. The unusual regional experience of Pedregal made the poverty of local rural life tolerable and permitted an on-going community system of protective, interdependent mutuality. These qualities of life in Pedregal resulted from and reinforced each other. To the extent that villagers knew about the revolution most surmised that it was something they wanted to avoid. They had some awareness that repression elsewhere was brutal and that revolutionary involvement increased one's vulnerability to repression. Villagers wanted to protect their tranquil corner and to survive the repression. They hoped that uninvolvement and ignorance of the struggle would help keep them safe. Not surprisingly, eastern Nicaragua comprised the weakest link in the revolutionary offensive against Somoza. This was true both militarily and ideologically.

Isolation separated most villagers not only from the regime but also from the revolutionary struggle. Guerrilla presence was low in the region, and most villagers were only dimly aware of an ongoing struggle. Most held little sympathy for the guerrillas and had not collaborated with the FSLN. Again, the two factors reinforced each other since low village sympathy for the revolution discouraged FSLN recruitment efforts there. Villagers were not so much anti-revolutionary as absorbed by their struggle for survival and oblivious to the politics of the outside world. Peasant comments describe the local atmosphere prior to 1979:

> I didn't collaborate with the Frente. I didn't know anything about that, and I didn't want to know. All I did was work.

I just worked all the time. I don't even know if there were others from the village collaborating [with the Frente]. That was none of my business.

I had a friend who was a combatant for the Frente. He came to my house fleeing from something. I hid him and helped him. I wasn't afraid because no one realized it [what I was doing]. But I never did anything else to help, only that. Before the triumph the Frente never came through here.

For the most part, villagers had no reason to become involved in a risky, bloody struggle and every reason to hope that life would continue in its present form. Although they did not look kindly upon the Somoza dictatorship, they had also escaped its worst effects. Some of the peasant contacts beyond the village, particularly with the medical community, even helped sustain life and community. Even more importantly from the village perspective, the Somoza regime allowed village life to proceed according to peasant preferences without destructive interference. Many peasant villagers are most content to continue with life free of external involvement or influence. This position is understandable given the extent to which village life has been finely tuned over many generations to protect life and provide adequate survival without any pretense at utopia or perfect egalitarianism. Life in prerevolutionary Pedregal illustrates how well this system can work to ensure life even when there are tensions and uncooperative members within the village and where poverty is endemic. Most villagers were unaware of the wealth and luxury that some Nicaraguans enjoyed, so they had few aspirations for a better life style. To the extent that villagers were dimly aware of life beyond village confines, they realized that they were far better off than most rural Nicaraguans.

Exceptions to the Rule: Activism within a Broader Ecological View

Within Pedregal, a handful of villagers were exceptions to the general rule of satisfaction and voluntary quiescence. These villagers became involved in the revolutionary struggle against Somoza. They attended meetings and talked with people about the need to support the revolution. They signed official petitions to the government protesting disappearances and massacres. These petitions sometimes addressed government treatment of specific persons and sometimes generally condemned human rights violations by the Somoza regime. Their actions were mild in comparison with the guerrilla activity of many peasants in other parts of Nicaragua (see, for example, Chapter 6), yet, viewed in the repressive context of the dictatorship, their choices were both dangerous and courageous. Unlike the guerrillas, their position against the regime was public, written, and potentially traceable. In prerevolutionary Nicaragua, petitions were extremely risky. In less isolated regions, peasants saw them as suicidal. The story of the villagers who participated in the revolutionary struggle is of interest because it illustrates how an ecological understanding of rural society and the world beyond influences political action.

Twenty percent of Pedregal residents became actively involved with the Catholic Church through a priest from a nearby town.[8] During evening Bible study, these peasants learned Liberation Theology and became Delegates of the Word, a distinction bestowed by the Church. As one villager expressed it, "The Church taught us that we had a right to live with more dignity, to work, to organize. It raised our consciousness and made us want to get involved in the [revolutionary] struggle." Marcos, an older member of the community and a deeply religious man, had been a delegate longer than anyone else in the village and had risen to a position of leadership among the delegates. In 1967, prior to becoming a delegate, he had been a member of the Conservative party and a loyal follower of the presidential candidate for that year. As a result of Fernando Agüero's pact with Anastasio Somoza that year, he became extremely disillusioned with party politics in Nicaragua and with the Conservative party. This is his story:

> We voted [prior to 1979] because they forced us to but also because we thought the Conservatives were an option. But they only deceived us, because Somoza always won. We followed Agüero, and the only thing he did was deceive us. There was a massacre the 22nd of January, 1967, thanks to him, and my father was killed in the gunfire. After that, we decided not to think about elections but to think about force.
>
> I have been a delegate since 1967, and the work that we did was to raise the people's consciousness. We showed the analogy between the slaves in the Bible and the way the people lived. Everything was very clandestine in Church seminaries. Those seminaries included representatives from the Frente. In some of those seminaries, there were even priests from the United States, although not from the government of the United States. Sometimes the Guard came [to the meetings] in civilian clothes to spy. We thought that what we were doing was not wrong, and we trusted in the protection of the Lord. We did it because of the poverty we lived in. We did it because others lived marginalized, and the work was badly paid. The boss paid whatever he wanted to. If the landlord gave money to a sick person, it was not a gift. He took it out of the sick person's salary. We gave all these examples to the people and explained what the landlords were like. We made skits to represent the government and the landlords. But that was dangerous, those skits, because it was illegal to talk about the government or represent the government that way. Even a child talking innocently about the skits could have betrayed us.

Other villagers followed Marcos's example and became involved with the revolution.

> I became involved to dedicate my life to the movement for liberation. We did it for the liberation of the people, for a change, to have something different.

> Father León organized us as delegates. He called us for meetings in the Curate House. I became a delegate because I was interested in discovering things

about Christ, and I liked it. I started as a delegate in 1975. I collaborated indirectly with the Frente, but I didn't want to become involved in the guerrilla war. The Frente met with us and some of us went to fight with them, but I was more of a follower and wasn't so involved as to go and fight. It was dangerous to become involved, to make that decision, but I did it because we had to advance. I opted for the civic struggle, for things like meetings. Once I participated in a denouncement of the disappearance of four-hundred peasants. We signed a petition denouncing that. I was not afraid because it was something just. It was more important to worry about what is just than about your own safety. If you worry too much about your own safety, you don't live very much.

These revolutionary activists were important exceptions to the village rule of quiescence. From a purely personal point of view they had as little to complain about as did their neighbors. In discussing their revolutionary activism, they were careful to explain that they had not become involved in reaction to personal grievances:

We, here, suffered nothing. Nothing happened here; it was very quiet. We joined because of what was happening to others. After all, we are all part of Nicaragua.

They didn't bother us here, but we wanted a change, knowing what was happening to other people outside of here. We realized that the Guard and the Somocistas were bloody people, and we wanted them to stop persecuting the young people as they did. Besides, you never knew when they would arrive here.

The behavior of these activists is particularly useful in illustrating the inadequacy of unidimensional individualist motivation in explaining political action. These peasants had no individual incentive whatsoever for their actions, and every individual incentive to remain quiescent. There was no economic gain to signing petitions, and the secrecy of their actions precluded even the rewards of status and power. In fact, from a short-term, maximizing perspective there was no logical reason for their choices. Their ecological perspective, however, and their consideration of the foreseeable consequences of action offer a more appropriate explanation for their activism. These quotations illustrate that religious involvement broadened the visible ecological system and made individuals aware of living within a larger world than the village alone. Religion allowed them to see that the pond of village life was actually a small lake of Nicaraguan society. Religious education interacted with the peasant sense of an ecological system and caused them to define community more broadly than did their neighbors. Through the church they became aware of system dissonance. They realized that Somoza's assaults on systemic harmony beyond the village posed a danger for village tranquillity as well as for community and individual survival. They acted to defend both the wider community and themselves within it.

The ecological understanding of these activists was not necessarily superior to that of their fellow villagers. Nor were they more intelligent. They shared the same political ecology that I am arguing belongs to the peasantry in general. The difference lies in where they placed the edges of the pond and how they defined the boundaries of community. Marcos and those who followed his example defined community as including Nicaraguans who did not live in Pedregal. They saw danger and injustice toward community members outside the village as ultimately a threat to Pedregal and to community members inside the village. At the same time pragmatism, individual concerns, and the need to preserve self by protecting community helped define their actions. In their activism these peasants took care not to place either themselves or Pedregal in any unnecessary danger. Village isolation allowed them to keep a fairly low profile while also taking some action in support of the revolution.

> The Guard never realized that we were going around having meetings and raising the people's consciousness. Father León always said we were just having religious meetings.

> I never had any problems with the Guard for being a delegate because there weren't many activities.

> The Guard never realized that we were having these meetings.

> We were always very careful. We always came and went with Bibles in our hands for protection and no one knew what we were doing.

Implications for Theory

An analysis of the data on political action within Pedregal and of political attitudes among the minority of activists confirms the description of the village provided thus far and illustrates how understanding the peasants' ecological perspective helps explain political action. Pedregal as a whole falls to the left of the spectrum of political activity presented in Figure 3.2. As was characteristic in all villages, the area of dissonance fell to the more assertive end of village experience and, in Pedregal, focused on petitions. Most villagers opted for quiescence, and all rejected nonviolent action such as demonstrations, strikes, and land invasion as well as violence. Disagreement surrounded the signing of petitions; some villagers favored it and others did not.

Given what villagers saw as the satisfactory nature of life in Pedregal, it is not surprising that economic and socioeconomic factors had no significant effect on attitudes about the signing of petitions that denounced the regime. The ownership of land and the size of land plot had no significant effect on the attitudes toward petitions. This finding is in accordance with what we would expect from a community system in which the land supports all villagers adequately and the landless have access to sufficient land for subsis-

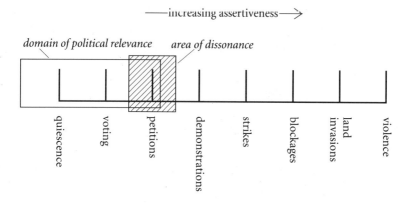

Figure 3.2. Pedregal: Spectrum of Political Activity

tence. Similarly, socioeconomic factors (experience with hunger, sibling or children's deaths to preventable disease, level of education) had no significant relationship to attitudes toward petitions. This finding supports the existence of an egalitarian community in which socioeconomic experiences do not differ substantially and where the level of living has been roughly equal among villagers.

The only independent variable that had any significant relationship to attitudes toward political action, and determined individual position on the area of dissonance (petitions), was the perception of injustice in the world around the village. In Pedregal, this perception was related to religious experience. Most respondents (76.7 percent), perceived no violation to their sense of community and a just functioning of the world, and most (80 percent) did not consider petitions an acceptable form of political action. The repressive character of the Somoza regime and the public record of one's name as a petition signer must have been a powerful disincentive even for those who perceived injustice around them. Among the minority who defined community boundaries more broadly and perceived injustice resulting from regime policies, the

Table 3.2. Pedregal: Acceptability of Petitions as Form of Political Action, by Perception of Injustice (N = 30, Missing = 0)

	Acceptability of Petitions (row percentages)	
Perception of Injustice	Acceptable	Not Acceptable
Yes	42.9 N = 3	57.1 N = 4
No	13.0 N = 3	87.0 N = 20

Note: Chi-square = 1.40916. Tau B = .0448. Confidence level = 95 percent.

inclination toward activism in the form of petitions was decidedly stronger. Among those who perceived no injustice, only 13 percent found petitioning acceptable; among those who perceived injustice, 42 percent found petitions acceptable (see Table 3.2).

The results presented in Table 3.2 are tentative because of the relatively low number of cases, that is, villagers interviewed (N = 30). However, results at a confidence level of 95 percent even with N = 30 are noteworthy and suggest a clear relationship between perceived injustice and political action in Pedregal.

Conclusion

The case of Pedregal makes a valuable contribution to the central argument of this book. Its story provides a grass roots example of the ecological community system to which most peasants aspire and hope to create, if given an opportunity. It also illustrates the political implications of an ecological sense of community. It shows how the peasant understanding of interdependence led many villagers to prefer nonparticipation when involvement was dangerous. An understanding of the peasants' ecological perspective helps us to see how, even within the same village, different definitions of community will lead to different choices of political action. In this case the peasants' ecological perspective explains both quiescence and deviations from quiescence among some villagers. The story of Pedregal underscores the efficacious political capacity of the peasantry even in an isolated village secluded from mainstream political life. In doing so, it raises questions about derogatory stereotypes of politically inactive peasantry that often appear in literature about the peasant class. The residents of Pedregal have taught us that quiescence need not result from fear, ignorance, false consciousness, or an inadequate and inaccurate world view. Rather, it may be a deliberate, thoughtful choice that reflects social and political reality. It may be the most appropriate choice in satisfactory circumstances in which protest would be unnecessary or counterproductive. Quiescence can thus be a deliberate political statement just as protest or resistance can be.

4 □ INTEGRATION AND ACCOMMODATION
San Luis, Alajuela, Costa Rica

Theories of peasant politics have been notably deficient in their treatment of collective nonviolent forms of peasant political action. For the most part, the field of peasant studies has ignored these activities, even though they are far more common than rebellion or revolution and far less costly for the peasantry. In the past, theories of peasant political action have focused heavily on violence and quiescence. The implication of such scholarly focus is that peasants are either rebellious or quiescent and that they are not capable of or interested in participatory political action. The assumption, it would seem, is that peasants seek either to destroy the current system or to withdraw from it entirely, but never to adapt to it and integrate with it in a realistic and modern fashion. This either/or theoretical approach flies in the face of numerous descriptive studies of the peasantry that find peasants to be an aware and involved sector of the population that wishes to integrate into modern society. Peasant political action results from peasant desires to maximize individual gain, protect community, and generally get a fair shake from society. It is more realistic, therefore, to view collective political action as part of the general repertoire of tactics that peasants use in their struggle for survival. In fact, in a modern and increasingly integrated world, political action that addresses and deals with the modern society seems, in most circumstances, far more likely to enhance peasant survival than either quiescence or rebellion.

The theory of political ecology is unique among theories of peasant political action in that it helps to explain collective nonviolence. It uncovers a peasant perspective on society in which peasants perceive themselves as participants, having both rights and responsibilities in the wider society. Since the theory recognizes peasants as participants in society, as opposed to the traditional view of them as outside of society, the theory of political ecology logically addresses participatory and reformist collective nonviolence that is neither withdrawn (as quiescence is) nor destructive (as rebellion is). The peasant perspective on interdependence extends beyond the village to include wider society and is both adaptable and flexible in the context of a changing, modern world. As a result, peasants willingly draw on both traditional and new forms of action in their effort to maximize survival chances. Collective nonviolent political action is particularly relevant to peasant survival today, at a time when the state and national economy increasingly touch the peasant world and peasant agriculture is integrated into society. Because it explains the choice of collective nonviolence as well as quiescence and rebellion, the theory of political ecology offers a more updated and realistic understanding of peasant politics than was previously available.

This next case study of nonviolent protest shows how the peasant ecological understanding of interdependence led the villagers of San Luis, Costa Rica, to see a need for collective nonviolent action of a certain kind. The theory of political ecology shows how these villagers perceived interdependence among themselves, their village, and their society. They became convinced that that interdependence was endangered and with it their own survival as a community and as individuals. At the same time, they saw collective nonviolence as more conducive to their own well-being than rejection or overthrow of the society as a whole. They sought to improve their position in Costa Rican society and thereby to improve the nation rather than to destroy it in a revolutionary sense. They wanted to reform the status quo in a constructive fashion rather than to reject it entirely.

The action they undertook, both as individuals and as a community, was motivated by both individualistic and communitarian concerns. Like the villagers in Pedregal, San Luis villagers did not act purely out of self-interest nor purely from altruism. The nature of the action and the reward in this story are both of the type that are most vulnerable to sabotage by free-riders in traditional rational-actor theory. In fact, free-ridership was not much of a problem in San Luis. Instead, peasants adopted a responsible rational approach because they perceived the value of helping to preserve community. Their calculations were based on foreseeable consequences as well as on considerations of immediate personal gain. Moreover, far from exemplifying adherence to tradition or a moral economy, their actions illustrate the capacity of an adaptable village successfully keeping pace with the modern world while also maintaining interdependence among villagers and maximizing the chances of survival. Although anger and moral outrage were clearly a part of the motivating force in San Luis, these peasants acted long before subsistence became threatened. In an integrated society, there was no need to wait until matters reached such a dire point. Instead, villagers acted as modern members of contemporary society.

With the San Luis story, this study moves away from quiescence and into the realm of organized political action; this chapter directly addresses the question of nonviolent protest action such as petitions, demonstrations, and strikes. The experience of San Luis, an activist peasant community, exemplifies the use of these tactics in an arena of democratic politics where certain rules and expectations define the limits and patterns of political action. Questions about nonviolent protest include what kind of community experience would elicit collective protest that was also carefully nonviolent? What kind of world view would cause peasants to deliberately place themselves in the middle of the political spectrum, between quiescence and collective violence?

Community Context

Although the concept of a "typical" Costa Rican village is nebulous and imprecise, San Luis comes about as close to that stereotype as is possible. Historically, it has been a village of family farmers growing Costa Rica's oldest national crop, coffee.[1] San Luis lay within the southern tip of Alajuela province, nestled among the mountains that surround the Central Valley. This is coffee country, and villagers had at least three generations of local experience as coffee-producing smallholders. Because staple crops (beans, corn, and rice) did not grow well at the village altitude, the profit from coffee went to purchase subsistence foods.

Public services in San Luis were indicative of the political, economic, and geographic centrality of the region and of the extent to which the village had been included in the process of national development. A paved two-lane road wound up the mountainside, crossed several cement bridges, and reached to the far end of the village. In the center of the community stood a church, a primary school (grades one through six), a canteen and local store, and a public telephone. Frequent bus service connected the village with the city of Grecia, which was seven miles away and had a health center, hospital, and secondary school (grades seven through eleven). Older children could use the bus to commute to secondary school. From Grecia, buses connected daily with all parts of Costa Rica. When the main Pan-American highway was only a winding mountain road, it cut directly through Grecia. Now a superhighway passes eight kilometers from the center of Grecia. Villagers traveled frequently between San Luis and either Grecia or the capital, San José. A few villagers had even sent children to live with relatives in San José while attending school.

The village was thoroughly integrated into the market economy. Although soil fertility was even greater in the past, land in San Luis was still highly productive for coffee. The elevation produced rich coffee beans, although the plants themselves took slightly longer to mature than they would at lower altitudes. Peasants sold their coffee to local cooperatives, from which it went to the national market or to national export houses. The living afforded by selling coffee and buying food was better than that enjoyed by staple crop producers elsewhere in Costa Rica. Peasants depended on the village store for groceries and on shops in Grecia for clothing. They purchased tools in San José or through local cooperatives.

More than one hundred families lived in San Luis. All but two family heads earned their living in agriculture working either their own land or that of others. I interviewed thirty heads of household, twenty-eight men and two women.[2] The majority were long-term residents; the most recent arrivals had been there more than ten years. Most respondents were members of families who had owned land in the village for several generations, and many community residents were related either by blood or marriage. Sixty-three percent of respondents owned their own land.

One threat to coffee farming came from the nearby volcano, Poás. In the early 1950s Poás spewed out clouds of ashes that spread over the mountaintops for miles around. In San Luis that was a time of hardship, unemployment, and forced emigration. After a few years, however, the peasants who stayed had revived the local coffee industry. In 1988, Poás again emitted a steady stream of gas and later ash although the quantity was less than in the 1950s. The gas killed the coffee tree leaves and caused substantial financial loss among some of the coffee farmers, primarily those located farthest up the mountain and directly downwind from the volcano.

Despite the threat of Poás, San Luis had led a relatively charmed existence. Atypical in Central America, San Luis had avoided elite land concentration and peasant landlessness. Yeoman peasant farmers settled in the village in the early years of this century, and this tradition has continued into the present. Over time the peasants had been able to collect a larger percentage of the profit from their crop. Four decades ago peasants sold their freshly picked coffee to merchants who transported it to processing houses. This buyers' market allowed the merchants to dictate very low prices and to sell the beans for prices far above those offered to the peasant producers. During the progressive administrations of José Figueres in the 1950s and 1960s, the state helped the peasants form processing cooperatives owned and managed collectively by villagers from San Luis and elsewhere. Subsequently, the peasants sold their coffee to the cooperatives and processed it locally, eliminating the merchant middlemen and improving peasant profits. The co-ops, however, were economic institutions and were constitutionally prohibited from participation in national politics.

Land plot size illustrated the extent to which small-holders prevailed in this village. Respondents owned an average of 11.5 manzanas.[3] Thirty-seven percent of the interviewees owned a land plot too small to support them. They supplemented farming with agricultural labor. Pressure on the land had increased gradually with immigration and population growth. Village landlessness went back less than a generation, and most landless villagers had migrated to San Luis from other areas of Costa Rica. Respondents' fathers had owned an average of 13.26 manzanas.

Rich soil quality and a profitable cash crop meant that the carrying capacity of the land was much higher than in Pedregal. Respondents estimated that a family needed 5.75 manzanas of village land to support itself.[4] This small amount would only be adequate, they qualified, if the peasant family used the land to grow and sell coffee and utilized appropriate levels of technology, particularly fertilizer. Even so, the low figure is excellent testimony to the fertility

Table 4.1. San Luis: Surplus/Deficit of Community Land Ownership (in manzanas)

Land needed to support average peasant family	5.75
Average village land ownership	11.5
Average surplus	5.75

of San Luis land. Comparing the average amount of land owned in the village (11.5 manzanas) with the minimum considered necessary to sustain a family (5.75 manzanas) we can see that those who owned land had no trouble making a living and could afford to share the product of their land with others. (See Table 4.1.)

Moving from Pedregal to San Luis affords quite a contrast, as San Luis was the most well-to-do village in this study. Although older respondents remembered that life in the past had been harder, San Luis residents had always fared well by peasant standards. Many houses were cement and the wood houses were solid and painted. Everyone wore shoes and most children had school uniforms. Forty-three percent of respondents owned at least one car or jeep, and 6 percent owned tractors. Thirteen percent had telephones in their homes, and 93 percent owned at least one TV. Only one respondent ever remembered going hungry. In the living memory of the village, the community had always had a school. All families can afford to keep boys as well as girls in school for six years, and social pressure had helped keep most peasant children in primary school. In addition, the Costa Rican school system takes its annual break during the three-month coffee harvest so that studies do not compete with that intensive labor period. As a result, only one respondent was illiterate and the average schooling was 4.5 years among all respondents. Forty-three percent of interviewees had completed six years of primary school. Medical care had improved in most respondents' lifetimes. Although 23 percent had lost siblings to preventable childhood diseases, only 10 percent had similarly lost children. Thanks to the national health plan established after 1948, all respondents received medical care at the hospital in Grecia. A comparison of socioeconomic indicators from childhood and adulthood revealed that some of those who had been among the community's poorest children were among the village "haves." The village was not rigidly divided along class lines and upward social movement was possible.

Ecological Interdependence

Unlike Pedregal, San Luis is thoroughly integrated into the national political, economic, and social system. For San Luis, national integration is extensive, desirable, and advantageous. Villagers pay taxes, vote, and participate in municipal and national politics. They sell their crops outside the village, have a stake in economic policy, and purchase most of what they need to survive. Social policies provide them with health care and education and maintain commendable public services in the village. Although a desire to maintain community caused most Pedregal peasants to choose quiescence, a similar concern for community has drawn villagers of San Luis into collective protest.

Life in San Luis is much less insecure than in Pedregal. Natural disaster could strike and the Poás volcano could erupt again, but villagers do not live on the brink of economic crisis. Unlike villagers of Pedregal, San Luis residents lived comfortably above the subsistence line. Their standard of living was high even among Costa Rican peasants, all of whom live better than peasants elsewhere in Central America. Each family individually and the village as a whole had more economic leeway than villagers in Pedregal. In addition public services reduced the cost of individual crisis. The road was good, and medical help was a twenty-minute drive away. The telephone usually works.

Despite relatively less threatening circumstances, residents of San Luis have still needed to maintain a cohesive, interdependent community in which residents support and depend upon each other. The fact that San Luis villagers have been able to maintain ecological interdependence in the context of extensive market integration and reduced insecurity is testimony to the depth of peasant commitment to an ecological system, and to the strength of rural understanding that individual well-being still depends on a vibrant, healthy community.

Landlessness and Interdependence within the Coffee Economy

Ecological interdependence in San Luis is complex and multifaceted. To maintain community in a changing world that has brought relative prosperity and full market integration, the village system must be adaptable, not wedded to inflexible traditional norms. Some aspects of ecological interdependence are built on age-old concerns for subsistence and relative egalitarianism, issues clearly addressed by the land management system in Pedregal. San Luis benefits from a somewhat similar scheme. Other aspects of community interdependence in San Luis address modern-day concerns arising from involvement in a market economy. In confronting these latter issues, village interdependence in San Luis has been creative and adaptable. Ecological interdependence has ultimately granted San Luis a resilience and durability that allows it to survive as a modern peasant community.

One potential problem for the tranquillity of San Luis and the region is landlessness and the economic situation of those 30 to 40 percent of families who own little or no land and work primarily as laborers. This problem has resulted from population growth and in part from migration. Respondents whose families have been in the village for two or more generations usually own land. Those whose families arrived within the past twenty years are more likely to be landless villagers with a limited number of employment options. The primary employment opportunities occurred during the coffee harvest from December to February and the cane cutting season, which starts shortly after the coffee harvest begins and also lasts approximately three months. The landless may also find temporary or permanent work on the farms of their neighbors, either in the village or in nearby communities. A fortunate few hold permanent jobs on one of the larger village farms. A final option for the landless is to seek work on the one large hacienda in the local area. Most landless villagers spend some part of each year unemployed.

In response to the plight of landlessness, village landowners share with less fortunate villagers by loaning land, offering wage employment, and providing payment to workers above and beyond wages. Some landowners loan out small land plots free of rent, although plots are smaller and the practice less extensive than in Pedregal. Others provide temporary or permanent work for landless villagers, who are paid the national minimum wage. Most also receive a number of extras from their employers in addition to wages: firewood for cooking, milk from farm cows, or interest-free loans. Permanent workers sometimes receive a rent-free house on the farm property which becomes theirs for as long as they work for the peasant landowner. One other non-wage payment that is extremely important to landless workers is social security benefits, or the payments that allow participation in the national health plan. Many employers make the monthly payments that include workers and their families in the national health plan and thus entitle them to free medical care which is available in Grecia. In return for work, wages, and non-wage extras, landless villagers feel a strong sense of obligation toward their peasant employers. The best patrons benefit from hard-working and devoted employees who stay with them over long periods of time and provide reliable labor during the critical harvest months.

The coffee economy, however, provides the most important way for landless villagers to be included in interdependence. Village dependence on coffee as the principal crop gives the landless three assets critical to ecological interdependence: income, power, and a stake in community. These assets mean that the poor are seen as central actors in village interdependence: they make an essential contribution to the economy, they can inhibit the enterprise if they are not included, and they treasure the coffee economy just as the landed do. Their involvement in the coffee economy, therefore, is based upon individual concerns and interests as well as upon knowledge of themselves as members of a community whose welfare is intertwined with others. The centrality of the poor is most obvious at harvest time. The labor shortage that has always been a problem in Costa Rica becomes acute during the coffee harvest. Women and children who do not normally farm join the men in the fields during the harvest and work long hours to bring in the crop. Even then, completing the harvest successfully is difficult under adverse weather conditions. During these crucial weeks, the conscientious labor of the village poor spells the difference between a successful crop and a disaster. Moreover, the quality of the contribution made by landless pickers reverberates into the following year, since only the trees picked with the utmost care will produce at an optimal level then.

This description illustrates that San Luis is not a utopian village where everyone shares, cooperates, and mutually supports out of the goodness of their hearts. Rather, they have a combined interest in cooperation. Although voluntarism, mutual concern, and a sense of community are clearly present, there are also rational, individual incentives to participate in village mutuality as well as traditional norms that encourage employers to treat employees in a decent fashion. The interdependence of coffee production results from a mixture of individual incentives, traditional norms, and the peasants' ecological perspective. In fact, the villagers do not separate these factors out as disparate aspects of village life. Opportunities to sustain community and the village economy through wage labor are also sources of income necessary for survival and points of leverage that can encourage landed producers to participate in community. Support of the landless translates into an available cooperative labor supply which will maximize profits. Thus participation in village interdependence sustains community and is economically profitable. Mean-spirited or exploitive employers defy traditional norms and undermine community but may also have a lower yield in next year's harvest as a result of careless picking this year or worker preferences to pick for better employers.

The profitability of participation in community is reinforced by the tools that the poor can wield to encourage the landed to participate in village interdependence. The most powerful such tool is the refusal to work during the crucial coffee harvest. Even a work slowdown can be an effective tactic when timing is critical. Carelessness during picking damages the trees and can substantially reduce yield next year and even in years thereafter. As in any village, the poor also have recourse to malicious gossip and character assassination. Even these mild sanctions are serious penalties in a small community where everyone knows everyone and word travels like wildfire. A good reputation will be indispensable when the next harvest season rolls around and competition for scarce labor is again fierce.

Village interdependence is thus integrated into and supported by the market-oriented coffee economy. Although only the landowners produce their own coffee, they cannot do so without the labor input of their landless neighbors. Coffee is a labor intensive crop, and the mechanization of coffee production has proceeded slowly. Throughout the year, landowners are dependent on the careful, conscientious labor of their landless neighbors who work deep in the coffee groves and are almost impossible to supervise. During the harvest, coffee producers are entirely dependent on the landless labor supply and would be economically ruined without the cooperation and support of the poor. Similarly, of course, the landless are dependent on the landed coffee producers for extensive employment during the harvest, for periodic employment during the year, and for non-wage extras that do a great deal to sustain life and health.

The peasants' sense of ecological interdependence that goes beyond a simple moral economy or bilateral reciprocity has adapted the village to the demands of a coffee-producing, market-oriented economy. Ecological interdependence includes land sharing and the redistribution of other basic goods. It rests on a coffee economy that depends on both the landed and landless for its viability and in return supports the entire village. It is sustained by both individual incentives and a concern for community. There are powerful economic reasons to be a good village citizen. It is equally true that the village economy is a community economy that is sustained by group effort.

The Social Safety Net

Reciprocal relationships of land/labor exchange contribute to and reinforce norms of ecological interdependence. The result of a huge network of exchange relationships through the coffee economy is a generalized sense of community and an awareness of individual dependence on others. As a result, ecological community extends beyond land/labor arrangements and the production of coffee into aspects of village life that are not directly related to the coffee economy. Villagers in San Luis subscribe to norms of ecological interdependence that protect life for all, within village means and short of generalized catastrophe. Medium landholders expressed concern for the living condition of their poorer neighbors, even when they themselves lived comfortably. This concern generalized to the community level manifests itself in a social safety net that protects all villagers so that no one is allowed to become destitute. This informal net provides minimum necessities to those in the worst circumstances without attempting to ensure that all live equally well. Thus relative equity prevails. No one enjoys extravagant wealth, and even the landless do not drop below a certain level of poverty. Subsistence needs are not a problem for anyone in the village.

Ely is one of the more affluent villagers in San Luis. His farm management exemplifies ecological exchange relationships typical of San Luis. He owns sixteen manzanas of choice coffee-growing land. He hires pickers during the harvest and runs the farm with two permanent workers during the rest of the year. His permanent workers, Carlos and Juan, live in rent-free homes on Ely's property. In addition to minimum wage, he pays their social security benefits, offers them free milk and cooking fuel, periodically makes them small interest-free loans, and allows them to till a corner of land for their family's use. Ely's workers labor long hours for him. When I visited his home, I often found them working long after most workers had quit for the day. Ely was one of the favored employers during harvest time. He always had pickers lined up long before the harvest season began. Ely spoke thoughtfully about his treatment of his workers: "They are good men; they work hard. I can depend on them to get a job done. Since I give them a house and other things, they feel an obligation to me. People know how I treat Carlos and Juan, and that's important. I guess I'm sort of a leader here so other people do what I do. That way the workers get treated well, and we can all live better here."

Neither individualist nor communitarian motives fully explain Ely's attitudes toward worker and social relations. Individualist concerns include the short-term loss to Ely of providing a house and other non-wage payments to his workers. Traditional rational-actor theory would expect Ely to press every advantage with his workers and offer nothing extra. Ely, however, has foresight that extends beyond the short term into the foreseeable future. There is an economic incentive for him to be generous, as his behavior pays off during the harvest and year-round. The moral economy theory, on the other hand, accurately grasps the nature of reciprocal exchange between Ely and his workers and is able to anticipate each behaving as they do. Yet it doesn't account for or even take into consideration Ely's additional focus outward, beyond his own farm to the maintenance of village community. His awareness of the consequences of his actions—the effect of a good example—is ecological and is expressed toward the end of the above passage. He himself lives better if other landed peasants on village farms also treat their workers well.

Miguel, an older respondent, could remember two occasions in which families had been held above the subsistence line by community action. One of these families was his own.

> When I was a boy, we were very poor. We had some very hard years. Sometimes we were hungry. I remember two years like that. There was a patron, my father's patron, who gave us milk and some other [food]. What he gave us was all we had for nine people. We were very poor. I always remember that because we probably would have died [otherwise]. Other families also gave us a little food and helped us when we were sick. . . . I remember one case of a mother and daughter who asked [the community] for a house and land. The mother was very old, and she had no husband. A group collected a lot of money to build a house. Then we all built the house together. It was very nice.

The social safety net provided real benefits to poorer villagers and extended a supportive hand to those who would otherwise be destitute. It rested in part on traditional norms of reciprocity, a village moral economy, and the peasant sense of justice that respects each individual life and subscribes to relative egalitarianism. Nonetheless, San Luis is not a village of altruistic souls morally superior to others. They simply saw their own interests as intertwined with others' interests. Villagers readily admitted that there was a rational self-interested purpose to the social safety net. When medium landholders expressed concern about the unemployment of their neighbors, their concern exhibited a prudent sense of self-interest as well as an altruistic concern for poorer neighbors:

> We have to help the poor. If not, they are dissatisfied and become a danger to us.

> We have to make sure the poor pan lives well, not that we're all equal, but that he lives well, something basic.

Thus village "haves" participate in village interdependence as much out of a sense of self-preservation as out of concern for others. In fact, they do not see a distinction between the two.

This combination of self-interested and communitarian motives illustrates the ecological awareness of the peasant and peasant understanding of individual/community interdependence. The respondent who is concerned about potential danger from destitute villagers is as much aware of his own dependence on community as is the poor family in need of a house. The village "have" who is concerned about community tranquillity because he wants to maximize profits from coffee production is no less important a preserver of community, because his concern for group life is, in part, a reflection of profit orientation. He has simply understood the rational economic incentives for preserving community. His support for community is much stronger than any support based solely on altruism or village tradition.

Excellent testimony to the successful function of the safety net is the acceptability of life among the landless. Many are unwilling to leave the village and the Central Valley even if given an opportunity to own land in a more isolated and less developed part of the country. One man who had been given the task of finding landless peasants from the region to settle on land in a distant part of Costa Rica could only find three takers. Even for the landless, the insecurity of landlessness and temporary unemployment do not outweigh the benefits of wages earned during employment, the receipt of paternalistic "extras," the convenience of living in a central region, and the informal insurance of village interdependence.

Ecology beyond the Village

Peasant awareness of ecological interdependence extended beyond San Luis to both the natural and social world of which the village is only a part. The peasants were keenly aware of their own dependence on factors external to and bigger than the village. Their discussions of agriculture and farming revealed close attention to the condition of the natural environment and awareness of the need to sustain the ecosystem, so that it could sustain them. Their choices about political action reflected their perception of themselves as members of a wider national community entitled to certain rights within that community. They saw themselves as contributors to and sustainers of their society and they expect the society, in turn, to sustain them.

Ecological Interdependence with Nature

As in Pedregal, the peasant awareness of ecological interdependence included the natural ecosystem. In San Luis, that awareness manifests itself first in attentiveness to the quality of the soil and second in attention to the behavior of the nearby Poás volcano. Their behavior and interviews reveal their awareness of their dependence on the soil and their willingness to take measures to maintain the soil at a high level of productivity. Their attention to the Poás volcano exhibits itself in their repeated mentioning of it and in their ongoing activity to combat the ill effects of it.

San Luis villagers are more fortunate than their counterparts in Pedregal in that the environmental difficulties they face are less severe, and they themselves have more power to combat the problems they do face. Not only does San Luis enjoy fertile soil that produces some of Costa Rica's finest and richest coffee, San Luis villagers have the financial wherewithal to afford fertilizer. They spend a large proportion of their profits on fertilizer and make every effort to use the best fertilizer available. Several respondents expressed concern that, despite these efforts, the soil is less productive today than it was one generation earlier. Many villagers try to improve soil quality through fertilizer rather than simply maintaining it at its present level. As economic problems have confronted these villagers, some of their fiercest political battles have been waged over access to fertilizer and their need to provide the soil with the best possible fertilizer blends. In the past the Costa Rican government has tried to restrict or eliminate the importation of expensive and high-quality fertilizer from Europe in order to force peasant producers to use the brand made domestically. San Luis villagers and other peasants nationwide opposed this effort and demanded access to the best fertilizer available on the world market. Their political battle with the government was thus heavily influenced by environmental concerns.

The peasants were largely successful. The government agreed to fertilizer imports for a period of time during which the domestic fertilizer producer, Fertica, was required to substantially raise its quality. After that grace period imports would decline if peasant producers were satisfied with Fertica's improved product. San Luis villagers informed me that Fertica had indeed raised its quality and that they were now sufficiently satisfied with it to substitute Fertica's brand for imported fertilizer.

Needless to say, San Luis villagers did not single-handedly engage in or win this struggle with the government. Rather, they were part of an organized, nationwide effort that will be discussed in more detail below. Yet villagers interviewed were very much involved in the struggle and remain committed to it.

> Yes, we won that one and now Fertica's product is pretty good. We have to keep an eye on them, though, because there is a lot of corruption in government enterprises like Fertica. If their fertilizer starts to deteriorate again we have a right to resume importation and to do it through the union so we get lower prices. Personally I most prefer the Dutch fertilizer, it's the best in the world, but for now Fertica is OK. You know we actually have our own people in there [in the factory] analyzing Fertica's product. That was part of what we demanded.

Respondents referred repeatedly to the issue of soil fertilization and protection and the need to remain vigilant about fertilizer quality. They made it clear that soil protection was a top priority for them and that the issue could again become a political battleground if the quality of Fertica's product declined in the future. They had made no binding promises on this score and had secured the political right to again purchase foreign fertilizer if soil protection required it. The peasant position on soil protection reveals the greater level of power enjoyed by San Luis residents as compared with the relative powerlessness of Pedregal villagers viv-à-vis the Somoza state. In San Luis villagers had parlayed their power into environmental protection.

The favored position of San Luis villagers relative to their counterparts in Pedregal is also illustrated with the issue of cooking fuel. Whereas Pedregal residents only have access to wood, San Luis villagers cook with gas, which is regularly delivered to the village in cylinders, trucked in over the paved road. Most residents can afford gas and have no need to cut wood. In addition, their houses are superior to those in Pedregal and keep them relatively warm, even in the chilly rainy season.

The peasants' awareness of their dependence on nature is not confined to the soil. The proximity of an active volcano is a constant reminder of human vulnerability and dependence on nature. It is also an incentive for village cohesion and mutual support. At the same time, villagers did not view Poás as an enemy but appeared proud to live so close to a famous national landmark. The volcano is a part of their natural surroundings, like the rain, sun, and soil. They saw it as something that offered problems to be dealt with but that also had advantages. The very altitude of the village that brings it so close to Poás also allows the production of rich coffee that commands excellent prices. Villagers boasted that they produced the best coffee in Costa Rica, thanks to the altitude. Even ash emissions from Poás have their advantages. Peasants who remembered the ash eruption of the 1950s also recalled that the soil quality had improved markedly thereafter, and the village had survived.

Village memory included several instances in which villagers had worked together to survive volcanic activity. The best example was in the 1950s when huge quantities of ash settled everywhere and destroyed the coffee crop for several years running. Some villagers had given up in despair, sold their land, and left. Most, however, had held on to their land and banded together to help each other through severe poverty. The village had also sent a delegation to the president to request relief for villagers. Miguel, whose story is described above, was a member of that delegation. He remembered being angry because the government did not provide enough relief quickly enough.

When I last visited San Luis in 1989, the villagers were again coming together to confront the latest volcanic activity. At that time Poás had emitted gas rather than ash. The peasants reported that the gas settled on the coffee trees and slowly burned the leaves to death. Again the peasants were working together and with the state to find ways of combatting this latest catastrophe and to obtain relief to enable them to survive a poor harvest. Villagers were disgusted with this problem, since they doubted it would have long-term beneficial effects as the ash had.

Ecological interdependence with the natural environment in San Luis illustrates both the peasants' awareness of their interdependence with nature and their collective ability to confront and solve the problems nature presents. In the areas of soil management and volcano activity the peasants have made great strides in reducing or eliminating the problems they confront. Yet these peasants do not view nature as their enemy. They perceive and act upon their responsibility to also protect nature.

Village/Society Interdependence

The story of political action in San Luis is not confined to the village but takes place in the wider political and economic context of Costa Rican society. The peasants saw themselves as citizens of Costa Rica as well as residents of San Luis, and they perceived themselves as making an important contribution to society through the hard work of coffee production. They were also dependent upon society and affected by political and economic decisions made at the national level. Their political action and attitudes reveal their conviction concerning their rightful place as Costa Rican citizens and their expectation that they be treated with respect by the wider society. The following section illustrates how their perception of community led them into nonviolent collective action that asserted their rights within the national community but also strove to protect that wider community as well.

Ecological Harmony Threatened

The context of economic problems and political action in San Luis is best understood by temporarily stepping back to consider the economic history of the village. In doing so we can see how the peasants have acted to preserve the ecological interdependence described above, and the ecological perspective has become political. The first coffee-producing peasants arrived in the area that is now San Luis in the early part of the twentieth century. They divided the land into plots of not more than one-hundred manzanas and worked their farms with family labor. As the price of coffee rose on the international market, these small producers made enough to survive, but the large export houses and middlemen siphoned off most of their profit. When the peasants formed cooperative purchasing and processing houses in the 1960s, they reaped a larger profit for their coffee. In the early 1970s, the international price of coffee rose dramatically, and the cooperatives allowed the peasants to partake in the bonanza. Village interdependence permitted even the landless to benefit from the economic upswing. Wages paid to coffee pickers in Costa Rica became the highest in Central America.

This time of economic prosperity did not last. With the international economic crisis of the late 1970s, the price of coffee remained stable while the cost of production rose dramatically. Imported inputs such as tools, fertilizers, and insecticides became much more expensive. Products produced domestically wcrc unsatisfactory because of their inferior quality, which resulted in lower productivity and less profit, making credit even more difficult to repay. The amount of credit available to small and medium producers decreased markedly, and interest rates soared from 5 percent to 23 percent by 1985. Following upon the heels of economic prosperity, the crisis appeared even more serious to the peasants. Suddenly they were no longer making the high profits they had made in the early 1970s. Even more threatening was the possibility of losing land when low profits rendered them unable to make their credit payments. Knowledge that some peasants had actually lost their land increased the anxiety level among all small and medium producers. The landless felt the crunch through the decreased availability of employment. Tasks that landed peasants would have paid to have done in 1970 they did for themselves in 1980.[5] Wages failed to keep pace with the cost of living, and for the landless the rising price of land erased all hope of ever becoming landowners.

Rising prices, falling profits, and the threat of land loss amounted to a decline in the living standard the peasants had grown to expect by virtue of their contribution to an export-dependent economy. Their sense of their place in the national economic community and the deserts they expected by right of that place all appeared violated or threatened. Their level of affluence, which villagers felt they deserved by virtue of their economic and social contribution, dropped and threatened to drop further. Society and the economic system, which they saw as represented by the state, no longer provided them the economic position they felt was their due. Dissatisfaction, fear, and anger reigned in San Luis.

In discussing the economic crisis, villagers frequently referred to the social and economic contribution they made to Costa Rica by producing high-quality coffee and bringing in badly needed foreign exchange and by paying taxes on the coffee they produced.

> We are the backbone of this country. With the taxes we pay we are carrying everyone on our backs. Now [1985] we can't even get a decent price for our coffee.

> We are producing for the country. It's a great benefit for the country. We deserve a good price for our coffee and to live in a decent manner, be able to send our children to school.

Collective Action: Unionization

In reaction to deteriorating circumstances and their fear that the situation might worsen still further if they didn't act, the peasants in San Luis began to organize. The crisis, of course, affected peasants everywhere, and San Luis residents joined a unionization movement that was cropping up across the country. Peasants in poorer and more isolated regions such as Limón had felt the crisis even earlier and begun organizing in 1978. Unionization began in

Costa Rica's Central Valley in 1981. In May of that year a peasant union was born in Cartago, historically the focal point in Costa Rica's Central Valley. UPANacional (National Union of Small Agriculturists) quickly became the largest peasant union in Costa Rica, boasting by 1985 a total of sixteen-thousand members, which was more than twice that of any other peasant union. Although by no means national in scope, the new union represented peasants from across the Central Valley region and expanded to include branches in several other regions of the country. In the organizing stage UPANacional encountered little outward opposition.

From its inception UPANacional (hereafter UPA) focused on the problems of the small and medium landowners. Union talk in San Luis centered upon the needs of the smallholders, who had lost ground since the early 1970s. Their goal was to avoid losing any more and, if possible, to regain some of the lost profit margin. Acting through their union in conjunction with landholding peasants elsewhere, landed and landless peasants launched a campaign for economic justice. The anger and determination they exhibited leaves little doubt that they were reacting to a situation which they perceived as a violation of their rights as peasants, as community members, and as Costa Rican citizens.

Through UPA the peasants addressed the Costa Rican government. Their attitude was that the state held an obligation to soften the impact of the economic crisis on very important citizens and national contributors such as themselves. An original petition to President Carazo in August of 1981 focused on problems of credit, imports, prices, marketing, and crop insurance. Although the state had allowed the peasants to organize and publicly present their demands, it failed entirely to respond to those demands at anything other than a rhetorical level. The peasants felt forced to take stronger measures. They organized a series of increasingly challenging, but organized, nonviolent measures designed to attract the attention of the government and satisfy the demands presented in the petition. The publication of the demands in *La Nación*, a leading newspaper, brought no results. A demonstration march between the legislative assembly, the president's house, and the central bank also received no response. Finally, they organized a major blockage of the nation's highways. Peasants turned out across the central region to stand and sit on all the major highways. No agricultural produce could reach the cities. Conservative political actors condemned the blockage and the media carried accusations of communism and antidemocratic tendencies, but despite the outburst, the state did not respond with repression. Faced with a food shortage in the cities and anger from a variety of commercial and popular sectors adversely affected by the blockage, the government moved to negotiate. It met with union leaders and listened to peasant concerns and demands. The state promised to meet a reduced number of the demands originally presented, and the peasants lifted the blockage.

These first few months of union activity established a pattern that would continue through 1984. When faced with specific problems, the peasants acted through UPANacional and requested remedies. They presented their requests to the government in the form of direct petitions and to the public through newspaper advertisements. When no response materialized, they organized demonstrations in San José. When demands were still ignored or promises unfulfilled, union leaders would again call out the region's peasants to block the highways. This final tactic invariably brought the government to the negotiating table and led to the satisfaction of many peasant demands. Gradually, the atmosphere of suspicion and hostility that the first highway blockage engendered softened to one of acceptance and mutual respect between the government and the peasants. Union organization allowed the peasants to halt the economic decline and launch a movement to restore economic justice, as they defined it. Although they continued to have enemies among the more politically conservative elements of the government and large economic interests, the level and frequency of criticisms died down. UPANacional began to win acceptance on the national political scene, as more and more people recognized peasant demands as legitimate. Although not thrilled to be faced with highway blockages and more demands on an economy in crisis, the state accepted the need to negotiate with and make concessions to the peasants. As one San Luis respondent aptly put it, "The government recognizes the peasants as a force to be reckoned with because there are a lot of us. If they completely close the door to us, we can turn against them and they know it."

By 1985, a new pattern in union activity had developed. The legitimacy of the peasants' demands and the reality of their ultimate threat of a highway blockage were such that the government proved willing to negotiate before a blockage. Progress on problems such as reimbursement for crop losses and the establishment of a union import cooperative continued. Newspapers treated these peasants' demands as legitimate, and accusations of communism diminished. Union leadership consciously maneuvered the organization into this more accepted position by adopting some of the state rhetoric about the value of Costa Rican democracy, national independence, and the importance of private property. Between 1985 and 1988, the union dealt directly with the state and got much of what it wanted through negotiations. Over time, however, members got less and less of what they expected and began questioning UPA's close ties to the government. Some claimed that the leadership had been co-opted. During a mass membership general assembly, the peasants voted out Freddy Murillo as their secretary general and replaced him with Guido Vargas, who pursued a more vigorous and demanding strategy vis-à-vis the state.[6]

By 1990, the peasants of UPANacional had achieved and maintained a position as legitimate political actors on the national scene. They had reinvigorated their union and continued to make progress toward alleviating the problems of middle and small landowners in the Central Valley. High-level negotiations had replaced mass protest action. Union leadership did not foresee the need for another blockage within the near future for the purpose of achieving union goals.

Union Limitations

Perhaps the most important criticism of UPANacional is that it has neglected the interests of the landless in the Central Valley. Although it began with the expressed intention of defending the landless as well as the small and medium landowners, the interests of the former soon assumed secondary priority. Through union membership, landless peasants benefit from (reduced) social security payments and thus receive medical care which would otherwise be unavailable to them and their families. For many landless peasants, this is their only reason for belonging to UPANacional, as they receive no other direct benefits from the union. A few participate in union cooperative projects that bring in low-cost work clothes and tools.

Rhetoric to the contrary, UPANacional has made no attempt to address the problem of landlessness, either by redistributing land within the central region or by working toward shifting the landless to land in other regions of the country. Moreover, given its stated respect for private property, its defense of the position of small and medium producers, and its adoption of governmental rhetoric, it seems unlikely that the union could undertake anything as structurally transformational as land redistribution without losing its present legitimacy on the national political scene and thus compromising some of the interests of middle and small landowners.

Nonetheless, landless peasants in San Luis do support UPANacional. Many turn out for demonstrations and blockages and are openly supportive of the union: "Yes, UPA does a little something for us, the workers. They have committees that try to see how they can help us. It's a good union. It helps the landless with membership in a cooperative . . . and other things. It helps [the landed] peasants and with that there is more possibility of work [for us]."

Miguel is a villager whose attitudes toward unionization and political action illustrate an awareness of individual/community interdependence that is the hallmark of the peasant ecological perspective. Barely literate, he is one of the poorest respondents from San Luis, and the only respondent who ever went hungry. On that occasion his life and the lives of his family were saved by community action. Miguel is one of UPA's strongest supporters in the village. His commitment to the union equals that of any of the landed producers who benefit directly from their membership. Yet Miguel is not a landowner, and given his poverty, he stands little chance of ever purchasing land. Miguel sees himself first and foremost as a village member and only secondarily as landless. His perspective allows him to grasp that the union and the village community are dependent on him just as his family relied on the village to survive when he was a boy. "I am very much in favor of UPA. It helps everyone and we have to help it. The more bodies there are [during a blockage], the stronger it is, the more power the union has. UPA benefits the whole village."

Miguel's attitude exemplifies the inability of individualist and communitarian theories to fully explain political attitudes in San Luis. An individualist or rational-actor theory would expect to find Miguel among the village's first and most determined free-riders because he derives no direct benefit from the union even when he does participate. Anyone who theorizes that Miguel will act in a self-interested, short-term maximizing manner misses his sense of individual/village interdependence and perception of the need for mutual supportiveness. Like individualist theory, a communitarian or moral economy theory would predict inaction from someone like Miguel. His subsistence is not threatened, and he exhibits no strong sense of outrage over threats to life. Yet Miguel is one of the most dedicated activists in San Luis. Miguel knows that he and the village are mutually dependent, and this knowledge explains his political action. The support of the San Luis landless for the union is largely attributable to village interdependence in which landed and landless are mutually supportive. Villagers live and work together too closely and are too interdependent for one group to make headway heedless of the plight of the others. Such headway would be short-lived indeed if it excluded the village landless on whom landowners and the village coffee economy rely so heavily. Some of the benefits that accrue to the landholders through UPA eventually trickle down into the hands of the poor. Because they make an important contribution to the village coffee economy, village landless can turn some of what the landed gain to their own benefit. With union success, employment has once again become more steady and secure. "Extras" continue even if they do not increase. A lack of effective union representation has not left the landless peasants of San Luis abandoned.

Political Action in an Ecological World

The village communities of Pedregal and San Luis offer examples of ecological peasant communities in vastly different political and social contexts. In Pedregal, perceptions of community led to choices of political action, and differences among villagers' perceptions explain differences in choices within the community. Perceptions of community also underlie choices of political action in San Luis. Unlike most people in Pedregal, however, the villagers in San Luis see themselves as citizens both of San Luis and of Costa Rican society at large. Furthermore, they see San Luis itself as a subunit of Costa Rican society, contributing to the society (in the form of coffee production), dependent on the society (on state policies on imports, exports, taxation, and credit), and ultimately vulnerable to problems in the wider society if crises develop and the state fails to handle them in ways that are favorable to smallholding coffee producers.

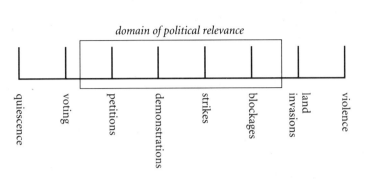

Figure 4.1. UPA: Spectrum of Political Activity

Community Citizens as Actors

These perceptions of their community and of their individual and communitarian place in society have led San Luis residents into political action. Unlike their counterparts in Pedregal, they have opted to act as a single group and, as a group, have chosen unionization. This choice illustrates their understanding of the advantages of nonviolent collective action and their skill in using it. The story of UPANacional reveals the political capacity of the peasantry within a system that permits mass mobilization and political participation. It also underscores the peasant preference for nonviolence where such tactics are an option and can be effective. This preference illustrates the need for social science to also address peasant nonviolent protest. UPA has demonstrated how effective organized nonviolent action can be. Its experience also illustrates the peasant ability to skillfully select among nonviolent tactics and to move from one to another as circumstances require. On the political spectrum shown in Figure 4.1, the experience of UPA and of San Luis villagers within it falls within a subsection of that spectrum running from petitions to blockages. As political actors, the peasants started with the least confrontational tactic that might also be effective: UPA began by petitioning the government. When that tactic failed, UPA moved up the spectrum and tried marches and demonstrations. When those also failed, the union blocked the highways. Later in its political experience, UPA moved back toward demonstrations and even petitions. The story of the union reveals a keen political capacity to move back and forth along the spectrum as political goals require.

At the same time that the peasants seek their own individual economic goals, they remain cognizant of the wider society, of the needs and vulnerabilities of that society, and of their own role and responsibilities within it. Accordingly, they studiously avoid violent actions that might undermine the

Costa Rican democracy. UPA pointedly rejects any actors or groups that it sees as advocating violence such as the Communist parties.[7] Union leaders also reject land invasion, again because they perceive it as a threat to the wider society and to themselves and their own interests within that society. We will see later that political opinion within San Luis is somewhat in disagreement with the union over the issue of land invasion. Nevertheless, the careful choice of tactics that are effective but that do not threaten the wider community illustrates the responsible, rational nature of these peasants. Coming from within a small community, they are trained to watch the ripple effect of their actions even as they step beyond San Luis and act politically within the broader society.

Community Perspective and Political Choices

For UPANacional the relevant area of political action begins with petitions and ends with blockages. These tactics are seen as acceptable, effective, and nondestructive. Most peasants thought that blockages, for example, were tense and time-consuming but necessary and productive.

> It brings us together and we feel encouraged to know that there are a lot of us and that we have the same problems. It breaks us out of our isolation.

> It was the first time I had been able to do something against the big people . . . the first time I had been able to defend myself. The peasant feels inferior next to these people [the state, national elites]. I feel satisfied to be able to fight for the interests of the people.

> It's an important opportunity if only to be able to say "Here I am!"

> You feel like you are defending yourself, that it's something just.

At the same time, these peasants reject quiescence and voting as ineffective in accomplishing specific gains.

> You have to pressure [the state]. If you don't pressure they don't do anything. Even if they make promises they won't keep them if you don't pressure.

> It doesn't matter which party you vote for. Both major parties are the same. Voting keeps us in a democracy, assures continuation of our system, but it resolves nothing for us.

> It's very important to vote. . . . Voting is a symbol of our liberty . . . And it's great fun, a big party. It's important to vote to preserve the democracy because it [democracy] is better, even if we have all these problems. Voting doesn't resolve anything but it makes things so we can continue the way we are. I don't have any respect for the major parties. They have no good platforms to offer. There's no hope for them. The campaign is a shameful farce.

Even if voting accomplishes nothing, at least it means we have a democracy. In a democracy we have the right to scream, to make noise.

Just as villagers are in agreement about the futility of quiescence and voting and agree that blockages are acceptable, almost all villagers in San Luis reject violence as a form of political action.

[Revolution] is not for us. It would ruin everything. You make a revolution when you have nothing left to lose. You say to yourself, "Yes, they can kill me, but so what? I have nothing to lose." But me, I have too much to lose. No, . . . not here, we have too much to lose.

I don't think we would ever have a revolution here because there is dialogue and respect between the people and the government. There are limits on the actions of each one.

There is no reason to use violence now. I don't really agree with what the government is doing, but at least we have peace and dignity, and we are living well.

Villagers in San Luis agree with the union's evaluation of most of these tactics and trust the union to be able to choose from among the acceptable tactics those that will be most effective in a given context.

With respect to land invasion, however, San Luis villagers are not necessarily in agreement either with the union leaders or with each other. Some villagers define land invasion as acceptable because they perceive it as potentially effective but not as dangerously threatening to the wider society. Those who feel this way are often village landless, who see their own landlessness as an unfair distribution of community (village or national) resources. Land invasion, on the other hand, is rejected by others, particularly the landed, because they see it as potentially threatening to themselves as individuals and destructive of the wider community: "You have to respect private property. If we [in UPANacional] don't respect private property, who will? Others will stop respecting ours." This speaker rejects land invasion both on the basis of his individual self-interest (he is a landowner) and on the basis of his society at large. He sees UPA as an example that will be followed by other political activists. Thus we see that on the political spectrum the area of political relevance for San Luis is broader than that for UPANacional, as illustrated by Figure 4.2.

Individual experiences in the context of community determine attitudes toward land invasion. When an individual perceives the ecological system as malfunctioning, he or she moves toward political action. The malfunction may be perceived as an economic or socioeconomic problem or as an injustice that violates moral values. In either case, it is a deviation from the correct ordering and procedure of the peasant's ecological system. A malfunction undercuts the contribution that any one participant makes to the system and consequently undermines the delicate balance of interdependence and mutual support between self, village, and wider society. In an effort to maintain eco-

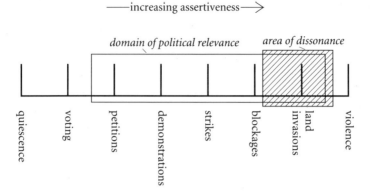

Figure 4.2. San Luis: Spectrum of Political Activity

logical equilibrium, political action is undertaken in an attempt to remedy the situation.

In San Luis, blockages are a common political tactic designed to remedy system malfunction. Petitions and demonstrations are also widely accepted because they have sometimes proven effective. These tactics yield results but do not endanger the national ecological system. They enjoy almost universal support among San Luis residents, and there is no variation in support along economic and socioeconomic lines or in perceptions of injustice. There is no statistically significant relationship between economic, socioeconomic, or injustice variables and support for petitions, demonstrations, and blockages or

Table 4.2. San Luis: Acceptability of Land Invasion as Form of Political Action, by Land Ownership (N = 140*, Missing = 0)

Land Ownership (in manzanas)	Acceptability of Land Invasion (percentages)		
	Low	Medium	High
0	40.0 N = 18	26.7 N = 12	33.3 N = 15
1–4	48.6 N = 18	29.7 N = 11	21.6 N = 8
5–9	38.9 N = 7	38.9 N = 7	22.2 N = 4
10 or more	67.5 N = 27	30.0 N = 12	2.5 N = 1

Note: Chi-square = 14.668. Tau C = −.227. Confidence level = 99.9 percent.

  *Figures on individual land ownership were available through the municipal authorities for all members of San Luis. Accordingly the N for this table is higher than for the others.

Table 4.3. San Luis: Acceptability of Land Invasion as Form of Political Action, by Educational Level (N = 30, Missing = 0)

Respondent Completed Grade School	Acceptability of Land Invasion (row percentages)	
	Acceptable	Not Acceptable
Yes	80	20
	N = 8	N = 2
No	55	45
	N = 11	N = 9

rejection of quiescence, voting, or violence. Villagers agree with each other about these tactics.

Acceptance of land invasion as an appropriate tactic varies among villagers and is related to economic and socioeconomic problems and to the perception of injustice. The data collected on economic and socioeconomic experience and on moral concerns about injustice reveal relationships between each of these variables independently and attitudes toward land invasion. These relationships are best explored through cross-tabular tests. (Tables 4.2, 4.3, and 4.4)

In San Luis, the peasant ecological perception of community places the village and its residents within a national context. They perceive the national economic crisis as violating the proper function of the larger society in a way that injures the village and its residents. That injury undermines villagers' capacity to support themselves and their community and also threatens the contribution they make to the national society. Ultimately, they see danger to themselves (high taxes, low productivity) as a threat to society, and a danger to society (such as communism) as simultaneously a threat to their village and to themselves.

Convictions about deserved standard of living among San Luis peasants differed markedly from those of the Pedregal residents. This is true both for

Table 4.4. San Luis: Acceptability of Land Invasion as Form of Political Action, by Perception of Injustice (N = 30, Missing = 0)

Perception of Injustice	Acceptability of Land Invasion (row percentages)	
	Acceptable	Not Acceptable
Yes	60.7	39.3
	N = 17	N = 11
No	100	0
	N = 2	N = 0

Note: Chi-square = .12560. Tau B = .20336. Confidence level = 86 percent.

what the two communities perceived as just and for their expectations. Because San Luis is closely integrated into the national social and economic scene, the peasants have ample opportunity to witness living standards outside the community and to compare them with their own. Their knowledge of the outside world and their experience a decade ago led them to place community boundaries broadly and to conclude that their right to a particular standard of living had been unjustly breached. In believing that they were entitled to live on a social par with non-peasants, villagers demonstrated their own subscription to peasant justice, including relative equity. While the foundations of peasant justice in Pedregal and San Luis are recognizably similar and include subsistence and relative egalitarianism, peasant notions of justice in San Luis have changed to keep pace with the growing affluence of national society and village integration into the national mainstream.

Land ownership and the size of land plot owned had a significant relationship to the acceptability of land invasion. Thanks to municipal tax record (based on land ownership), landownership status is available for all 140 families in San Luis. Landless peasants and those with insufficient land are significantly more inclined to find land invasion acceptable than peasants who own enough land or more than enough land to live on.

The positive social experience of San Luis meant that there was little variation in most socioeconomic indicators and no significant relationship between most of them and attitudes toward land invasion. For example, hunger is not a relevant experience for San Luis residents because most have never experienced it. Similarly, deaths of siblings and children to preventable childhood diseases were too rare to show any significant relationship to attitudes toward land invasion. Almost all villagers have attended school and are literate, leaving no variation in literacy. Only the successful completion of grade school, as opposed to fewer than six years of education, held any significant relationship to attitudes about land invasion. Peasants who had successfully completed grade school were more likely to find land invasion acceptable than were grade school dropouts.

This relationship is particularly interesting because the significance of landownership correlates in the opposite direction. Landownership conveys a relatively more favorable economic position that could be reflected in having successfully completed grade school. Yet those who have completed grade school are more likely to view land invasion favorably than those who have dropped out. This finding would seem to indicate that education predominated over economic status and that grade school completion is related to a favorable view of land invasion regardless of landed status.

Results of statistical tests of the relationship between the perception of injustice and attitudes toward land invasion are surprising and do not exactly parallel what we would expect from the predictions of the political ecology theory. In a cross-tabular bivariate test, the perception of injustice is clearly related to a positive attitude toward land invasion. However, the relationship is not a statistically significant one. (See Table 4.4.)

It is, of course, difficult to achieve statistical significance with a small sample size (N = 30) and this alone may account for the low level of significance of perceptions of injustice. Because the relationship indicated in Table 4.4 is in the predicted direction but not statistically significant, a similar test on a larger sample might very well find that the relationship between perceptions of injustice and attitudes toward land invasion appears at a statistically significant level.

Conclusion

The experience of San Luis is evidence that rural dwellers and village life can survive into contemporary times and yet retain the characteristics of peasantry and the cohesive, interdependent, rural community. At the same time, national integration has required the community to change and adapt if it wishes to survive and participate in the national economy. If it had abided by only the traditional norms of the moral economy the community would have already been destroyed by modernization. But the peasants' ecological perspective has allowed them to see changes coming and to respond to them. Integration has combined with peasant notions of ecological interdependence so that villagers now see themselves and their village within a wider national community that is the national society. This perception has produced political action and attitudes that are designed to preserve both self and community within the wider society. The unique circumstance and national integration of San Luis also illustrate peasant skill at using collective nonviolent political action. The experience of these villagers shows how crucial these tactics can be and how effective they are at accomplishing desired goals. In the San Luis story we see why peasants might choose nonviolent collective protest, and we learn how community vision can make such tactics the best possible choice.

A theory that will explain the survival of San Luis and the political action of its residents must account for the peasant understanding of ecological interdependence among themselves and between their village and the outside world. Peasant political action is not unidimensional and is neither solely self-interested nor purely communitarian and altruistic. It is, in fact, both. Political action in San Luis is indeed premised on calculations of immediate benefit, in that there are substantial economic incentives to union membership. Yet if short-term self-interested concerns were the only motives, San Luis would be plagued by free-ridership, and unified action would be impossible. Because union benefits accrue to all peasant producers and coercion is not available to force peasants to participate, the self-interested short-term perspective would lead almost all villagers to become free-riders. Free-ridership would be especially prevalent among village landless, such as Miguel.

But, as the theory of political ecology predicts, short-term personal gain is only a part of the peasant calculus. Peasants also factor in responsible rationality, foreseeable consequences, and interdependence between the group and the individual. This perspective explains the strength of collective action and the fact that some of UPANacional"s strongest supporters are among the village landless. In San Luis rationality is more responsible than free-ridership. The truly rational peasant perceives the extent to which the individual economic position is bound up with community welfare. Free-ridership is both irresponsible and self-defeating.

At the same time, action in San Luis is hardly traditional and moves far beyond any guidance that might be obtained from traditional norms alone. Tradition offers a starting point for defining social life in the village. Tradition stresses norms of reciprocity among villagers and sanctions against those who refuse to participate in such exchanges. Tradition encourages a moral economy that protects subsistence. But tradition does not cause villagers to look increasingly outward, to become angry over injustices at the national level or to engage in collective nonviolence that addresses the state. Tradition does not explain the sophistication these peasants have attained in participating in the market economy, becoming environmentally aware soil specialists, or maneuvering through the pitfalls of political interaction with the state. Traditional norms and sanctions, such as those of a moral economy, do not account for the social interaction among villagers surrounding the production of coffee or the political demands made of the state in the context of coffee production. Traditional norms protecting subsistence do not explain peasant perceptions that they deserve a living standard substantially above subsistence. Tradition neither predicts nor explains unionized action in San Luis.

Having chosen action that protects individual and community survival together, the peasants have found that collective action itself reinforces their convictions of interdependence and their need for each other. In political action, as in economic production, the peasants need each other. Their unionized struggle for better working conditions has not been easy, and no single one of them or subgroup of them could have done it alone. Political action confirms that their individual and collective well-being is itself dependent on their ability to work together. Thus the peasant political ecology led San Luis villagers into political action and is itself reaffirmed by that action.

Nicaragua: oxcart hauling water during the dry season

Nicaragua: revolutionary village of Quebrada Honda, peasant children. These are the children of Jose, quoted in Chapter 6.

Nicaragua: peasant making basket

Nicaragua: peasant village of Pedregal. This photo illustrates the rocky soil that played an important role in the village's political story.

Nicaragua: peasant family. The young man with the hat was killed by the Contras one year after the photo was taken.

Costa Rica: a relatively affluent peasant family and their wooden home

Costa Rica: a peasant family and their cement home

Costa Rica: main road in La Lucha village. Sign gives the name "La Lucha." Use of that name is part of the peasants' struggle against the government and the IDA.

Costa Rica: La Lucha, one-room wooden shack of one of the poorer peasant families in the village

5 ▫ ECOLOGICAL COMMUNITY
El Hogar and La Lucha, Costa Rica

Between quiescence and rebellion lies a whole series of collective nonviolent actions that allow peasants to participate in their modernizing societies in a constructive and integrated fashion. These types of political action are becoming increasingly common among the peasantry, and it is essential to have a theory that explains their usage as well as that of quiescence and rebellion. The previous chapter began to explore how the theory of political ecology explains peasant usage of certain mild forms of collective nonviolence. This chapter continues that exploration but addresses more assertive forms of protest, particularly land invasion. In the stories of El Hogar and La Lucha, Costa Rica, we see how the peasant understanding of interdependence led these villages to petition, demonstrate, block highways, and ultimately invade land, all in the effort to ensure interdependence and therefore survival.

The theory of political ecology presented in Chapter 1 suggests how political action grows out of an ecological perspective that peasants acquire from village life. Previous approaches and theories restricted their attention and explanations primarily to life within the peasant village and to relations among villagers. Yet, as we saw in Chapter 4, as peasantries become more and more integrated into the modern world, participating in national societies economically and politically, a theory that takes into consideration peasant perspectives beyond the village becomes necessary. This chapter uses the theory of political ecology to explore relations within two Costa Rican villages and the political action that grew out of intravillage relations. The story here is particularly useful in seeing the political implications of the peasants' ecological perspective as it includes more than one village and an additional form of political action.

Like their counterparts in San Luis, the peasants in El Hogar and La Lucha chose demonstrations and highway blockages as ways of preserving community, but they chose to continue their struggle with land invasion. The story of El Hogar and La Lucha demonstrates a keen awareness of interdependence not only within one village (El Hogar) but also between it and another village

(La Lucha) which peasants from the original community helped to establish. As with San Luis, the story of these two Limón communities illustrates the implications of the peasants' political ecology for society at large. In El Hogar, villagers attempted to sustain themselves through interdependence. Over time, however, their best efforts proved fruitless and even interdependent support could not keep a second generation of villagers at an adequate living standard. The villagers looked beyond the village for possible solutions to their poverty. La Lucha, the second village in this case study, arose from the vision of former El Hogar residents. These former residents of El Hogar could no longer survive within El Hogar and were joined by landless peasants from other villages who also found themselves unable to survive in their own villages of origin. The story of these two villages demonstrates the extent to which the sense of ecological community stayed with these peasants, even when they no longer lived in a village community on a daily basis.

Community Context: El Hogar

Villagers in El Hogar are much poorer than their counterparts in San Luis. Before the founding of La Lucha, economic problems in El Hogar were so severe that many landless villagers could not survive in the community. This situation is quite typical of rural Limón province, and the problems of El Hogar exemplify those of many long-standing villages in Limón. Exclusion of villagers by the practical reality of poverty, however, did not deny the landless a place in the peasants' political ecology which is inclusive, egalitarian, and resistant to subordination. It recognizes the needs of all rural dwellers, whether or not the village land base can support them, and it led peasants from El Hogar and elsewhere to invade land and establish a new community of interdependent individuals where none existed before.

Like San Luis, El Hogar is a cohesive community, despite extensive integration into the market system and Costa Rican society. That cohesion is evident in the nature of village relations and in the form of political action taken on behalf of the landed. It also appears in village support for the landless and in an ecological perspective that extends beyond the village. El Hogar is a very small village of not more than forty families and is located in the interior of Limón province, four kilometers outside the small town of Guacimo. Village land originally belonged to banana companies, and the original path into the jungle was the railroad track. As banana plants died of the Panama disease in the 1920s and 1930s, the banana company sold off its Limón land and abandoned the province. Peasants who purchased the abandoned land hiked over the railroad tracks into the site that is now El Hogar. The tracks that the companies had laid for shipping out bananas were originally the only means of access to El Hogar.

Those same tracks still connect the village with Guacimo, but now a dirt and gravel road parallels the tracks, passing through El Hogar and moving

Table 5.1. El Hogar: Surplus/Deficit of Community Land Ownership (in hectares)

Land needed to support average peasant family	15.7
Average village land ownership	11.5
Average deficit	-4.2

deeper into the jungle to the next village. Public services in El Hogar indicate that the village has been more economically integrated than publicly served. The only public transport is a small train that runs from El Hogar to Guacimo once each morning and evening. The entire village has running water, although many homes lack flush toilets. Only houses along the track have electricity. The community has a small grocery store, a one-room elementary school, and a public telephone. However, neighboring Guacimo is a small commercial center connected by bus and train to other parts of Costa Rica. It boasts a church, a Red Cross outpost, and a small agricultural technical school. The nearest hospital and high school are in the city of Guapiles, nine miles away.

Village land is rich and fertile, perfect for maize, beans, and yucca. Over time, corn and yucca became both cash and subsistence crops. Today corn is the primary cash commodity. Villagers produce vegetables and raise animals for milk, eggs, and meat. Although the land is superior, the village economy is similar to that of Pedregal. Peasants grow much of what they need for home consumption but also sell certain products commercially on the national market. Unlike Pedregal, however, where only some residents engaged in limited market activity, in El Hogar all landowners are both commercial and subsistence farmers and have extensive market ties. Furthermore, peasants have easy access to Guacimo markets, where they can purchase items not produced at home.

Most El Hogar families own land and grow maize, beans, and yucca. A few villagers who own insufficient land to support themselves supplement their income with rented land or by working for neighbors. However, such possibilities are extremely limited, and most villagers who are land short have been forced to leave the village in search of work elsewhere. I interviewed fifteen peasant farmers in El Hogar, all of whom owned at least some land. The average landholding among respondents was 11.5 hectares. Villagers estimate that a family needs 15.7 hectares to support itself. The figures reveal the inadequacy of the average landholding and show that village land has already surpassed its carrying capacity. (See Table 5.1.) There is no surplus to support landless villagers as there was in Pedregal and San Luis. Forty-seven percent of villagers own so little land that they cannot survive without renting from their neighbors or working part-time as laborers on the neighbor's land. Even then, the living is poor by Costa Rican standards. El Hogar's economy has stretched as far as it can to accommodate as many adult children of the first generation as possible, but most of the second generation have had to leave the village.

In the 1930s and 1940s, the peasants sold their corn and yucca to wholesale buyers who traveled in and out of El Hogar along the railroad tracks. These merchants hauled the product to market in mule-pulled wagons fitted to run along the tracks. They paid poorly for the grain and charged the peasants the transport cost. The peasants knew the grain commanded a much higher price in San José but had no other method of getting it there. Isolated, disorganized, and almost unable to sell their grain otherwise, the peasants took what they were paid without argument.

Chronic Economic Problems and the Peasant Response

The peasants were not the only group who suffered at the hands of the wholesale grain purchasers. The arrangement also produced very high prices on basic foodstuffs for the Costa Rican consumer. In 1943, the government established the National Production Council (CNP), which became the sole buyer of staple crops. The CNP was designed to ensure both peasants and consumers a fair price. Despite laudable intentions, the CNP soon succumbed to corruption, which undermined its purpose. At their own expense, peasant sellers transported their corn long distances to a handful of CNP processing plants. Upon arrival, they often stood in line for days in all weather conditions. CNP officials weighed the corn and priced it by weight. The price was reduced if the corn was insufficiently dry. Peasants were responsible for bringing the corn in dry, and CNP officials ran laboratory tests for humidity. Peasants reported that the weighing and testing practices were inaccurate and corn prices unfair. They said that the scales underestimated weight, and the tests overestimated humidity. They had no way to check the evaluations made by CNP officials and no recourse if they felt they had been cheated. Moreover, peasants received payment by check and often found there was no cash in the bank to cover the checks. They frequently lost more productive time after they had sold their crop, waiting around the bank in Guacimo for funds to arrive.

Peasants felt that under the CNP system they were little better off than they had been with the private wholesale merchants. The price they received for their grain was still barely enough to live on. There was neither space nor tolerance for protest within the corrupt CNP system, and individuals who protested went to jail. This situation continued into the 1970s.

General indicators of life quality expose the human side of the poverty these peasants endured. Forty percent of all respondents reported having lost siblings to preventable childhood diseases or to hunger. One older resident of El Hogar remembered that of sixteen children in his childhood home, only the four youngest had survived to adulthood. Twenty-eight percent of respondents had lost children to childhood diseases, and 43 percent remembered going hungry during childhood. One respondent said that four of his siblings had died of hunger. Fifteen percent had suffered hunger in adulthood, and 15 percent of the peasants interviewed were also illiterate. The median level of schooling among all respondents was three years. Medical care is a recent gain that most respondents have achieved only in the past fifteen years. Thanks to effort made by the local peasant union (UPAGRA, different from UPA discussed in Chapter 4), 87.5 percent now have access to some medical care. Although only one respondent had a car and only three had motorcycles, 40 percent owned battery-operated televisions and 55 percent had radios.

Peasants who leave El Hogar and other villages because they cannot attain enough land to live on usually do not leave Limón. They seek employment in the banana industry or in nearby urban centers and retain ties to their home communities. Departure from the community does not deprive them of a sense of interdependence between themselves and the village or wider society. As peasants, they retain a sense of their own right to join equally in the wider society. Most dream of becoming landowners and of returning again to the smallholding life style. The life of the landless who have left peasant communities such as El Hogar is an important part of the village story. Their story illustrates the presence of the peasants' ecological perspective even among those not living in a village and not running a family farm. The experience and opinion of the landless is also crucial to understanding the background of La Lucha.

Limón province has a serious problem of landlessness. Landownership is concentrated, in that the banana companies and other economic and political elites who live in San José are the major landowners. The landless condition of second-generation members of El Hogar and other similar villages is exacerbated by migration to Limón from other parts of Costa Rica. Many landless peasants wish to work for the banana companies but find that such employment is only temporary. The companies fire workers at age forty when they are defined as having passed their physical prime. This policy thrusts a generation of workers onto society without retirement benefits and many years before they can retire. The loss is increased by the fact that banana work is all these people are trained to do. Many peasants prefer to avoid banana work entirely because it will not solve their problem of landlessness but will deprive them of their most physically productive years.

Life for the landless is very difficult. These people are among the poorest in Costa Rica.

> When I was a boy, my father was a laborer and earned 75 cents a day. Life was harder then. They [employers] paid really badly and there was work only two or three days per week. We were hungry, as hungry as animals. As an adult I was always a laborer and we never had land. . . . Life was worse than now, really terrible and with hunger. We ate monkeys, bananas, and coconuts, whatever was on the trees. I always remember my youngest son almost died of hunger, and we had to make him eat monkey.

> My family was abandoned by my father, and we survived by theft. I left home as soon as I could. I married and continued work as a laborer. We went hungry

often when I was a child, but then as an adult, we didn't go hungry. I worked as a laborer in San Carlos and that was worse than here because there was less work and the wages lower, but we still never went hungry.

One woman whose husband had worked for the banana companies remembered what that life had been like:

> When I lived with my father, we lived OK, but once I got married, we lived much worse because we had no place to live. It was horrible working for the banana company. Every so often they moved us from one house to another, where ever they sent us and the children had no place to play. The children only had one room. I went hungry living with my father and also living with my husband.

In the communities of Pedregal and San Luis, the village economies have each sustained life among all villagers including the landless. There the small difference between average landownership and the plot size needed to sustain a family resulted in a surplus that has been partially indirectly redistributed to village landless. Exchange relationships of land, labor, wages, and goods have allowed landless villagers to find a home within these communities. The existence of reciprocity systems in these villages rests on a foundation of individual economic incentives, traditional norms of egalitarianism and resistance to exploitation, and upon an ecological sense of interdependent community.

El Hogar differs from Pedregal and San Luis in that its economy has no surplus that can be redistributed to village landless. Even landed villagers are struggling to make ends meet on plots that are too small to fill a family's subsistence needs. There is no land that can be redistributed through rent or land/labor exchange relationships. Aside from the land shortage, structural factors mitigate against material exchange relationships of interdependence in El Hogar. First, corn does not require the intensive harvest labor that many cash crops demand. Barring inclement weather, peasants can collect their crop more slowly using family labor alone. This arrangement deprives village landless both of the economic leverage over landowners they have in San Luis and of the opportunity to participate in and sustain community by contributing to the village economy. Corn provides neither social nor economic avenues for including the landless in the productive life of the village. Second, unlike coffee, corn is not a lucrative cash crop planted for the large profits it will bring. It is primarily a subsistence crop that peasants can also sell to urban consumers. Its low cash value and its restriction to the domestic market make the living it affords much poorer than that derived from coffee production. Corn production has historically meant that El Hogar residents are very poor and generally cannot afford to hire workers even when they need supplemental labor.

Although interdependence surrounding agricultural production is less in El Hogar than in San Luis, and this has somewhat reduced peasant awareness of interdependence, it is nonetheless remarkable that the peasants' ecological perspective is still as prevalent as it is even without support from the practical necessities of farming. Even when the poorest villagers, the landless, have left the village and their need for support is not evident on a daily basis, awareness of their condition and of generalized interdependence remains. Moreover, the village landed are sufficiently poor to recognize their own potential dependence on the community for survival. Thus reciprocity and mutual exchange remain in El Hogar even when not directly related to production. For example, residents exchange small amounts of temporary labor. They return labor help in kind so that neither party needs to use scarce cash in payment. Those selling food may give some away or sell it at reduced prices to those in need. Yet villagers are aware that they have little surplus to share among themselves.

Villagers see the world and the condition of their village in interdependent terms. Landowners who still live in El Hogar worry about landlessness even though they themselves own land. Luis, for example, owns a fine land plot in El Hogar and has been able to maximize its productivity. His level of education allows him to learn new agricultural techniques that improve his income. He is one of the few El Hogar residents who owns a tractor. Luis is unusual in that he is a second generation resident of El Hogar. He explained his position as follows:

> We [in El Hogar] have problems of landlessness here. I don't know what we are going to do about them [the landless] in the future. We don't have any more land for them. I'd like to have more of my friends here in El Hogar, but there isn't enough land. The problem is that the big guys [the large landowners] own so much land that there isn't any more for us.

Luis uses the words "we" and "us" even though his own family has enough land to support itself, and the problem he worries about affects others more severely. Yet he sees landlessness as a problem that belongs to the community and not only to the individuals affected. Many of his boyhood acquaintances who might stand by him in crisis have been forced to leave El Hogar. Both physical distance and poverty reduce their chances of being able to help Luis should he be in need. Luis' neighbors also repeatedly expressed concern for the landless and worry over what the community can do for them.

As Luis's comments illustrate, the awareness of landlessness includes an understanding of interdependence between individual and community. The peasants' comprehension of the causes of landlessness reveals an understanding of the village place in a wider ecological community. The villagers know that soil fertility is high in Limón and that local land could easily support the population if peasants had adequate access to it. They know that the poverty which results from landlessness or tiny land plots is not due to poor soil quality or to a population level that has exceeded the soil's carrying capacity in the region. Rather, it is due to the fact that large expanses of land are inaccessible to the peasantry because they are privately owned. The traveler through Limón cannot help but note the open expansiveness of the province that is so different from central Costa Rica. Much of this land is not farmed. It lies fallow, is sparsely used for cattle ranching, or belongs to national forests.

Peasant notions of justice preclude the extensive ownership, without use, of scarce resources. In the context of poverty, peasants perceive land concentration and fallow fields to be an injustice. In their view, the arrangement fails to recognize either the peasants' right to an adequate and comparable economic place in Costa Rican society or their contribution to the national economy. Awareness of landlessness and the perception that landlessness is unnecessarily imposed on the local peasantry by an unjust social and economic system is part of the ecological perspective in El Hogar. This view is also in evidence outside the village among the landless. The perception that the ecological system is unnecessarily off balance affects political attitudes and action in El Hogar.

Organization in Response to the Problems of Production

Discontent over inadequate land access, low crop prices, and the corrupt practices at the local CNP corn processing plant finally boiled over when economic crisis hit Costa Rica in the late 1970s. Regional poverty meant that the crisis hit Limón's peasantry first and was felt most cruelly. The Limón peasants became the first in Costa Rica to unionize. In 1977, Rolf, a local school teacher from Guacimo, was disturbed by witnessing the treatment peasants received at the Guacimo processing plant. This is Rolf's story.

> I was a teacher at the agricultural high school in Guacimo. I always talked with my students, and they told me what life was like in the countryside, trying to produce corn and live off what was produced. I wasn't married then so I spent a lot of time hanging around downtown Guacimo, talking with the peasants. Some of them were the parents of my students. I learned what a hard life they had, how it was such a struggle to produce, and in the end they barely earned enough to live on. The price paid at the CNP was really low and they had all kinds of ways of ripping people off. One day I was standing outside a local cantina, and I saw they were taking a guy away in handcuffs. They had him handcuffed and were taking him down the middle of the street. They just treated him in a rough and humiliating way. Everyone was staring at him, and he couldn't do anything to defend himself. I felt really bad to see this man treated that way. I felt terrible. It really made a big impression on me. Then I started to get angry. I got more and more angry, and I started to think about a way the peasants could defend themselves. I thought that maybe they could form a peasant organization that could defend them against injustices like these.[1]

Previous efforts to organize Limón's peasants had been led by urban dwellers from San José, students, or members of the Communist party. These ventures had failed, and the Communist party in Costa Rica had decided that it was impossible to organize the peasantry. Unlike earlier organizers, however, Rolf was not an urban "outsider." His occupation had placed him within the peasant community, and he was liked and respected by smallholders and the landless alike. Rolf began his efforts by looking for peasant organizers in El Hogar, which soon became the hub of union activity and political support. He began with a small group of landless and land short peasants who lived in El Hogar or had family connections in the village. This group met frequently, decided to form a union, and began traveling to more isolated villages to rally support for the new organization. Once contact had been established, peasant enthusiasm kindled easily.

In late 1977, the peasants christened their new union UPAGRA (Union of Small Agriculturists of the Atlantic Region). By early 1978, Rolf and the peasant leaders agreed that, united, they had enough strength to act. As with UPA-Nacional, UPAGRA's initial attention was to the needs of landed peasants. They focused their energies locally rather than appealing to the state apparatus in distant San José. In that they considered the local CNP to be their principal problem and primary enemy, they decided to combat perceived injustices and corruption perpetrated by the local CNP officials. The tactics chosen by the new union demonstrate the peasants' awareness of the wider society and of their rights and responsibilities within it. Regional history includes extensive use of unionization, petitions, and numerous other kinds of nonviolent collective tactics. The peasants also knew that they needed the CNP. They depended on it as the principal purchaser of their product. Their goal was to reform the CNP, not to undermine or eliminate it.

Several weeks prior to the harvest the peasants presented a petition to CNP officials at the processing plant in Guacimo. They wanted to reduce lines by increasing personnel and establishing longer hours of service during harvest season. They demanded weighing and testing methods that could be followed and verified by the peasant seller. They requested that outside experts should be permitted to inspect the scales and correct them for inaccuracies. For several weeks, the CNP ignored the petition, hoping that the peasants would forget their demands and give up. The peasants, however, sought publicity for their cause and, through the newspapers, warned the CNP that the new union would take stronger measures if a response was not forthcoming. When harvest time arrived, the CNP opened its doors; no improvements in weighing, testing, or pricing practices had been made. The peasants' petition had been disregarded. The tactic was designed to break union unity. The CNP calculated that some peasants, anxious about crop spoilage, would soon sell their grain at CNP prices. They calculated that other peasants would see that the protest was in vain, and would eventually bring their grain to be sold.

The peasants, however, proved equal to the challenge. Support was sufficiently strong and widespread that most did not yield to anxiety and temptation. Instead of stampeding to sell their grain, peasants left their corn at home and moved to the highways. They set up highway blockages on all of the three major roads leading into Guacimo. Local villages, including El Hogar, no longer had access to Guacimo. Leaders estimated that at least one thousand peasants turned out at each blockage point. Peasants who would have broken ranks and brought their grain in for sale were physically unable to get into town. Traffic not carrying corn could continue along the roads but no corn could reach the CNP receiving station in Guacimo. Faced with the possibility of having no corn for Costa Rican consumers, the CNP yielded. In negotiations, the peasants won all of the points they had demanded. That season, corn sales proceeded under new conditions.

The peasants had won their first major victory. From then on, the CNP would take them and their new union more seriously. Although some problems with the CNP remained unsolved and local officials were still not above attempting to cheat the peasants in new ways or at new receiving stations, the situation would never again become as extreme as it had been in 1977. In the aftermath of the 1978 highway blockage, UPAGRA did not even attract the negative publicity that UPANacional would draw after its first blockage several years later. The state made no attempt to repress or disband UPAGRA or to silence its leaders. As long as UPAGRA worked within the established economic system, it would be reluctantly accepted on the national and local political scene.

Although individuals obviously had economic incentives for political action and unionization, the short-term reasons for free-ridership or inaction were even stronger, and individualist motivation alone cannot explain the political action described here. The peasants were angry at the CNP, but anger cannot explain their perception of themselves as part of a large ecological system that included the CNP as well as the village. The establishment of UPAGRA epitomizes the political ecology of the peasant because it illustrates the ways in which concerns about a viable interdependent system extended beyond the village itself and had political effect. Neither the peasant perspective nor their political action was confined to the village. Their perception of agrarian problems reflected a keen awareness of the connection between events beyond the village and circumstances in El Hogar. The peasants understood the link between local poverty and the wider society. Problems imposed from beyond the village came in the form of both the CNP processor and extensive land concentration. At the same time, once the peasants looked outward and discovered the extent of the political opposition to their efforts, their need for and commitment to each other increased even further. In this way political action and the opposition it received increased the peasants' awareness of ecological interdependence among themselves. UPAGRA thus reflected but also reinforced its members' ecological perspective of poverty and local economic problems in the context of the wider society. That perception caused villagers to act as part of a cohesive group that went beyond the village boundaries.

Union Response to the Problems of Landlessness

Even after the peasants' initial victory against the CNP, the ecological perspective of peasants within El Hogar still caused them to worry about the plight of landless peasants beyond the village. Villagers in El Hogar are not the first peasants in this study to perceive their community as part of a wider society. The ecological perspective of peasants in San Luis also placed that village in economic and political interaction with the wider natural and social world. Yet, given a balanced relationship with the outside world, the survival of the villagers in San Luis could be accommodated within the village itself. Unlike the central valley, however, the world around El Hogar was so ecologically unbalanced, so divergent from the peasant sense of justice, that the victory with the CNP only marginally redressed the problem. Even as CNP practices improved, former members of El Hogar and the children of village residents still could not be accommodated within the village. The peasants' victory with the CNP was incomplete in the wider context of ecological interdependence, and although the problems of landed peasants seemed at least temporarily addressed through UPAGRA, the injustice of land tenure in Limón province continued. El Hogar and other villages like it still could not sustain its own members. This unaddressed problem led landless peasants from El Hogar and elsewhere to contemplate land invasion. Landed villagers such as Luis and even nonpeasants from the local area supported this idea. Their ecological perspective led many peasants to countenance an effort to address imbalance that only indirectly affected themselves.

Near El Hogar lay a plantation of five thousand hectares, whose absentee owner lived, worked, and owned other property in San José. Although cattle grazed a small portion of this land, it was mostly unworked, either forested or lying fallow. From the peasants' point of view the land was abandoned, unworked, and unproductive. In view of their own need for land, the situation seemed unfair and a violation of their own standards of social justice and relative equity. These standards exist in part to preserve interdependence within the community. The unjust pattern of land tenure violated ecological interdependence by imposing unnecessary and avoidable poverty on the neighbors and children of landed peasants in El Hogar and other villagers. The poverty of these neighbors and children in turn undermined their ability to contribute to and sustain community and family life. Parents whose children were landless carried an exhausting economic responsibility that could never be entirely fulfilled within the context of the village. Families whose nieces, nephews, and neighbors were far away on the banana plantations or struggling to make ends meet without land found their community support system impoverished. Dependence on their own resources in the context of poverty prevalent in El Hogar left villagers in an extremely precarious position with almost no group insurance to depend on. Landless individuals could barely support themselves and could offer nothing to neighbors or help to maintain a supportive community. Individually and socially, landlessness in El Hogar and in Limón province as a whole was costly, risky, and unacceptable.

The existence of landlessness when nearby land lay fallow violated traditional peasant norms which include a code of relative egalitarianism and resistance to the subordination of one person's needs to those of another. Extensive wealth side by side with local poverty violated norms of relative equity. One person enjoyed luxury while most suffered poverty that was extreme by Costa Rican standards. Land tenure arrangements in the area violated peasant norms of resistance to subordination. The large landowner subordinated the interests of one group of people to his own. Peasants felt that the basic needs of many people should not be subordinated to one person's desire for luxury. Peasants were aware that their poverty was not a part of the natural order. Landlessness was obviously neither inevitable nor due to unavoidable population pressure, as land was plentiful nearby. This inequitable arrangement undermined the ecological balance in which community and individual survival depend on each person's being able to contribute to production and the maintenance of community. The peasants expressed their perception as follows:

> If there are people who need it [land] and there is abandoned land, it is just [justo] that they should take it because then there is more production for the people and for the country. The country needs producers, and there are plenty of people who want to produce.

> The people who have no land have to invade [land]. There is a lot of land that is not being used and people who have nothing.

> It is an injustice that they [large landowners] do not work the land. If they have it abandoned like that, invasion is justified.

A number of landless and land-short peasants, many of whom had lived in El Hogar, decided to invade the plantation that lay fallow almost next door to the village. With the assistance they requested from UPAGRA, they recruited landless peasants from other villages, and gradually a large group formed. Most lived in the general area from which the highway blockers had come in 1978, and some of the key leaders were natives of El Hogar. There was substantial local support for the invasion, even among nonpeasants, including local merchants and shopkeepers who lent support. The peasants hoped to bring in Costa Rica's inert agrarian reform institute IDA, then ITCO, to purchase the property. Landed supporters of the invasion understood that they would not qualify for land under IDA's guidelines if and when the invasion became successful but that the landless would.[2]

In March of 1980, the peasants invaded the land to establish a new community. They went in as a group of eighty or more with their entire families, congregating in an area that is now the site of the La Lucha primary school. They coordinated their efforts and worked the land together rather than dividing it into individual plots from the outset. They constructed small shanties of cardboard, wood, metal, and other portable scraps and camped out in lean-to shelters and cooked over open fires for months on end. They planted corn, beans and other vegetables. Within a few weeks of the initial invasion, the Costa Rican Rural Guard forced the peasants off the land at gunpoint and burned the shanties and the newly planted crops. One of the squatters explained, "They fell on us like on pigs. They surrounded us with guns in a big circle. I was scared to death. We never raised a hand against them but went quietly with them." Yet as soon as the public authorities left, the peasants once again entered the property and started from scratch to rebuild homes and replant crops. This scenario was repeated a second time as the struggle stretched out over most of 1981.

Finally, the Rural Guard took stronger action. It threatened the peasants with M-16s, shooting into the air and trees above the small community. Once again, the peasants were driven off the land. More than one hundred of them were imprisoned in Guapiles and Limón, where conditions were punishing: "We were in jail thirteen days. The food was terrible, just little rocks of rice, and there was glass in the food the last day we were there. There was a judge who arrived and defended us and forced the kitchen to make some more food. He said we weren't criminals, we hadn't done anything."

Up to this point, IDA had remained uninvolved in the conflict even though the institute is supposed to reduce the problem of landlessness in Costa Rica. The peasants felt that the invasion was not succeeding and that repression against them was growing worse. They decided to confront IDA directly and attract national attention to the cause. Several hundred landless peasant families and local supporters rented buses and went to San José, where they occupied the IDA building, machetes in hand, and refused to allow personnel to leave.

In the face of such clear determination, the government began to yield. Through their union, the peasants had learned what IDA regulations required for the receipt of land. They demanded that IDA purchase the land from its owner and distribute it to the landless invaders according to IDA's own laws concerning land redistribution. They presented a list of peasants who had continuously participated in the invasion and who qualified for land according to IDA's own regulations. While IDA processed the claim, the peasants were allowed to remain on the land and began to feel like a real community. After eighteen more months of bureaucratic delay, they won their battle for the land and established the La Lucha community. Albeit at great cost and on only a small scale, they had succeeded in establishing an ecological peasant community. They would not forget the difficulty they had encountered nor the reluctance with which IDA had redistributed the land. From the peasants' point of view, the IDA officials had been reluctant, deceptive, and evasive throughout the process and had only conceded because the peasants had forced them to do so. This experience proved to be a portent for relations between IDA and the new community.

La Lucha

The story of La Lucha in the first years after IDA officially recognized it (1982–88) exemplifies the peasant struggle for interdependent community. Although IDA officially acknowledged the new village, its de facto policies fell far short of treating it as a legitimate peasant community. For almost a decade after its establishment, IDA sought to control La Lucha, to undermine its autonomy and self-direction, to undercut its capacity for mutual support, and to maneuver it into extensive dependence on IDA. In response, the village has fought back, standing again and again as a tiny but determined unit against the power of a major state institution. Far from undermining peasant cohesion and community, the struggle against IDA has reinforced and strengthened the process of reestablishing ecological community. The very ferocity and duration of the struggle has underscored for the villagers the extent to which they need each other and must act as a group if they wish to survive individually and as a whole. Symbolic of the invasion and the subsequent effort, villagers and locals christened the new community "La Lucha," "The Struggle." Also symbolically, IDA has refused to recognize this name for the community. Instead, IDA refers to it as "Santa Rosa," even though pedestrians in the village and nearby urban centers, when asked for directions, have no idea where Santa Rosa village is located.

The peasants date the establishment of the La Lucha community from 1981, although IDA still had not granted all land titles even by 1987. La Lucha is a larger community than El Hogar and consists of over one hundred families. As a result of IDA administration, village land is divided into standard parcels of fifteen hectares. The vast majority of La Lucha residents own one of these parcels, no more and no less. Respondents estimated that an average of 13.48 hectares was sufficient to support a family, leaving a surplus of value that may be redistributed to less fortunate villagers as time passes and landlessness reappears. The figure indicates that the peasants and IDA agree on required plot size and that IDA is correct in parceling out La Lucha land in fifteen-hectare plots.

Public services in La Lucha are worse than in El Hogar and poor by Costa Rican standards. The community is twenty-seven kilometers from Guacimo and seven kilometers from the small town of Rio Jiménez. The road from Guacimo to Rio Jiménez is paved, but the road leading into La Lucha from Rio Jiménez is dirt and gravel and of very poor quality. It winds through the entire community, crossing two dangerous bridges, one of which consists only of loose wooden boards nailed together. No train tracks pass through La Lucha, but a bus runs between the community and Guacimo twice each day.

A primary school (grades one through six) and a general store stand in the center of the community. La Lucha lacks running water; residents use wells. There is no electricity or telephone service, and the nearest public telephone is in Rio Jiménez, which also has a general store and a canteen. La Lucha residents must travel to Guacimo for Red Cross services and forty-one kilometers to Guapiles for a hospital or to attend a regular high school. In La Lucha, I interviewed twenty-five adults, twenty-two men and three women, each of whom owned a standard fifteen-hectare plot in the community. Most interviewees had participated in the 1980–81 land invasion and had lived in the community ever since. Some were former residents of El Hogar.

Although newly landed status has substantially improved living standards and levels of security among La Lucha residents, between 1982 and 1987 life in La Lucha continued to be troubled with conflict. Involvement with IDA offered the only possibility of permanent land access, but IDA has also demanded administrative control over village life in ways that would never be acceptable in other Costa Rican communities. IDA's control and involvement resemble the control a landowning boss might exercise over a community of sharecroppers who depend on him for survival. If allowed to succeed, IDA's efforts would undermine the entire purpose of the invasion, which was to regain the capacity for self-support and ecological interdependence among a group of landless and formerly dependent peasants. In view of the destructive effect of IDA's efforts, it is not surprising that La Lucha residents have fought against the institution and for community with energy and determination.

IDA's first efforts were directed against UPAGRA. Peasant loyalty to the union conflicted with any potential feeling of obligation to IDA, and UPAGRA offered an alternative rallying point. Unfortunately for IDA, most members of the new village were also supporters of UPAGRA. Instead of welcoming the opportunity to work with such an organized and widely supported community force, IDA saw UPAGRA as a competitor and set out to destroy support for the union within the new settlement and to prohibit any type of peasant organization outside of IDA's control. This effort attacked the loyalty of most members of the community to UPAGRA. IDA and the media accused UPAGRA of terrorism and communism and tried to frighten away peasant support.[3] In 1986 one man who had been elected to community office told this story:

> We tried to elect a [development] committee. We invited Marcos [IDA's administrator in La Lucha], but he didn't come. We had elections without him and the people elected me president and Juan vice-president. As soon as Marcos found out, he said the elections were void because he had not been there. So we had another meeting, and this time he came. We had elections again, and once again the people elected me president and Juan vice-president. Marcos said he couldn't accept the outcome of the elections because that meant the committee had been "infiltrated" by UPAGRA. [Juan is an UPAGRA leader.]

We didn't see why we should overturn the vote just to please Marcos when the people had twice voted Juan in. So then IDA started calling me a communist as well as Juan. All I want to do is work for my community so if that's communism then communism is good. The only thing I know about communism is that everyone works, which sounds OK to me. Now the committee is pretty much paralyzed because IDA won't accept it, and it can't act with IDA blocking its path at every turn. And we don't see why we should have elections a third time. It's good to have Juan in office because he can call the people out to work and get them to work for the community, and when IDA calls them, no one does anything.

The conflict and IDA's refusal to recognize, much less work with, community leaders made all developmental efforts within the community extremely difficult. Whenever the residents, working alone or through UPAGRA, pushed for a specific improvement, IDA balked and offered excuses. The peasants found themselves forced to struggle repeatedly against IDA in order to make any improvements in the community. IDA opposed the building of a school and outlawed the felling of village trees for that purpose. Despite threats of arrest, the peasants chose a day, gathered in a prearranged spot, and built the school together. Likewise, IDA opposed the arrival of public transport. The villagers approached the bus company together and negotiated a route. When I last visited La Lucha in 1989, the peasants were struggling with the national electric company to bring electric service to the village, all without the involvement, much less support, of IDA.

Throughout its interaction with La Lucha, IDA has shown no sympathy for or understanding of the peasants' ecological perspective. The peasants in La Lucha have rejected IDA's efforts at community control in favor of a more realistic vision that accords with rural reality. They know that a community cannot support itself and protect its members if it is dependent on outsiders who control village life but lack any notion of village reality. The peasants' own involvement with agricultural production grants them an awareness of interdependence and cooperation that IDA, as an urban institution of state bureaucracy, lacks.

IDA's credit program for peasant producers within La Lucha exemplifies its lack of ecological understanding. It has no sense of the way in which actions by some farmers can affect the circumstances of others such that coordination is necessary. The peasants, by contrast, know how cognizance of interdependence should inform any credit program. IDA's program rejects their knowledge and perspective so that, over time, all villagers have left the IDA credit program and sought scarce credit elsewhere. Rosendo entered IDA's credit program for planting squash. His story illustrates IDA's lack of understanding of the peasants' ecological perspective:

IDA told me they would give me credit to plant squash. They told me it would sell really well because the market in squash was very good, and there wasn't enough [squash]. Everybody wanted to buy squash. They said I would be able to sell at a good price and pay back the loan. Yesterday I got an ugly surprise. I harvested my first crop of squash. I rented a truck and filled it full. I took it to market, but the man there said he didn't want the squash. He says everybody is trying to sell squash this year. I tried all day long to sell the squash. In the end I had to bring it all back home. There it is sitting out there in the sun spoiling. So I had to pay for renting the truck, but I got nothing for the squash. I don't know what I'm going to do now because that was only the first part of the harvest. There will be more next week. If I can't sell the squash, I'll never be able to pay back the loan.

I think IDA told everyone the same thing they told me. "Plant squash. It'll sell well." But they never plan anything. They just talk, and they don't know what is happening out here in the countryside. They don't know anything. They are a bunch of fools talking nonsense, and we get trapped.

Rosendo's story evidences his perspective on ecological interdependence among peasant producers, a perspective that IDA lacked. The credit program called for self-interested, individualized behavior and only rewarded maximized production by each person. Responding to credit program incentives, each peasant produced as many squash as possible. The theory was that each person would earn more—and could take out and repay a larger loan—by planting more. In fact, however, the behavior of each peasant producer had consequences for all the others. Maximized individual production only produced a surplus of squash on the market, a glut that caused prices to plummet. Rosendo feels that a credit program that reaches large numbers of producers should also have a sense of how the activities of those producers are interdependent and affect each other. If designed with an awareness of interdependence and foreseeable consequences, such a program would assign a production level to each peasant, keep market prices at a level that allowed individual profit, and make loans that peasants could repay out of the profit earned.

By responding to IDA's incentives and overproducing, peasants overrode their own more appropriate ecological understanding of the rural world. One might argue that the peasants should have known better but placed unwarranted faith in IDA. They have, however, learned from their error and no longer trust IDA to run a workable credit program. IDA's behavior is particularly problematic as it also aggressively pursues peasant debtors such as Rosendo who have failed to repay loans as a result of their inability to market their crops. When loans are outstanding, IDA sends collectors who threaten to foreclose on peasant land plots if loans are not paid. The peasants find this threat particularly infuriating after they have fought so hard to obtain the land and when they consider IDA responsible for the collapse of the market. By 1989, most La Lucha residents had learned to avoid dealing with IDA as much as possible. They preferred to work with almost any other agency or institution. They find the National Bank of Costa Rica a more reasonable and trustworthy creditor.

In the end, the determination and unity of the villagers seems to have paid off. By the time of my last visit to La Lucha in 1989 the conflict between the community and IDA had subsided somewhat, leaving the peasants feeling relatively successful. IDA had promoted the administrator who had been so uncooperative and divisive within the community and so critical of UPAGRA, but, although villagers scoffed at the promotion, at least they no longer had to deal with him. La Lucha residents continued to develop their community, mostly without either help or hindrance from IDA. UPAGRA survives as a strong union, and La Lucha residents support it. As this study ended, La Lucha villagers had joined their counterparts in El Hogar in the struggle for better production conditions. In the past, economic incentives, moral concerns, and above all the ecological perspective led them and their supporters toward land invasion. Fortunately for them, their own landlessness is no longer a concern. Now that same perspective leads them to join landed peasants elsewhere who confront the problems of smallholding production found in San Luis and El Hogar.

Despite their successes on several fronts, the peasants of La Lucha have not lost their sense of ecological interdependence; success has not caused them to forget that they still need each other. In fact, the pressure and opposition they have faced from IDA has reinforced their sense of interdependence and reaffirmed their ecological perspective. By seeking to undermine peasant unity IDA has had the opposite of its intended effect: it has strengthened the peasants' commitment to each other, to their village, and to their union. As landholders with a strong sense of interdependence, they continue to participate in union activities and to act politically through UPAGRA in defense of small production.

Political Attitudes in El Hogar and La Lucha

This chapter has treated the two villages, El Hogar and La Lucha, as two halves of the same story. La Lucha is an outgrowth of the experience of El Hogar and other villages similar to it, because the ecological perspective of peasants in El Hogar and the local area was responsible for their decision to establish La Lucha despite the difficulties involved. Because of the close interconnection between the two communities, the analysis of political attitudes that follows examines the data from both villages together. Peasants in both villages have repeatedly participated in petitions, demonstrations, and blockages. They have learned through their experience with UPAGRA that these tactics can accomplish many of their goals without threatening the wider system. Landlessness, socioeconomic experiences of poverty, and concerns about injustice explain the villagers' decisions to undertake political action. Their experience has also created cohesiveness of opinion about most of the politically relevant

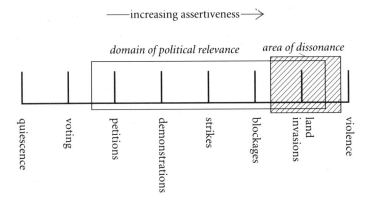

Figure 5.1. El Hogar and La Lucha: Spectrum of Political Activity

tactics of these villages. That cohesion means that these opinions exhibit no variation in relationship to economic, socioeconomic, or moral variables that can be statistically demonstrated. These villagers agree that petitions are unacceptable because they have little effect; demonstrations and highway blockages have proven useful and are widely accepted. In discussing demonstrations, one respondent explained, "You have to pressure the government by demonstrating. If you don't demand things the government won't do anything." At one point when I was present during an UPAGRA highway blockage one participant commented, "Up to now, they have conceded nothing. They have us humiliated. If they don't respond we'll have to do something different. And we will, too. I may be poor and humble, but I'm determined!" After that same blockage, another participant explained his feelings: "You feel happy and triumphant. You feel like you're defending yourself. After a blockage I feel physically exhausted but morally proud that we have demanded, not requested, our rights."

There are, however, two tactics about which villagers are not entirely in agreement. The first of these is land invasion. It is the area of dissonance both for El Hogar alone and for the combination of data when both villages are viewed together (see Figure 5.1). Landlessness in Limón province has been a central aspect of the story of these villages. Landlessness and peasant poverty in the context of local land tenure arrangements violate the ecological expectations of interdependent support and contribution. A landed resident of El Hogar explained his attitude toward land invasion:

> As long as the land belongs to a large landowner, land invasion is very good because they [large landowners] are always trying to take our [the peasants'] land. They go and take land and never record it on their title. They are just thieves and don't need all that they have. They like to take land just to have it

Table 5.2. El Hogar and La Lucha: Acceptability of Land Invasion as Form of Political
Action, by Land Ownership (N = 168*, Missing = 0)

Size of Land Plot (in hectares)	Acceptability of Land Invasion (percentages)		
	Low	Medium	High
0	41.7 N = 20	27.1 N = 13	31.3 N = 15
1–4	44.2 N = 19	30.2 N = 13	25.6 N = 11
5–9	47.5 N = 10	33.3 N = 7	19.0 N = 4
10 or more	60.7 N = 34	25.0 N = 14	22.6 N = 8

Note: Chi-square = 6.35219. Tau C = .0101. Confidence level = 99 percent.
  *This information is available for most members of both villages.

and never use it. We have to fight very hard against that because there are people who have nothing.

Some landed villagers in El Hogar, however, do not agree that land invasion is an acceptable tactic. The relationship between landlessness and the acceptability of land invasion as a political tactic is illustrated in Table 5.2. Landless respondents are significantly more inclined to favor land invasion than are landed respondents. Furthermore, the acceptability of land invasion increases as plot size declines.

The other independent variables examined here—socioeconomic experience and the perception of injustice—also bear a significant relationship to attitudes about land invasion in the two communities (see Tables 5.3 and 5.4). Although the perception of injustice can be measured in the same way in both villages, the differing levels of past poverty make the relevant socioeconomic variable different. The statistical test of the political effect of socioeconomic experience must examine that experience within the historical context of each village and tailor the socioeconomic variable examined to reflect that context (see Appendix). The pattern found with the socioeconomic data and the data on injustice confirms that of the data on land ownership: poorer peasants are more likely to be positive about land invasion than are the less poor. The socioeconomic experience of poverty in El Hogar is evident in the loss of siblings to preventable childhood diseases. El Hogar is an older village than La Lucha, both in the years of its existence and in the age of its inhabitants. When these villagers were children, medical care was much worse in the province than it was when they were adults with children of their own. Accordingly, sibling deaths to preventable disease occurred much more often

Table 5.3. El Hogar and La Lucha: Accceptability of Land Invasion as Form of Political
Action, by Socioeconomic Experience (N = 39, Missing = 1)

Socioeconomic Experience*	Acceptability of Land Invasion (row percentages)	
	Acceptable	Not Acceptable
Neither	25.0 N = 2	75.0 N = 6
Either	68.0 N = 17	32.0 N = 8
Both	100.0 N = 6	0 N = 0

Note: Chi-square = 8.84074. Tau C = .44707. Confidence level = 99 percent.

*This independent variable is a composite of the relevant socioeconomic experience in each of
the two villages for which data are combined here. For El Hogar the relevant socioeconomic experience is either hunger or sibling death to preventable childhood disease or both. For La Lucha the
relevant socioeconomic experience is either hunger or illiteracy or both.

than did children's deaths one generation later. Villagers who had experienced
either hunger or sibling deaths are the poorer villagers in El Hogar, and they
are significantly more likely to find land invasion acceptable than those who
have not.

The experience of poverty in La Lucha is also evident in rates of hunger or
illiteracy. The significance of hunger is similar to that found in El Hogar. Sibling deaths, however, is not a significant independent variable in La Lucha because there is little variation in the experience of it: most La Lucha residents
had lost siblings. However, illiteracy, which was generally low in El Hogar, was
a significant indicator in La Lucha. Unlike landed residents of El Hogar, most
formerly landless members of La Lucha have had a much more mobile existence and have not had constant access to a school during childhood. Illiteracy thus becomes a significant variable in La Lucha whereas it was not in El
Hogar.

Table 5.4. El Hogar and La Lucha: Acceptability of Land Invasion as Form of Political
Action, by Perception of Injustice (N = 40, Missing = 0)

Perception of Injustice	Acceptability of Land Invasion (row percentages)	
	Acceptable	Not Acceptable
Yes	67.6 N = 25	32.4 N = 12
No	33.3 N = 1	66.7 N = 2

Note: Chi-square = .32076. Tau B = .18905. Confidence level = 90 percent.

Table 5.5. La Lucha: Acceptability of Violence as Form of Political Action, by Socioeconomic Experience of Hunger or Illiteracy (N = 24, Missing = 1)

Experience of Either Hunger or Illiteracy or Both	Acceptability of Violence (row percentages)	
	Acceptable	Not Acceptable
Neither	0	100
		N = 8
Either	40.0	60.0
	N = 6	N = 9
Both	100	0
	N = 1	N = 0

Note: Chi-square = 6.57479. Tau C = .0075. Confidence level = 99 percent.

While land invasion is the tactic over which there is disagreement both in El Hogar and between the two villages together, within La Lucha the disagreement is over the acceptability of violence as a political tactic. La Lucha is the only Costa Rican village in this study where at least a few villagers find political violence acceptable. Although they have not engaged in such action and are very careful to qualify the circumstances under which it might be acceptable, some villagers are still extremely alienated from the system and would not find it supportive of ecological interdependence under certain circumstances. If the current system were to move any further in the direction they feel it has already gone, then ecological interdependence might be better served and sustained by eliminating the current system and establishing another.

> I remember being afraid of the Guard when they ran us off this land. But I also learned who they are. I was only afraid because I didn't have a gun. I think if they have guns, and use them, well, I have a right to have one too, and use it too.

> If they ever try to take my land or my house I will fight as hard as I can with whatever I have. If they use violence against me I'm willing to do the same.

Tables 5.5 and 5.6 illustrate the relationship between the acceptability of violence and either socioeconomic experience or perceptions of injustice in La Lucha alone. The vast majority of residents in both villages remarked that they perceived injustice in the world around them. As the interview data indicate, that perception explains their decision to take a variety of political actions against the production and marketing problems of the landed and against land tenure arrangements in the area. Ninety-three percent of all respondents mentioned injustice as a reason for taking political action. However, the perception of injustice was so universal that the significance of the relationship between injustice and action is not evident in statistical tables that

Table 5.6. La Lucha: Acceptability of Violence as Form of Political Action, by
Perception of Injustice (N = 25, Missing = 0)

Perception of injustice	Acceptability of Violence (row percentages)	
	Acceptable	Not Acceptable
Yes	100	0
	N = 8	N = 0
No	60.0	40.0
	N = 9	N = 6

Note: Chi-square = .04895. Tau B = .20229. Confidence level = 84 percent.

demand variation in the independent variable.[4] The ethnographic data in the
form of peasant interview responses support the assertion of the theory of political ecology about the central importance of perceptions of injustice and
concern for the ecological system in explaining political action. Paradoxically,
that support is so strong and invariable that it cannot be reflected in statistical
tests. The sample size for La Lucha alone is very small, and these data should
only be considered as indicative of a relationship that might be more positive-
ly confirmed by more data. In general, however, even peasants who have
struggled against state institutions such as the CNP and IDA know that they
have survived within the Costa Rican system. They do not view lightly the
possibility of violence against the state but see it only as a last-resort method
for preserving their ecological world. Their preference is to avoid violence if at
all possible.

Conclusion

The stories of El Hogar and La Lucha show a broader applicability of the theory of political ecology than was evident from Pedregal and San Luis alone.
Taken together, these accounts examine forms of political action unique within this study and largely ignored by previous research on peasant political action. They illustrate yet another manifestation of the peasant political ecology
and provide a broader knowledge of the perspective it brings on interdependence within community and within the wider society. The experience of El
Hogar illustrates the strength with which peasants hold convictions about
ecological interdependence in that they continued to work for ecological community even when poverty had seriously undermined supportive capacity
within the village and forced many to leave El Hogar. The political ecology
proved to be a sustaining force both in the creation of La Lucha and for peasants who lived there after the invasion. It brought them through an exhausting political struggle for the land and allowed them to withstand IDA's persistent efforts to undermine their new village. It permitted them to re-create the
ecological community that had been lost to poverty in El Hogar and other vil-

lages in the local area. As a result of their determination they are now producing for their community and contributing to the wider society as well as supporting themselves and each other within the ecological village.

Although there were economic incentives for the political action studied in this chapter—both the struggle with the CNP and the land invasion—individual self-interest alone does not explain what took place among these peasants. As in San Luis, short-term self-interest cannot explain unionized collective action such as blockages when short-term individual rationality in the sense of the classic rational actor would encourage peasants to become free-riders. In retrospect, knowing that the land invasion was successful, we can see rational economic incentives for the landless to participate in the land invasion. Yet land invasion is usually not successful in Costa Rica, and failure was far more likely than success; still the participation rate was high. Even now, knowing that the invasion was successful, individual incentives cannot explain the support for land invasion provided by landed peasants who stood to gain no land from the action. Individual incentives also cannot explain peasant criticism of IDA's credit policies when short-term maximization of individual reward (albeit calculated incorrectly) would have led peasants to behave precisely as IDA's program encouraged them to.

Similarly, communitarian interests and altruistic concerns about peasants as a group explain a part but not all of the political action in this story. Peasants saw CNP prices and certain aspects of national economic policy as morally wrong and unfair for everyone, quite apart from the individual impact such policies had on each of them personally. The action taken was clearly in the interests of the entire peasant sector and of separate communities as well as of individuals. In fact, the gain to the group was greater than the gain to any single individual, and individuals knew this when they expended tremendous effort and lost productive time in the struggle. This communitarian concern was even more evident with the landless participants in the effort against the CNP than it was with the landed. When the CNP raised purchase prices and improved standards of fairness, the landless gained only indirectly and only somewhere down the line in the form of higher wages and more steady employment. Thus participants in the struggle against the CNP acted for altruistic reasons, but these were not their only motives. No one participated entirely out of a concern for others. Every participant, even the landless, stood to gain both individually and economically from their actions.

Anger over the violation of community norms such as the moral economy also play a partial role in explaining the story told in this chapter. Anger over an injustice, even when subsistence was not threatened, was an important motivator to political action, both against the CNP and in the land invasion. Furthermore, reciprocity and interdependence are traditions that were increasingly threatened by village poverty. Anger over the destruction of those traditions and the social safety net they represented was part of the political motivation among villagers. Yet tradition alone cannot explain the full story.

Village tradition cannot account for the way in which villagers looked outward toward the wider society and interacted successfully with that society. Tradition cannot explain how or why villagers envisioned a new community as a solution to their problem.

Individual incentives, altruism, and tradition each played a role in the political choices made in this case study. Yet each is only a part of the story. Peasants participated in blockages because they had economic grievances to address, because they were angry at the CNP and worried about the group, and because traditions of reciprocity were seriously undermined within El Hogar and elsewhere. But the peasants' ecological perspective subsumed all of these concerns and also stressed interdependence among the peasants, their villages, and the wider society. That perspective allowed them to move beyond tradition and to undertake actions not used before, including land invasion. That perspective stressed survival and demanded new and innovative responses to a changing world in order to ensure survival.

Although the story of these two villages differs from that of San Luis in its specifics, it is similar at a broader and more theoretical level. Like their counterparts in San Luis, peasants in El Hogar and La Lucha have retained a strong sense of ecological community and interdependence despite integration into the national economic and social life of Costa Rica. That perspective has allowed the villagers to adapt and change as national integration requires it and to remain politically engaged with their society. The ecological perspective has encouraged peasants to develop and use new political tactics that increase their chances of survival in a changing world. The use of these tactics has reaffirmed the peasants' ecological perspective because opposition to such collective action has drawn the peasants closer to each other and underscored for them the extent to which they and their political success are dependent on each other. Collective nonviolent tactics play a key role in such adaptive survival. Like the San Luis story, the experience of these two Limón villages underscores peasant skill in using collective nonviolent tactics and the critical contribution these tactics can make to individual and group survival. The ecological perspective shows how and why villagers might use and prefer these tactics and how the tactics fit with peasant goals of survival. Through these examples we can observe that a multi-dimensional approach to understanding and explaining political action among the peasants is necessary, because peasant society and politics are far more complex than any single motivation can account for.

6 □ PEASANT REVOLUTION
Quebrada Honda, Nicaragua

Peasant revolution is a tactic to which theories of peasant political action have paid close attention. In fact, it is the only political tactic for which we have an extensive theoretical literature on motivation. The preceding chapters have amply illustrated that unidimensional approaches, for example those that stress rational choice, anger, or tradition, do not fully explain the political stories in Pedregal, San Luis, El Hogar, or La Lucha. In fact, a unidimensional focus on the individual, the group, or tradition cannot even fully capture the way peasants see their world, much less explain their political actions within that world.

A multidimensional ecological approach to peasant revolution is a better and more complete method for understanding this extreme tactic than is any theory relying on a single dimension of the peasant experience. The theory of political ecology makes as unique a contribution to understanding peasant violence as it does to explaining collective nonviolence and quiescence. The story of Quebrada Honda shows how villagers' understanding of ecological interdependence led them to revolution. It illustrates how the same ecological perspective that led to quiescence in Pedregal, to blockages in San Luis, and to land invasion in Limón province also led to revolution in Quebrada Honda. These villagers perceived interdependence among themselves, their village, their natural environment, and their society. They became convinced that interdependence was endangered and with it the survival of their community, their environment, and themselves. Over time and with growing experience, they became convinced that constructive participation was impossible. Violence was a last resort, chosen only when every other path was closed and all other alternatives fruitless. From the peasants' perspective, they stood no chance of survival at all, without revolution.

Political violence by popular groups is an extremely costly and risky strategy, particularly when directed against the state or powerful elite groups. The risk and cost involved make political violence unattractive for the peasantry under most circumstances. As we have seen, peasants may use numerous forms of collective nonviolent action and prefer these tactics when they can be successful. Yet peasants can also use violence and will do so if they see no other way out. Just as their perspective of ecological interdependence showed the peasants that collective nonviolence maximized their chances of survival in a Costa Rican context, it also showed them that nonviolence was suicidal under a regime like Somoza's regime in Nicaragua. Accordingly, the peasants' ecological perspective in Quebrada Honda led villagers toward revolution in the effort to maintain interdependence and facilitate survival.

Quebrada Honda's experience of politics under the Somoza regime differs substantially from that of any village in this study. The regime destroyed the peasant way of life in Nicaragua so extensively that the political ecology of the peasant was in crisis. From the perspective of most Nicaraguan peasants in the 1970s, ecological interdependence had become impossible. Peasants were systematically excluded from political participation and separated from the land and the wider natural environment. The ecological village structure crumbled, and many of Nicaragua's peasants reacted to this extreme situation in an extreme fashion by choosing political violence.

The village of Quebrada Honda provides an opportunity to view the pre-revolutionary peasant experience in Nicaragua in detail. Quebrada Honda experienced the destruction of the ecological system at the individual and village level. Located in an area of prime farming land, it epitomized the peasants' exclusion from normal interdependence with their land and the natural environment. The peasants were also excluded from meaningful participation in the social, economic, and political life of the nation. Quebrada Honda's central location underscored the injustice of such exclusion because its centrality should have allowed the peasants to participate fully in national life.

In response to these circumstances, villagers in Quebrada Honda joined the revolution. They joined early; they exhibited an unusual depth of commitment; and they acted as a cohesive unit. They replaced the normal relations of ecological interdependence that society had denied them with a stronger form of cohesion—an ecological interdependence under siege and in war. Their interdependence became that of soldiers in battle or of a society resisting an occupying force. They became peasant revolutionaries and in the process contributed to building a new, more inclusive ecological system at the national level.

Community Context

The defining characteristic of Quebrada Honda is its proximity to the social, economic, and political mainstream of Nicaraguan life. The village lies thirty-three kilometers from Managua and eight kilometers from the city of Masaya. Its geographic position had an important influence on the political experience of the village, in that Managua was the center of national politics, and Masaya the center of revolutionary conflict. Managua was the hub of Somoza's political rule; Masaya was a national hotbed of guerrilla activists, supporters, and sympathizers. Quebrada Honda's location would normally have resulted in the inclusion of its residents in national life. Instead, villagers were marginalized in every conceivable way. They were ostricized from national political, economic, and social life and denied any meaningful place in their society. Ultimately, marginalization became so extreme that the village became the focus of intense levels of repression, and its centrality became a deadly circumstance.

Despite the village's proximity to two major cities, under the Somoza government there was no public transportation from Quebrada Honda to either Masaya or Managua. A dirt road in from the main highway became six to nine inches of powdery dust at the height of the dry season and a sea of mud as soon as the rains began. Horse and oxcart travel were extremely difficult but possible except during the height of the rainy season. On foot, the hike took ninety minutes; bicycle and car travel was possible only during the dry season, when wealthy elites drove through the village frequently on their way to a private resort. The National Guard also used the road to bring army jeeps, trucks, and tanks into the village. Access to the city allowed village women to visit the Masaya market weekly, where they purchased what they could afford and sold vegetables or snacks.

Public services into Quebrada Honda were as poor as the public transport. Prior to 1979, there was no electricity. The peasants made small lamps, but Anastasio Somoza outlawed even these, claiming that they facilitated illegal meetings. No water was piped into the village nor did families have wells. Water was available only from the wells of two large farms just outside the village. Both were owned by members of the National Guard, who sold the peasants water by the barrel for an exorbitant price. Peasants had to supply their own barrels and traveled daily by oxcart to purchase water. The exhausting trip took between two and four hours, depending on the condition of the road and the length of the line at the well, and each oxcart carried only two barrels. The closest telephone was in Masaya. Some years before the revolution and long before the repressive height of the Somoza regime, the villagers built themselves a tiny schoolhouse, which was inadequate for the village size by 1979. It was open only sporadically and stopped at grade four. Most peasant children were unable to attend school because they were busy earning a few pennies to help support the family by selling handicrafts or snacks and by picking coffee or cotton during the harvest season. Houses in Quebrada Honda were tiny, dilapidated shacks of corrugated tin, plywood, and cardboard with dirt floors. Families lived eight and ten members to two or three rooms, and children slept four or six to a bed. Furniture consisted of a few stumps or logs and perhaps a wooden table.

In 1986, Quebrada Honda consisted of 180 peasant families, all of whom had lived there prior to 1979. Before the revolution, survival had been extremely difficult. None of the families had owned enough land to live on, and very few could even rent land on which to make a living. They had survived by combining a number of activities. They planted a few corn or bean plants on any tiny corner of land they could find. They grew a fruit tree or two, subsisted as much as possible on fruit such as oranges and avocados, and sold whatever fruit they could in Masaya. Men, women, and children over eight years of age worked as migrant laborers on the coffee and cotton plantations during the three-month harvest season each year. A few periodically found employment in a nearby craft shop or earned a few córdobas selling handicrafts in Masaya. Unemployment and landlessness prevailed in Quebrada Honda, and many villagers had no income for as much as nine months of every year. I interviewed thirty peasants, twenty-four men and six women. Most had suffered chronic unemployment and landlessness and had hung on each year waiting for the harvest season to arrive.[1]

Quebrada Honda was a microcosm of the national pattern of elite land concentration and peasant landlessness. Land ownership in Nicaragua under Somoza was so concentrated as to make landlessness in Limón look mild by comparison. Outside of exceptional circumstances, such as the extreme isolation of Pedregal, the Nicaraguan peasantry had been reduced to almost total landlessness. The plains between Masaya and the town of Tipitapa have some of the richest land in Nicaragua. Fathers and grandfathers of respondents from Quebrada Honda had owned land on those plains. Gradually, they had lost that land to wealthy elite supporters of the Somoza regime.[2] The new owners had driven the peasants off the plains and into the steep hills outside Masaya. The land in the hills is heavily eroded and broken by stream beds and deep gorges that fill with rushing water during the rainy season. The name Quebrada Honda means "deep gorge." This land is practically impossible to farm. One or two fruit trees took hold on each tiny house plot, and some peasants found room for a row or two of beans or corn alongside their shacks.

The most common national method of taking land from peasant families was by predatory loan-shark practices. As landlessness increased and plot sizes shrank, peasants were less and less able to make ends meet and survive. They borrowed small sums from loan sharks, who charged exorbitant rates and demanded the land as collateral. Unlike their counterparts in Pedregal, villagers of Quebrada Honda had no access to low interest rates or bank loans.

> The lawyer was a usurer. That's what we called him. From ¢5,000 ($709.72) that I borrowed, I had to pay ¢8,000 ($1134.75) at the end of one year (interest rate = 60 percent). . . . If you didn't pay after two years, the person who lent the money sent his lawyer and they took your land.[3]

> My father borrowed ¢2,000 ($283.69) and at the end of the year he owed ¢3,500 ($496.95; interest rate = 75 percent). It was very unjust, and they were part of the law. You couldn't argue with them.

> We borrowed ¢3,000 ($425.53) and had to pay back ¢4,000 ($567.38) after one year (interest rate = 33 percent).

Stories such as these were endless. Interest rates went as high as 80 percent in one calendar year. After peasants had lost their farmland and were living on a small house plot, lawyers still required the use of the house and plot if money was borrowed for subsistence. Families were reduced to homelessness.

> If you borrowed, they took away your house. The people who lost their houses went to live next to the street on land that belonged to the municipality. They lived there covered by dust from the street. The lawyers had all the power, and they were always happy to lend so that later they could take away everything.

Families fought hard to retain their land, and its loss had important political impact. Juan José, one of the community leaders, remembered his family's loss of land when he was still a boy.

> I was ten years old when we borrowed ¢500 ($70.92) from a lawyer, and we used our two manzanas as collateral. After one year we owed ¢600 ($85.1). We tried for five years to repay the loan, and after five years the lawyers came and took our land. I felt very sad. That was the land we had worked. You feel abandoned. Everybody cried, my father, my mother. I really remember that because my father cried. And then we didn't have any place to work. We became peons and the level of life went way down. I always remember that.

Among all respondents, the average plot size was 0.9 manzanas. Respondents remembered that their fathers had owned, on average, 3.8 manzanas and that their grandfathers had owned an average of 6 manzanas. Taking into account the high quality of the nearby land, peasants calculated that an average minimum of only 7 manzanas would have been sufficient to support a family. Although villagers had been without an adequate land base for more than three generations, total landlessness was a more recent phenomenon. By the 1970s, the amount of land they were able to farm was far below the minimum they calculated was necessary for survival via subsistence farming alone (Table 6.1).

Observations about the quality of life revealed the poverty that comes of total land loss. Seventy-seven percent of respondents said that they had suffered hunger prior to 1979. A few respondents said they had primarily been hungry during the cotton and coffee harvests, but 60 percent of all respondents said that chronic hunger had been part of their lives.

> We were hungry a lot, especially on the plantations. The landlords gave food but it was very little and only half-cooked. They gave us one tortilla and a

Table 6.1. Quebrada Honda: Surplus/Deficit of Community Land Ownership

Land needed to support average peasant family	7.0
Average village land ownership	0.9
Average deficit	-6.1

handful of beans three times a day. On some haciendas, there was water available, but on others, we had to drink dirty rain water.

Yes, we were hungry often. The cotton did not feed us. We also went hungry to pay the debts or to keep from losing the land. We were hungry all year.

The worst is when your children are hungry, and you feel you are ready to do anything.

Among all respondents, 67 percent had lost siblings to childhood diseases, and 47 percent had lost children to similar illnesses.[4] No respondent had ever owned an automobile, and only two had owned a television prior to 1979. Fifty percent had owned a radio.

Educational levels in the community reflected poverty, exclusion from society, and child labor. The average schooling among respondents was one year. Most had worked instead of attending school.

We had to work to live. I couldn't go to school.

We had to work in the sun all morning and afterwards go to the school, tired, in the afternoon. You can imagine how little we learned. Often we were too tired to go at all. I completed two years, but it took me six years to do it.

When asked about his children's school attendance one man explained,

They went officially, but they didn't learn anything because the school almost didn't exist. First there was a mobile school that moved from one house to another. Then we from the community built a school. The children went, but a lot of times the teachers didn't.

Like education, medical care was almost unavailable, and most villagers relied entirely on herbal medicine.

There were no [medical services], and for that reason, I lost a child. My wife had [gave birth to] the children in the house, and there was no telephone service and no doctor when things went wrong. That's why so many children die.

Unlike their counterparts in most other villages in this study, residents of Quebrada Honda had virtually no access to rented land. When they did rent land, the terms were so unfavorable that they were likely to end a season deeper in debt than they had started. In contrast to rental arrangements in Pedregal and San Luis, rental agreements in Quebrada Honda were so exploitative that they were almost no option at all. Peasants were required to pay cash in advance of the season. Failure to pay resulted in loss of one's house, no matter how poor it was. Landlords provided no inputs or support. Peasant farmers were required to assume all risk inherent in agriculture and got nothing back if the harvest was poor or was lost. Aside from the unequal distribution of risk, the cost of renting land was high and increased steadily. Peasants remembered that land had once cost four hundred córdobas per manzana per year to rent. Between 1973 and 1979 it had gone from five hundred to six hundred córdobas per manzana per year. If a peasant family had rented the seven manzanas necessary to support itself at ¢600 per manzana the cost would have been ¢8,400. Only two respondents had been able to rent land at this rate. For most peasants, the option of renting disappeared as the cost rose. Landlords were increasingly influenced by a national atmosphere that freed them from any obligation to share resources with the peasants even for a price. Landlords would make more money or at least suffer less inconvenience by simply refusing to rent at all.

The situation of landless peasants was worsened by the scarcity of wage labor. There was no industry to absorb the uprooted peasants, and crafts and service professions could not provide the needed employment, so stories of extreme poverty were numerous.

> We were extremely poor. We lived in a house of bamboo and cane with palm leaves [for a roof]. The beds were of sticks lashed together, and on one of those I was born. I had clothes for the first time when I was twelve years old. We ate once a day, and there was a lot of hunger. There was malnutrition. There was plenty only for those who had money.

> We were very poor. My parents were so poor that they raised us naked. We didn't even have clothes. There was never even one single month in which we had enough to eat.

> There really wasn't any land to work. There was no work and no possibility of studying. We lived very poorly. There was no work anywhere. There was a farm near here, but they didn't work it. We ate fruit from a tree. We bartered the fruit for meat or other food because we had no money. We were hungry.

> We were *poor*. There was nothing to eat. It never got any better. We lived completely dominated by poverty. We were always hungry. I was thirteen when I got my first pair of shoes.

The only exceptions to these sad stories were the accounts given by community residents whose families had worked for the National Guard as spies.[5] These few were the only ones who had not gone hungry or who had obtained access to medical care. The following description of prerevolutionary life comes from Miguel, whose family worked for the Guard. Although his words contrast sharply with those of his neighbors, Miguel was careful not to reveal why he was so much more fortunate, and I learned of his Guard connection from other villagers.

> Life was not bad. There were possibilities of buying shoes, clothes, according to your own taste. You put on whatever clothes you liked. There were more things because there were fewer people and the land was better, less eroded. The government never gave us anything nor even asked what we wanted. But there was always enough to eat.

Quebrada Honda is by far the poorest village in this study. As the above stories indicate, village life hovered at the subsistence line, and survival was an open question for all. Some, particularly children, died of malnutrition. Because survival within the village as subsistence farmers was no longer possible, villagers had used every resourceful technique to keep themselves and their families alive. The extreme poverty undermined the ecological system, threatening community and individual survival. Individuals who could barely keep themselves alive had no material surplus to share with others. The supportive systems of land/labor exchange relationships and of medical support found elsewhere were unavailable to villagers. There was no land to redistribute, rent, or share, and no money to pay for wage labor. Circumstances were so extreme that people lived in perpetual and simultaneous crises. In addition, land tenure arrangements deprived peasants of supportive interaction with nature. The land itself could easily have supported the peasantry, but they had no access to it even through rent or labor exchange, much less through ownership. Even limited land access would have altered the life situation of peasants in Quebrada Honda, but the economic system deprived them of land.

Economically, morally, and ecologically, the situation in Quebrada Honda defied peasant notions of justice in every conceivable way. Landlessness denied peasants any means of self-support within the village context and violated longstanding traditions of relative egalitarianism and resistance to subordination. The national economic system condoned extreme luxury for some at the price of poverty, landlessness, and even death for many. The political system mandated subordination and repression. National and local circumstances eliminated any possibility of the interdependent support that the peasants knew was necessary for survival and that they saw as their basic right because of their Nicaraguan citizenship. The cruel imbalance that favored some and threatened most with death outraged the villagers. The violation of norms of subsistence, relative egalitarianism, and ecological interdependence incited fury within Quebrada Honda. In response the peasants turned to political violence.

Ecological Imbalance beyond the Village

Nicaragua's agrarian system did offer one limited and ultimately inadequate source of employment for the nation's landless majority. Two of the country's major export crops, cotton and coffee, required labor-intensive harvesting. Landlessness and chronic local unemployment left most peasants with no choice but to migrate annually to the coffee or cotton regions. There they found three months of hard labor at scanty wages. Driven below the subsistence line by village economic conditions, most peasants were forced into harvest labor and took their entire families with them to maximize the opportunity.[6]

Harvest employment did not, however, provide much help in the desperate struggle for survival. Wages were so low that families could barely live on

Table 6.2. Migrant Labor Wage Earnings (Nicaragua, 1970–1979)

Land needed to support one family (peasants' own estimate)	87 manzanas
Yearly cost of 7 manzanas in 1978 at ¢600/manzana or ¢1,200/man/year*	¢ 8,400
Cotton Harvest Wage	
Average daily wage	¢ 21
Average weekly wage	¢ 126
Average monthly wage	¢ 504
Total harvest wage (one average man)	¢ 1,512
" (two average men)	¢ 3,024
" (three average men)	¢ 4,536
" (four average men)	¢ 6,048
Coffee Harvest Wages	
Average daily wage	¢ 33
Average weekly wage	¢ 198
Average monthly wage	¢ 792
Total harvest wage (one average man)	¢ 2,376
" (two average men)	¢ 4,752
" (three average men)	¢ 7,128
" (four average men)	¢ 9,504

*There are two harvests per year. Peasant estimates of 7 manzanas needed assume two harvests per year, but rent is charged per harvest, not per year.

them even for the three months of the harvest, much less during the rest of the year. On the cotton plantations the highest-paid worker might earn ¢60 per day ($8.51) while the slowest and least-skilled worker, probably a child, might labor all day for a mere ¢8 ($1.13). The average daily wage was ¢21 ($2.98). At that rate, one adult worker might hope to earn ¢126 ($17.87) in a six-day week, ¢504 ($71.49) in a month, and ¢1512 ($214.47) in total during the three-month harvest. Work on the coffee plantations paid slightly better, although again wages varied with skill, strength, and speed. Among respondents, the average daily wage was ¢33 ($4.68), although the best worker might earn ¢50 ($7.09) in one day and the slowest only ¢10 per day ($1.42). Calculating from an average of ¢33, an adult worker might hope to earn ¢198 ($26.95) in a six-day week, ¢792 ($112.34) in a month, and ¢2376 ($337) during the three-month harvest.

Unfortunately for the peasants, the two harvests overlapped almost completely, so that most workers had to choose between one and the other. Some simple arithmetic indicates the gap between what a family might earn and what they would need to rent enough land to subsist (Table 6.2). Starting with the peasants' own estimate of a minimum of seven manzanas needed to support a family and assuming that this much land were available to rent, it would be almost impossible to make ends meet. The full wages of the male household head during the coffee harvest (₵2,376) would not even have paid half the cost of renting the land, and two full wages from a coffee harvest would just barely have amounted to half of the necessary ₵8,400. Although women and children worked, their wages were less than those of men. At the cotton harvest even the wages of four men would not have covered the land rental cost for one family, and most families could not count on the wages of four men.

Peasant expectations of mutual support, contribution, and participation between individual and wider society were extensively violated by harvest work conditions. Whereas harvest labor offered landless peasants in San Luis a chance to participate in the interdependent village economy, harvest work offered the peasants of Quebrada Honda no such opportunity. Employers treated the Nicaraguan peasantry as expendable—useful as labor machines but not to be included in society in any meaningful fashion. The accounts of harvest labor are reminiscent of slavery.

> It was horrible. They treated us like horses. They gave us rotten beans and nothing to drink. If you had a strong stomach and could swallow that stuff, you could work more. And you always had to go [to the harvest] in order to save the house and pay [one's debts]. They treated us very badly, and the food was rotten and raw. We were hungry, and if we protested they fired us or threw us in jail. We were always hungry. . . . They gave us sour rice and beans that were badly cooked. They paid us every fifteen days, and it wasn't enough even to be able to eat until they paid us again.

> It was always horrible. They were landlords who didn't care about us. They fired us for any little thing. You had to stay quiet and humiliated because you had to eat and you had to work to eat. They didn't give us any food. We had to bring everything we ate. They woke us up at 1 A.M. so we could start working then.

In addition to undermining community cohesion by temporarily separating villagers, the labor system often pitted peasants against each other. Juan José, who remembered his father's tears over the loss of the family land, was one of the swiftest cotton pickers.

> They used me to speed up the other workers even beyond their endurance. They placed me at the head of the line and paid me ₵7 per quintal instead of the standard ₵5 per quintal they paid everyone else.[7] For that extra wage I had to lead the line and set the pace for everyone who followed. Everyone who came after me had to cut as much as I had cut or else not even receive the normal ₵5 per quintal. I hated to be the lead picker in that way but I had to stay there because my family needed my wages so much. We would not have survived without me. But, I learned to hate the landlords for that system. I saw how they used me and my poverty to hurt my friends and neighbors.

Thus in the wider society as well as in the village context, peasants were exploited, excluded, and denied every opportunity to participate in or contribute to their society in any meaningful way or to draw support and sustenance from citizenship. Landlessness, local unemployment, and the cruelty and inadequacy of harvest labor meant that the peasantry only barely survived economically. The desperate situation forced all family members, even the youngest children, into service. Peasant life was brief and brutal.

The final outrage to the peasant political ecology was the National Guard. This paramilitary force loomed as an ominous shadow behind all economic hardships, a deadly discouragement to any thoughts of protest. Peasants who dared to protest the usurious interest rates, the loss of land, or the slavelike plantation conditions suffered imprisonment, torture, and perhaps death for their impudence. Respondents were perpetually aware of the Guard's presence and the danger of protest in the face of that repressive force.

A private lake resort in the hills near Quebrada Honda symbolized for the villagers the extent to which they were absolutely excluded from Nicaraguan society. It also illustrated the role of the National Guard in maintaining the injustice and inequality that surrounded them. The Laguna de Apoyo lies within the bounds of Quebrada Honda itself. This crystal-blue lagoon fills the basin of an inactive volcano at the entrance to the community. Its cool clear water invites the hot and dusty traveler to take a break from the stifling heat of the road. Yet peasants from Quebrada Honda were forbidden to approach the lagoon. It was open only to the very wealthy. Smooth, paved highways forked off from the dusty peasants' road and swept down the mountainside to the shore which was lined by huge mansions surrounded by immaculate green gardens. Stations manned by National Guard soldiers with machine guns stood at each entrance to the private park. Peasants dared not enter on pain of death.

Revolution

The situation in Quebrada Honda and in most of Nicaragua violated the peasants' political ecology in three interactive ways: it made economic survival almost impossible; it breached every conceivable expectation of rural justice; it undermined any possibility of a normal ecological relationship among individual, village, natural environment, and wider society. In reaction the villagers of Quebrada Honda joined the revolution both as individuals and as a unified whole. The movement toward violence was generalized and virtually unanimous. Such cohesion is remarkable given the risk of political action and the overwhelming presence of a repressive military force. Their generalized support for violent action is testimony to the villagers' pervasive desperation and outrage.

Quebrada Honda's virtual unanimity in action also exemplifies the peasants' determination to re-create community interdependence and to reassert their own right to participate constructively in Nicaraguan society. The peasants' choice of violent political action can best be explained as the resurgence of ecological community despite every economic, political, and military effort to undermine it. At the same time, the villagers' revolutionary activism itself regenerated their own commitment to each other and even strengthened it beyond what it would have been in normal times. Thus, as in the cases in earlier chapters, political action itself contributed to the ecological community and confirmed the peasants' sense of their need for each other.

When Quebrada Honda began to move toward revolution, several villagers led the way. These leaders were distinguished by their youth—typically they were under twenty—and their relatively high level of education, two to four years. They joined the revolution early, reacting to the economic and political injustice around them and the extensive violation of community norms. Most of these villagers were killed in the revolution. Two were still alive in 1986 and 1987 when I studied the village. Their stories are evidence that these villagers chose violence as a response to what they perceived as a massive and unacceptable violation of the community's political ecology.

Ramón came to the Sandinista revolution through his grandfather, who had fought with Sandino against the U.S. Marines between 1927 and 1933.[8]

> He told me stories about Sandino's struggle. He told me that Sandino was a peasant and that the rich people did not like him because he wanted to take the land away from the rich and form it into cooperatives for the poor. And that Sandino wanted schools for the children and that Somoza betrayed him. Later as an adult, I was interested in the Church and became a Delegate of the Word. But I decided that man had to try to change his own world. I decided that God was not going to do it for him. Waiting around for God to change things was the same as what the Evangelists do and that accomplishes nothing. Life showed me what our society was really like and what place I had in it.
>
> My first experience with the National Guard came when I was thirteen. I went to harvest cotton on a plantation of 9,000 manzanas that belonged to a Yankee. It was so big it had an airport. There were fifty Guards there. You had to get up at 5 A.M. but there were very few eating facilities. In order to be able to eat before 5 A.M. you had to be in line from 1 A.M. on. I was sleeping in the line, and I left the line to relieve myself. When I returned to the line one of the Guards told me I was cutting into the line, and he said a lot of obscenities to me. From that day on, I started to hate the Guard. I always hated the Guard and I always talked about my hate. I talked with everyone trying to demonstrate to them how obscene the Guard was. Whenever I saw the Guard, I reminded myself of what they had done. It was like a job I was doing unconsciously trying to turn people against the Guard. Then another time I was at a different plantation. The landlord didn't even come but instead sent someone to pay us who came with five Guards. He came in a big beautiful car. It was white. I had never seen a car before, and I went over close to it and stood looking at it. Then a Guard came over and told me to get away from the car because I was sick and dirty, and I was going to give the car an infection.

Later I worked three years as a gardener for a lawyer. He paid me ¢70 per week, which was nothing. I had to do everything for him, even cook his food for him. I lived with him on his plantation, and I saw how he lived while I was so poor because he paid me so little. Every two weeks he had a party with lots of people and drinks and food and luxury. One day he accused me of theft and threatened me with a .22 caliber pistol. After that I didn't want to work for him anymore. I told him I wanted to quit. I started to organize people on the plantations, trying to raise their consciousness and organize them to strike. I tried to turn them against the Guard. It was during my work organizing strikes that I met the FSLN. They arrived to organize strikes also. They gave orientation meetings. I started working with them, trying to organize strikes to get the landlords to raise the salaries or improve the food. We had some success on the coffee plantations because we struck when the fruit was ripe. Then the landlords responded because they knew they would lose their crop if we didn't work. It was one way that the people increased their power and confidence little by little. I organized the strikes but I always maintained a low profile. I never went to negotiate with the landlords for better conditions. That way the landlord never figured out who was behind it all. In all those years of organizing, the landlords never figured out who I was nor what I was doing, and I never had trouble getting a job on the plantations.

Later I started collaborating with the Frente. We acted as messengers. If the Frente was planning to attack the Guard, we gathered information about the Guard and delivered it to the Frente. I was twenty-five when I started doing that (approximately 1970), and I also continued organizing strikes. Another tactic that we had on the cotton plantations was to pick it [the cotton] early in the morning when it was still damp with dew. That way it weighed more and we earned more because of the weight. They tried to stop us from picking so early, but we had a lot of success with that tactic. I also gathered information about the Juez de Mesta, here in Quebrada Honda. I never acted as a combatant, but we gave away a lot of food to the combatants, and we helped by building barricades over roads so the Guard couldn't get past.

One wonders how Ramón had arrived at the decision to begin working for change when he was in his twenties and no one he knew was similarly involved. His explanation was that "the decision is born out of your poverty, the misery that one sees and lives and also from seeing the way they [the rich] live and all the luxury they have. I saw what they were doing with my money, money that should have been mine. I have a place in this society too. But they didn't allow me to have it. I wanted to be part of the society and treated like I belonged there." Ramón is speaking retrospectively about events ten to thirty years in his past. His memory is no doubt imperfect, and specific details may be clouded or inaccurate. The general picture, however, is clear. Ramón's expectations of ecological interdependence between himself and the world around him were extensively violated by his experience. The core of this story is Ramón's memory about his years as a gardener, when he lived in abject poverty while his boss enjoyed luxury and refused him a decent wage. That situation violated his belief in relative egalitarianism. He was angry and indignant at the unjust accusations leveled at him, and his inability to defend himself violated his natural urge to resist subordination. The acute contrast between the circumstances of the two human beings so outraged Ramón's sense of justice and decency that he began his struggle even alone against impossible odds. The world was so far removed from his sense of justice and correct ecological interdependence as to warrant such an effort.

Juan José, who has appeared already in this chapter, became a guerrilla. He was friendly with Luis, one of Quebrada Honda's revolutionary casualties. Juan José related how he and Luis, as teenagers, had begun thinking and reading together and had independently arrived at the conclusion that change was needed in Nicaragua.

> In the beginning, I doubted the Frente and did not believe the FSLN was the answer at all. I thought they were all communists like they [the Somocistas] had told us a hundred times. I thought they made soap out of old people and that they would take away our land and our children and that they wouldn't pay us anything but would only give us food, nothing else. But, Luis began to read newspapers from Mexico. He had more education than I. He had been to school seven years, and I only four. Out of curiosity, we read about Mexico and Cuba and other countries, and we learned what life was like in other countries. We read about Zapata and the agrarian reform in Mexico, and we read about the high levels of nutrition and education in Cuba. We read out of curiosity and because we had a need to fight against the Guard. Later we began to listen to Radio Sandino and Radio Cuba because Luis had a shortwave radio. We talked and thought a lot together but alone because we didn't know anyone from the Frente at all. Later we got together a group. We collected literature from socialist and communist parties. Then one day I met two men from Masaya. They offered to meet with us. About twenty of us met with them, and they explained to us the struggle that the FSLN was waging. They told us that it had to be an armed struggle because that was the only way to make a new society. They explained to us that much of what was called communism was not really communism and that what was said about communism was lies. So we joined the struggle. We worked during the day and went out to help the Frente at night. There was a lot of support among the population. They gave everything they could. I never felt afraid. Early on, the Guard came here to my house and talked with my mother and told her to talk with me and to keep me from getting in trouble. She promised to talk with me but it never made a difference for me. The Guard came here because I had been denounced, but I never felt afraid. I first heard of the Frente in 1972, but I didn't know what it was. Luis and I started looking for those pamphlets and reading. I was fifteen. When I first joined the Frente, I helped by painting slogans on walls and by giving out

pamphlets. In 1976, I started making bombs and supporting during the [military] taking of institutions. I also went around collecting money for the Frente. Later, I became involved in recovering arms from the Juez de Mesta. We turned the arms over to groups of guerrillas. I began as a combatant in 1977. I had a .38 [pistol], and some bombs and in the [last few months of the] insurrection I carried an M-16 that I had taken from a Guard. I killed a lot of Guards in my time as a combatant. I was in battles in Grenada, San Marcos, La Concepción, and Masaya. I was away from home in the mountains five years and during two of those years I never went home even once. Everyone at home thought I was dead. They killed two of my friends and two of my brothers in the battle of Monimbó. They also killed Luis there. I felt sick with fury. After those deaths, I felt even more furious. You don't even feel sad, only furious.

Juan José has a strong sense of himself within a community and as part of a larger whole. "We are all in this together," he said. "Either we were all going to die together or we were all going to make a new world together. I just couldn't stand to see the people suffer any longer." Juan José's story conveys his outrage over the loss of friends and family as well as a concern for his community and people as a larger whole. His decision to join the revolution reflected a reaction not only to a situation in which he and his family were economically unable to survive, but also to an extensive violation of traditional norms of justice, egalitarianism, and the centrality of basic needs. Taken together, these elements constituted a breakdown of Juan José's world. His village was unable to support him except by joining him in revolution. Juan José chose violence in an effort to re-create a just ecological system in which he could contribute to and be supported by his village, the land and natural world, and society as a whole.

Between the years of struggle in the early 1970s when Ramón and Juan José joined the FSLN and 1978, the rest of Quebrada Honda joined the revolution. By the eve of the revolutionary triumph in July 1979, community participation had reached 90 percent. One by one, individuals made the decision to support the FSLN. Some went looking for the organization themselves. Others knew Frente members in other contexts and were brought in by those friendships. Frequently new participants were goaded into action by some individual experience. Although later converts to the revolutionary cause may have been less visionary or courageous than Juan José or Ramón, they also felt compelled toward violence by the disappearance of the ecological system they needed for survival. In discussing their decisions to join the revolution, they emphasized poverty and repression, both of which undermined community and any possibility of mutual support.

As more and more villagers joined the struggle, repression and revolutionary activism reinforced each other with ever-increasing intensity.[9] Revolutionary activism quickly achieved a critical mass: as more and more villagers joined, those still uninvolved became the obvious (and perhaps uncomfortable) minority. Before 1978, the village had lost three beloved sons and community leaders. These deaths and the deaths of family members in other communities drew more residents of Quebrada Honda into the fray. Villagers frequently described their actions as a response to Guard brutalities, including the arrest, torture, and murder of friends and family; the processions of tanks and armed convoys through the community; the ransacking of homes; and the murder of defenseless people, particularly unarmed women, including pregnant women, and children. These actions were a direct attack on community and the ecological system as well as on individuals.

New participants were resourceful and imaginative. Although these later revolutionaries engaged in all the same activities mentioned by Ramón and Juan José, women, children, and the elderly were particularly innovative in finding new ways to help. Their support for the struggle is remarkable given the conditions of poverty that prevailed. Women carried food for the combatants into the mountains after dark, or into Masaya where a battle might be in progress. Often they delivered food under fire. Young women and children repeatedly made the ninety-minute foot journey into Masaya to participate in the growing number of illegal demonstrations. Children often carried vital food supplies or messages under fire or in situations where only a child could appear sufficiently innocent to escape the Guard. Sometimes even these children failed to escape detection by the Guard and were killed. Older men left their homes at night to fell trees across the roads or otherwise build barricades protecting the community from tanks. The following respondent illustrates his support for political violence even though he did not carry a weapon.

> I carried messages four or five kilometers between Frente battalions. The battalions each needed to know what the other was doing for coordination and attack. I traveled at night, on foot, over territory I knew well so I could travel without a light. It would have been very dangerous to have a light. I always traveled alone. I carried the messages in my head, nothing written down. If confronted by the Guard I was to try to escape but if captured I was to endure whatever torture they gave me but never to tell them what my message was. It was better for me to die in torture than to tell the message and cause a whole battalion to die. Once a whole battalion of thirty-three boys died because some messenger talked.

In Quebrada Honda, the National Guard had been corrupt thieves as well as repressors. They commonly ransacked peasant homes on the pretext of looking for weapons and carried off any valuable items no matter how small. They imprisoned peasants and charged their families exorbitant sums for the prisoner's release. Peasant families were hard-pressed to raise these amounts but tried to do so even if it meant going into debt for years or losing land, because most of those arrested were tortured or killed. One young man who had been arrested and had miraculously survived imprisonment told me the following story:

When they were taking me away in a truck, we met a boy on a motorcycle. He was coming from school in Jinotepe, and on that day he was wearing student's socks.[10] Those socks identified him as a student, which was the same as belonging to the Frente. So the Guard beat him to death with the butts of their rifles. I had to watch while they kept hitting him in the head. They told me they were going to do the same to me. When the boy was dead and all bloody and had his head broken and his face beaten in, they told me to break his spine so I could stuff his body in a sack. I had to break his spine and stick him in a sack. I will never forget that. Then they put the sack in the back of the truck with me. Who knows what they did with him after that? I felt horrified, and I wanted to cry, and I felt like throwing up. I had started collaborating [with the Frente] in 1976, and I was primarily moral support for them. I hadn't done much when they [the Guard] captured me, and I saw them kill that boy. They tortured me for six days. They tied my hands behind my back, and then strung me up by my hands and almost beat me to death. They stuck sticks in my ankles and legs and cut up my hands so badly it took years for them to recover. The day they took me, they also took an old man because he refused to betray where his sons were. He figured he had a better chance of surviving under torture than his sons because sometimes they were easier on old people. He was right because he survived. Another day they killed a friend of mine here in the community. After that, we decided we had to continue the fight because if we didn't the Guard would just keep getting stronger and would eventually kill us all anyway. We would never be able to live in peace with the Guard like that.

Older villagers who could not withstand the physical hardship of combat or underground work did what they could from their homes. In the process, they maintained an appearance of normality within the village that allowed those who still lived there to carry out the daily struggle for survival. Juan José's father, for example, allowed the guerrillas to convert a storage shed next to his house into a clandestine training school and meeting place. It also served as a temporary hiding or storage place. Although almost all villagers eventually became involved in the struggle, they had very little specific knowledge about the activities of others until just a few months before July 1979. Having less information made one less vulnerable to arrest and torture and less likely to injure others if broken under torture. Mutual protection lay in secrecy. Even family members could not afford to know the nature or extent of each others' participation in the revolutionary struggle until a few months before the triumph.

The secrecy and need to fight without full knowledge of others' involvement is strong testimony to the sense of interdependence and mutuality underlying the peasant struggle. Peasant revolutionaries fought for community and to reestablish an ecological system even without knowing which neighbors they were actually working with. The opportunities and incentives for free-ridership as described in the rational actor model are unlimited in such a situation. The extent of revolutionary participation despite such incentives and the lack of free-ridership underscore the limited utility of a rational actor explanation and the importance of community interdependence as a political motivator.[11]

Ecological Survival

The peasants of Quebrada Honda faced a threat to their ecological system on a scale unparalleled in this study. Possibilities for self-support, interdependent support between self and community, and sustaining interaction with the world beyond the village were all precluded by the extreme political and economic circumstances. To fail to rebel and at least try to protect individual and community interests was to voluntarily accept what the regime had imposed. The situation had become so desperate that failure to act could mean death through starvation or at the hands of the National Guard.

The villagers responded with a level of determination and anger that corresponded to the magnitude of the threat they faced. Fueled by moral outrage at the extensive breach of norms of peasant justice, their reaction was also a conscious attempt to hold on to what was left of the ecological community. It reflected a willingness to risk all to reestablish an ecological system that included but was not limited to the village. The very act of rebellion restored part of the cohesion and mutual support that had been eliminated by material privation, labor migration, and repression. Indeed, when so many elements sought to destroy the ecological village system, rebellion offered the only possibility both of retaining some remnant of mutuality and of re-creating an ecological system both within the village and beyond. Rebellion thus arose out of economic privation, moral outrage over violated norms, and out of the conscious vision of a foreseeable future. It was motivated by individual economic grief, concern about the community as a whole, and a dream of creating a more ecological future.

In the following pages, the peasants explain why they joined the revolution. Their words reflect desperation over poverty and moral outrage over injustice. These are individual concerns of poverty and general anger over injustice toward the group as a whole. Yet these are also elements of an overall belief in the necessity and correctness of an interdependent system and a determination to do what they could to restore a balanced political ecology in Nicaragua. The peasants' motives were individual, community-oriented, and interactive, in sum, ecological.

I collaborated with the Frente because there came a moment when I could not stand any more. Suppose you have a family with a mother and a father, and you are one of two *brothers*. And the father is the government. And if you are hungry or have some other need, he has to give you what you need. He can't just let you die of hunger. But what happens if the father only gives food to one son and lets you starve? How would you feel to see one son with so much luxury and you with nothing? Well, that's the way it was here. Seeing that makes you furious! *We are all Nicaraguans here, all equal people,* but some had everything and the rest of us had nothing, nothing! First it was one thing and then another and then another, and there comes a time when you can't stand it anymore. It was a struggle for justice!

You look at the injustices around you, the injustices we lived, how we lived like slaves, without clothes, without food, without work. You get involved to eradicate the poverty. My decision came from me. No one ordered me to do what I did, no one forced me. . . . It wasn't just to be a rebel. The government didn't care if I lived or died. All it cared about was its capital. I wanted to be a combatant, but as a combatant I probably would have died, and I had a wife and young children. So the Frente told me to remain underground to stay alive so I could raise my family. But if they had called me, I would have gone. They never called me.

I got involved because you couldn't do anything else. There was nothing else for us to do [in that society]. They arrested all those who spoke out at strikes and later all those who even went to strikes. They kept them and killed them later.

I got involved looking for a new society, some peace and quiet so we could live in peace and produce. I have always wanted just to work the land and produce. That's the only thing I know. But I couldn't do that with Somoza. The Guard wouldn't let us live in peace. They [the Guard] were very obscene with us. They shot people just for looking at them. The Somocistas could run you over with their cars, and you didn't even have the right to say a word. We just didn't have any place in their world at all. So I joined the revolution, trying to make a new society. This one didn't work anymore. I was just going to die anyway, watch my children die. I decided to fight, even if I had to die fighting.

In this woman's explanation one can see the reappearance of community and mutual support in the struggle itself.

We became involved because of the extreme injustice which existed here and because of the repression. The Guard was a bunch of criminals, murderers. They killed children. You make a decision, and you become ready to give up your life, to die. It was a people's struggle, our struggle, and you never felt alone.

One young man was motivated by the efforts of the guerrillas to protect Quebrada Honda.

I was really impressed that the Frente came to the community to try to protect us against the Guard. You feel like you have to do something also.

This was our struggle. It became part of the people, part of the village, part of the people everywhere. It was the only way to survive, maybe, if you were lucky. It was our only hope of making a new world where we could live in peace and produce, work the land and raise our children, be who we are.

These quotations illustrate the extent to which most villagers restored their sense of community by joining the revolution. They talk about the struggle as a group effort and underscore the mutuality of it. This is not to say, of course, that all villagers became unswerving revolutionaries. A few were tempted by financial reward into becoming informers. Some joined sooner; others joined later. Yet once revolutionary participation became the majority position, revolutionary effort defined the community and became the way to participate in the political ecology of the village. Some peasants may have joined the revolution for the same reasons that their counterparts in Pedregal contributed to the medical support system—their own protection lay in joining group efforts. It is also true that villagers may have exaggerated the extent of their own participation just as villagers in Pedregal and San Luis may magnify their own contributions to those community systems. Giving (or at least arguing that one has given) a lot to the insurance system strengthens one's right to fall back on that system in time of need. Yet these imperfections actually underscore the importance of community interdependence and of being part of the community, rhetorically as well as in political motivation.

This chapter has focused on how the need to restore a balanced political ecology led the villagers of Quebrada Honda into revolution. Yet as Chapter 2 made clear, the Nicaraguan peasantry did not begin their struggle with revolution. Rather they chose political violence after a long process during which they found all other forms of political action to be not only unacceptable and dangerous but also ineffective.[12] In comparison with the unusual situation in Pedregal, events in Quebrada Honda more nearly represented the typical political experience of the Nicaraguan peasantry during the years of the Somoza dictatorship. Villagers from Quebrada Honda concurred that quiescence and collective forms of nonviolence would never save the ecological community and were in fact suicidal. The area of dissonance in Quebrada Honda is, therefore, political violence, and there was not a great deal of dissonance even about that (see Figure 6.1).

Despite the fairly widespread belief in the acceptability of violence as a political tactic, there are some interesting patterns evident in the relationship between that dependent variable (area of dissonance = violence) and the independent variables: economic factors, socioeconomic factors, and the perception of injustice. (See the Appendix.) Although landlessness and poverty were principal motivators for political action among these villagers, statistical methods preclude examination of the relationship between landlessness and violence because there is no variation in the data on land ownership among

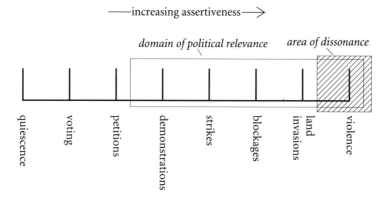

Figure 6.1. Quebrada Honda: Spectrum of Political Activity

these villagers. None of them owned enough land for subsistence prior to 1979. The ethnographic data indicate, however, that landlessness violated the peasant sense of justice as discussed in Chapter 1. The perception of injustice, which includes anger over violations of norms and over the destruction of ecological community, is the most significant single indicator of the acceptability of violence in Quebrada Honda (Table 6.3).

Among the socioeconomic indicators, the experience of hunger and of sibling death to preventable disease had a significant relationship to the acceptability of violence (Tables 6.4 and 6.5).[13] Once again, the theory of political ecology is supported by statistical tests on the data from Quebrada Honda. First, motivation is multidimensional —the result of several different kinds of concerns. Second, a concern for ecological community as reflected in a perception of injustice bears the most significant relationship to political action —in this case revolution.

Table 6.3. Quebrada Honda: Acceptability of Violence as Form of Political Action by Perception of Injustice (N = 30, Missing = 0)

Perception of Injustice	Acceptability of Violence (row percentages)	
	Acceptable	*Not Acceptable*
Yes	100.0 N = 25	0 N = 0
No	20.0 N = 1	80.0 N = 4

Note: Chi-square = 16.67308. Tau B = .0000. Confidence level = 100 percent.

Table 6.4. Quebrada Honda: Acceptability of Violence as Form of Political Action, by Experience of Hunger (N = 30, Missing = 0)

| Experience of Hunger | Acceptability of Violence (row percentages) | |
	Acceptable	Not Acceptable
Yes	100.0 N = 23	0 N = 0
No	42.9 N = 3	57.1 N = 4

Note: Chi-square = 10.62291. Tau B = .0001. Confidence level = 99+ percent.

Conclusion

Quebrada Honda is the first case in this study in which villagers saw revolution as offering the greatest chance for individual and community survival. Violence offered the only way to support ecological community for oneself and to re-create it for one's children. These villagers confronted a situation in which the national political and economic system had all but destroyed the ecological community within the village and disallowed ecological interdependence beyond the village. The peasants could not accept this situation because it threatened their survival and would not accept it because it defied their conception of justice. Instead they acted. They seized upon the only way

Table 6.5. Quebrada Honda: Acceptability of Violence as Form of Political Action, by Number of Sibling Deaths to Preventable Childhood Disease (N = 30, Missing = 0)

| Number of Sibling Deaths | Acceptability of Violence (row percentages) | | |
	Low	Medium	High
0	22.2 N = 2	22.2 N = 2	55.6 N = 5
1	14.3 N = 1	0 N = 0	85.7 N = 6
2	12.5 N = 1	12.5 N = 1	75.0 N = 6
3	0 N = 0	0 N = 0	100.0 N = 4
4	0 N = 0	0 N = 0	100.0 N = 1
5	0 N = 0	0 N = 0	100.0 N = 1

Note: Chi-square = 5.06362. Tau C = .0442. Confidence level = 96 percent.

they knew to preserve what was left of their ecological community. That way was revolution.

Their motives for revolutionary participation were thus individual and community-oriented, and therefore they were ecological. And because they were ecological neither a rational actor model nor a moral economy model can explain peasant choices in this case. A rational actor model that relies on short-term individual incentives is particularly inadequate in explaining peasant violence here. Violence was certainly a response to economic privation, and individual survival was definitely threatened by that privation and by the severe repression. Moreover, concerns for family were indeed important in peasant motivation to join the revolution. Yet the most influential economic concern was the poverty villagers already faced and not promises of economic reward yet to come, as a rational-choice perspective would emphasize. Although residents of the village have gained economically as a result of the revolution, the fact of economic gain was far from assured when these villagers joined the revolution, and many of those who joined never lived to see their reward.

In fact, the personal danger of revolutionary involvement was so great that the incentives for everyone to become free-riders would have been predominant if everyone had been limited by short-term self interest. Revolutionary participation offered no short-term personal advantages either economic or otherwise. Instead, revolutionary participation was more likely to result in arrest, torture, or death. The benefits of a successful revolution were by no means assured and in any case were at least as likely to accrue to others as to the revolutionaries themselves.

But villagers were responsible rational actors. They perceived their own dependence on community as well as the extent to which the revolutionary effort and everyone's survival depended on each individual contribution. As the peasants themselves testified, they turned to revolution of their own accord and in a situation where the fact and magnitude of their contribution was largely unknown or only partially known to their neighbors at the time. No one peered over their shoulders making certain they were good revolutionaries. No one held out incentives of power and prestige to draw them into the revolution. Such an explanation for their action borders on the absurd. It also underestimates and dishonors the self-sacrifice and generosity of spirit with which these peasants acted.

This is not to say, however, that individual concerns did not motivate Quebrada Honda's revolutionaries. Instead theirs was the motivation of responsible individuals who saw their own and their families' survival bound up with community survival and who acted to defend community, knowing that an ecological community would be more able to protect their families if not themselves. Such ecological motivation steps beyond immediate self-interest in the rational-actor sense and reveals instead a responsible self-interest and a concern for the foreseeable future. Such responsibility meant that some revolutionaries would lose their lives in the collective struggle and would not survive into the future they had foreseen. Yet their sense of their own ecological connection to the community and their desire to be responsible community citizens motivated them to sacrifice immediate self-interest—and in some cases even their lives—for the individual reward of protecting the community.

Indeed, the process of political action itself helped the peasants re-create the ecological interdependence that ensured survival. It allowed them to partially enact their own notions of justice. Juan José, for example, who objected to being forced to compete against his neighbors in the cotton harvests, found a way to work with them in revolutionary political action. Ramón, who had been so outraged by his employers' unfairness, could move toward his own definition of fairness through being a revolutionary. Revolutionary action allowed the peasants to re-create some semblance of ecological interdependence among themselves within the village and between themselves and the wider society. The sense of fellowship fortified by mutual suffering provided a village cohesion that allowed peasants to act together all the more successfully. Random violence by the state against neighbors could and did stir peasants to action almost as readily as violence against their own families. As one respondent remarked, "It might just as well have been me!" Indiscriminate state violence underscored the interdependence of villagers and the extent to which they were all in the same boat.[14] In this way political action itself reinforced and strengthened the peasants' political ecology in Quebrada Honda just as it had in earlier villages in this study.

The importance of individual concerns, albeit of a responsible, rational kind, and the way that political action helped re-create ecological interdependence within and beyond Quebrada Honda illustrate how a moral economy explanation is also inadequate in explaining this case. A moral economy or communitarian theory has typically been most convincing when explaining cases where subsistence is threatened and rebellion results, such as Quebrada Honda. Certainly many elements of the Quebrada Honda story fit a moral economy model, and the latter explains far more about this case than does a traditional rational actor approach. Moral outrage is clear in the peasants' testimony, and anger over subsistence violations is obvious. Moreover, the role of altruism is more apparent here than in any of the previous cases. These peasants, particularly those who died, were and are heroes, even if they are also individualists.

And here is where a moral economy or communitarian explanation falls short. For these revolutionaries were also individualists acting in their own particular interests, and their testimony makes that clear. The moral economy model never spells out the role of such concerns and in failing to do so it incorrectly (if inadvertently) delegitimizes those interests and renders itself less than fully realistic. A communitarian explanation also fails to capture the way that peasants sought to re-create interdependence within and beyond the community and how political action both grew out of and fed back into that effort. Finally, a communitarian explanation for rebellion relies on peasant traditions and defines the peasantry, even in rebellion, as always harkening backward toward an earlier, more traditional time when a more moral and precapitalist economy prevailed. That harkening backward is conspicuous by its absence from these peasants' responses. Indubitably they are looking forward and hoping to restore ecological interdependence not only within their village but also in a new Nicaragua that will include them fully and fairly in a participatory national society with which they will be interdependent.

This case, then, is unique in the way that it moves the theory of political ecology into the realm of explaining violence. From another perspective, however, the circumstances of Quebrada Honda only extend the story begun in Pedregal and followed through three Costa Rican villages. Quebrada Honda is simply another example of the peasant political ecology in action. In Pedregal, where villagers enjoyed a supportive ecological community, political quiescence appeared to maximize the chances of community and therefore individual survival. In San Luis, collective support for the coffee-growers union offered the greatest chances of village survival and of a continuing place within the village and societal system for each villager. In El Hogar, landlessness and poverty forced the ecological perspective outward toward finding a solution beyond El Hogar because there was none within it. That solution lay in the tactic of land invasion and the new village of La Lucha. In Quebrada Honda, the peasants' ecological perspective led them to believe that individual and community survival depended on individual support for revolution in defense of community and the reestablishment of a more ecological national system.

Thus in Quebrada Honda, as in every village studied so far, peasants brought to politics an understanding of the ecological nature of their world. Individual and community survival in each case were so intricately bound up with one another that the survival of one was inseparable from that of the other. That understanding was reinforced in Quebrada Honda on a daily basis as peasants fleeing from the Guard were hidden by neighbors, guerrillas were fed by community members, and individuals felled trees and built bombs to keep tanks out of the village. The peasant understanding of ecological interdependence led each previous village to select the political strategy most likely to preserve community and protect individual survival. In Quebrada Honda that strategy was revolution.

7 ▪ FROM QUIESCENCE TO REBELLION

Pikin Guerrero, Masaya, Nicaragua

The previous chapters offered a broad understanding of the political implications of the peasants' ecological perspective of the world across a variety of cases and tactics. They gave insight into peasant motivations in choosing quiescence, collective nonviolence, and violence. Yet none of these villages experienced the rapid movement from quiescence to rebellion that is often the subject of theories of rebellion and revolt. Villagers in Quebrada Honda, the only other revolutionary village in this study, evolved slowly toward revolution during a ten-year period. The village of Pikin Guerrero, by contrast, moved rapidly in the last months of 1978 and the first half of 1979 from seeming quiescence to revolutionary support. How and why this happened sheds important additional light on the motivations and process underlying peasant political action. The jump from quiescence to rebellion in Pikin Guerrero was inspired by both individual and community concerns. It represents another effort to preserve ecological community and thereby ensure survival both for the individual and for the group.

In the story of this last village, peasants found that the tactics most likely to preserve peasant community changed fairly suddenly with the deteriorating national political situation. In Pikin Guerrero, as in all the other villages studied so far, villagers strove to preserve community life and individual life within the community because they saw the two as interdependent. In the years prior to 1978, despite a developing social revolution, quiescence was the political tactic most likely to meet these goals. As the level of violence increased in the nation, political quiescence became outmoded and dangerous, and the village was threatened with destruction if it continued quiescent.

Community Context

Pikin Guerrero has qualities in common with several of the villages examined so far. Economically, the village lies in between the other two Nicaraguan communities. Prior to 1979, it was economically better off than Quebrada

Honda but worse off than Pedregal. Villagers did have a land base, in contrast to Quebrada Honda residents, but average land-ownership was lower than in Pedregal, and a larger proportion of villagers lacked access to land. Pikin Guerrero is also similar to each of the two Nicaraguan villages at different stages in its political history. For most of the prerevolutionary years, Pikin Guerrero was a politically quiescent village. Although fear played a greater role here than in Pedregal, the village choice of quiescence up until the end of 1978 closely resembles the choice in Pedregal. In the last six to eight months prior to the revolutionary victory in July 1979, however, the villagers of Pikin Guerrero joined the revolution. In that decision, they were more similar to the villagers in Quebrada Honda. Like San Luis, Pikin Guerrero is a coffee-producing village. Both were populated at least in part by smallholding coffee producers and the exigencies of the village coffee economy had a similar effect on social relations in both villages. Village mutuality and ecological interdependence in Pikin Guerrero bore a striking resemblance to relations in San Luis.

Pikin Guerrero is located southwest of Managua on the border between the departments of Masaya and Carazo. It is about four kilometers from the small town of La Concepción and about fifteen kilometers from the small city of San Marcos. This part of Nicaragua is hilly, but not mountainous. The rolling hillsides are cooler than most of western Nicaragua and are adequate for growing coffee. Although most of Nicaragua's coffee country lies far northeast of Managua in the departments of Esteli and Matagalpa, in the prerevolutionary years a somewhat inferior coffee bean was also grown around Pikin Guerrero.[1]

The road into Pikin Guerrero slopes gradually upward into the hills leading away from La Concepción. The dirt road is wide and passable by car and oxcart as well as by horse, bicycle, and foot. The torrent of water that runs down the hillside in the rainy season is not well channeled into drainage ditches and tends to pour down the road and into La Concepción, turning the road into a sea of mud. However, even during the rainy season, passage is not prohibited for long, for the road dries quickly. Prior to 1979, there was no public transportation into the village, but the outskirts of Pikin lie only two kilometers from La Concepción, so that peasants could travel to town, accomplish their errands, and return all in one day.

As with Quebrada Honda and Pedregal, Pikin Guerrero's relationship and relative proximity to urban centers affected its political experience and village political action. For Pikin Guerrero, that relationship was characterized by relative tranquillity and a live-and-let-live political atmosphere which continued throughout most of the years of revolutionary battle and disappeared only in the seven or eight months prior to July 1979. Pikin is closer and more accessible to La Concepción than Quebrada Honda is to Masaya. Yet this proximity did not bring either the political centrality nor the repression that peasants in Quebrada Honda experienced. Although Masaya is a major urban and political center, La Concepción is only a small town, uninvolved in mainstream politics in Nicaragua, and, unlike the road through Quebrada Honda, the road into Pikin was a dead end, not a main thoroughfare for elites that led to a major resort area. As a result, Pikin Guerrero's proximity to an urban area did not result in the repression found in Quebrada Honda.

In the prerevolutionary years, Pikin Guerrero enjoyed better utility services than either Quebrada Honda or Pedregal. Parts of the village had electricity. Villagers relied on wells for water, although during the dry season lack of water became a source of hardship as wells ran dry. The only source of water during these times was several large tanks built near La Concepción by Somocista elites. These elites filled the tanks by collecting rain water during the rainy season and sold the water at high prices during the dry season. Building their own storage tanks to collect rain water would have been an ideal solution for the peasants, but most lacked the resources to make such an investment. Peasant respondents resented this profiteering off the scarcity of water and claimed that one family in particular had become rich and built a beautiful house on the profits made from selling water to the villagers. The villagers felt they were unfairly penalized and cheated by the elites, both for their lack of financial wherewithal and for the unavoidable hardships of the dry season. Water, they claimed, was a universal resource that should be equally available to all.

Villagers in Pikin Guerrero were more fortunate than their counterparts in Pedregal and Quebrada Honda in having some limited access to health care in La Concepción. The clinic was closer than the ones available to villagers in Pedregal and could be reached by foot or on horseback. Very ill persons could also often be taken to the clinic by car, as the road into Pikin Guerrero was passable to auto traffic, except during and after a severe rainstorm. Health care in the clinic was not free, but peasants could generally afford the pennies charged for the service. Some preferred to rely on home remedies because of the lower cost, but in an emergency most could afford to visit the clinic.

Although the village has grown considerably as newly landed families settled there in the 1980s, in prerevolutionary years Pikin Guerrero consisted of approximately 150 families. I interviewed thirty household heads from among these families, twenty-seven men and three women. Villagers reported that in the 1920s and 1930s, the principal crop grown in and around the village was sugarcane. Beginning in the 1940s, large and small producers began planting coffee, and gradually sugarcane was phased out. The 1950s and 1960s marked the heyday of local coffee production. Trees and soil were at their maximum productivity, and the problems that would plague the industry later had not yet appeared. Coffee was very profitable during those decades. In the 1970s, 60 percent of villagers owned land. Average landownership was 3.9 manzanas, although villagers estimated that an average of 5 manzanas was necessary to support an average family producing coffee (Table 7.1). The deficit between average landownership and the average needed for self-sufficiency was com-

Table 7.1. Pikin Guerrero: Surplus/Deficit of Community Land Ownership

Land needed to support average peasant family	5.0
Average village land ownership	3.9
Average deficit	-1.1

parable to the gap between land needed and land available in El Hogar, Costa Rica. The difference in Pikin Guerrero was the coffee economy, which required surplus labor, whereas corn production in El Hogar did not.

The land in Pikin Guerrero is of medium fertility. It had been quite productive during the sugarcane decades and had been profitable for coffee farming in the 1950s and 1960s, but by the 1970s it was no longer prime Nicaraguan farmland. The country's best coffee land was to the north, and land in Pikin Guerrero was not suitable for cotton, Nicaragua's other principal agricultural export in the 1970s.

Landownership in Pikin was also more uneven than in either Quebrada Honda or Pedregal. The village included several families who owned between thirty and one hundred manzanas of productive land. By national standards these families were small landowners who certainly could not be included within the ranks of elite landowners surrounding the Somoza regime, but by village standards, these were large landowners. The distribution of landownership indicates greater inequality in Pikin Guerrero than in Pedregal or, ironically, Quebrada Honda, where most owned only a house plot. Inequality in landownership and in economic status in Pikin Guerrero most closely resembled land tenure arrangements in San Luis. There, as in Pikin, the village economy depended on coffee, but only some owned land and produced coffee. In both Pikin Guerrero and San Luis, landless and landed villagers were all involved in and dependent on the coffee economy.

Villagers survived using a variety of methods. Large and middle landowners grew coffee but could not farm all their land with family labor alone, and so they employed landless and land-short villagers as laborers. Those with small plots supplemented their farming with part-time year-round work and temporary harvest work on the community's larger coffee farms. As in San Luis, employment on coffee farms was available with fair regularity during much of the year, and that employment opportunity partially absorbed villagers who could not survive by working their own land. In addition to farming and wage labor, some poorer villagers rented land from wealthier villagers and paid either in cash at the start of the season or in kind after each harvest. Rental land was more available in Pikin Guerrero than in Quebrada Honda, although it was not accessible to everyone. Paying for rental land was also still possible in the former village when prices had made it impossible around the latter. Land rental thus offered another option for at least some villagers. Many village landless worked full-time as laborers or migrated periodically in search of plantation work. Experience with migratory labor was as harsh for

Pikin Guerrero villagers as for residents of Quebrada Honda, but the number of villagers who migrated was much smaller. During two months of each year, unemployment prevailed among those landless who did not become migrant laborers. A few village farms were large enough to have foremen, particularly when the landowner lived away from the village for some of the year. Such positions provided relatively secure full-time positions to a few villagers who were also allowed subsistence plots on the farms they managed.

Villagers remembered that life had not been too bad prior to about 1978.

> We got along. As we didn't have land, we always had a rough period each year, and we had to struggle to make ends meet then. But we managed, picking fruit or cotton away from here.

> We got along pretty well. My husband worked as a foreman for many years. The owner was good to us. He paid us and let us grow food on his farm. He even lent us money when my daughter got sick, and it was so expensive, the medicine.

Socioeconomic indicators for Pikin Guerrero suggest that poverty was roughly comparable to that found in Pedregal, endemic but not overwhelming. In addition, the village poor avoided the worst disasters of poverty by drawing on help from wealthier villagers. Although many villagers lived in unpainted wood shacks with dirt floors, some had sturdy wooden homes, and a few lived in cement houses. Villagers worked hard and had no luxuries, but life was not in jeopardy, even during the off season and the months of unemployment. Among all respondents, 57 percent had suffered hunger. Forty-seven percent had lost siblings to childhood diseases, and 40 percent had similarly lost children. There was no adequate school prior to 1979, and consequently only 37 percent of respondents were literate. Among all respondents, 23 percent had owned a vehicle, 23 percent a television, and 60 percent a radio.

The Ecological Perspective

Coffee was critical to political, economic, and social relations within Pikin Guerrero and was the basis for an ecological community. Its production required the input of most villagers at least part of each year and of everyone during the harvest season. The general impact of the coffee economy was to reinforce and protect the ecological community within the village even while mutuality and interdepent support were rapidly disappearing from the social scene in most parts of Nicaragua. In Pikin Guerrero coffee contributed to a particular set of social and economic relations that bore more resemblance to patterns in San Luis than to economic relations prevalent elsewhere in Somoza's Nicaragua.[2] This unusual village experience extended the duration of political quiescence beyond what would normally have been expected from a village so close to Managua. When Pikin Guerrero did ultimately turn to revolution, the social cohesion founded on coffee contributed to political cohesion in revolution.

Coffee as a Basis for Ecological Community

In the decades when coffee was Pikin Guerrero's principal crop and the basis of its economy, village landed (60 percent) could not manage production without the labor input of their landless neighbors. This was as true of large landowners (thirty to one hundred manzanas) within the village as it was of smallholding producers (five to twenty-nine manzanas). The coffee economy meant that all but the smallest landowners depended on the landless and land-short for labor. Affordable rental land was an unusual phenomenon in prerevolutionary Nicaragua, but that option remained available to villagers in Pikin Guerrero right up until July of 1979. In addition to land rental, a number of villagers lived well as foremen for larger farmers. Among Quebrada Honda respondents, two former foremen had bitter memories of their former positions. In contrast, those who had been foremen in Pikin Guerrero gave positive accounts of their experiences. One woman described the following relationship.

> We lived well working the farm for the Mister. He gave us a little house right there on the property, and we lived in peace, worked hard, raised children. When he wasn't living at the farm, he lived in the big city. Then he would come down here every weekend on his horse. He'd just ride on up here, and he always stopped at the house. He would talk awhile, have some coffee, play with the children. Then he would go on up to the big house. When he was here, he didn't get too involved in the farm. He just left everything up to Juan. Then once in a while, he would give him a raise, tell him he was doing a good job.
>
> While Juan worked the coffee, I planted some corn and beans outside the house. And some vegetables, and we lived like that.
>
> But all that time, we saved a little money every year, saved a little bit, and then another little bit. Then when the children were big we bought this house here and this little farm. When we got ready to go, the Mister came around and said he was sorry to see us go, asked us if we were sure we wanted to leave. And I felt a little sorry to go. He had been very good to us, very good. But we always wanted to own our own land, have our own house, so here we are.

The economic importance of these landless villagers gave them political and economic advantages that were not available to villagers in Quebrada Honda, for example, or to landless members of El Hogar. The importance of the labor they provided gave them leverage that they could use to extract access to land, decent wages, or any number of small favors or concessions from village landed. Among the landed, of course, one way to retain the labor force was to allow them a very small land base that would keep them tied to the local area most of the year but would not provide them with an independent subsistence.[3] Although this arrangement was hardly ideal from the perspective of the landless, it provided them with a livelihood that was far preferable to the desperate circumstances suffered by most of Nicaragua's peasant class and exemplified by the experience of Quebrada Honda.

The best economic evidence of the relatively fortunate position of landless villagers in Pikin Guerrero was the land tenure arrangement already described. As a result of that arrangement, some landless villagers gained access to land without being landowners themselves. Options available to the landless included land rental, foreman positions, permanent wage positions, harvest labor, migration, and any combination of these. The presence of these options symbolized and facilitated ecological relations in Pikin Guerrero, which were unusual in prerevolutionary Nicaragua.

Among land rental, farm foreman jobs, permanent farm jobs on the larger coffee farms, harvest labor, and migration, most landless and land-short villagers could survive without extreme hardship. Only a few villagers had to migrate regularly. This contrasts with Quebrada Honda, where everyone was gone for the full harvest season every year. In Pikin Guerrero, migration might even be local, as fruit orchards located near the village provided an additional source of temporary harvest income and a periodic option for some. Although these opportunities did not safeguard everybody against unemployment, as a series of stopgap measures, they kept the landless generally above the subsistence line and far better off than most peasants in Nicaragua.

Dependence on the poor caused landed villagers in Pikin Guerrero, like their counterparts in San Luis, to contribute to the welfare of the poor. The larger their plantation, the greater their need for skilled, cooperative, careful laborers to maintain high tree productivity and to run economically viable, productive farms. Even the largest village landowners were not major economic elites who could pay overseers to round up and import labor from elsewhere in Nicaragua. On a farm of one-hundred manzanas or less, such an investment in labor did not make good economic sense. Thus, even among the largest village landowners, profitability and individual economic gain depended on being a community member in good standing. There were personal as well as economic incentives for a supportive attitude toward the poor. Violent sanctions of cruel landlords were not unheard of in Pikin Guerrero. Both economic loss and personal danger stalked those who failed entirely to participate in village mutuality.[4]

The material manifestations of interdependence were not restricted to land tenure arrangements and the mechanics of coffee production. A myriad of interactive relationships crisscrossed the village. Beyond the asymmetrical relationships between village haves and have nots, village landless helped each other regularly with loans and by sharing food and tools. Because employment was usually temporary, employed landless villagers helped the unemployed landless so that they could draw similar support when the situation was reversed. Landed villagers also joined this network, making small loans to unemployed landless villagers and helping them purchase medicine during medical crises. In exchange, landless villagers were loyal and careful workers. One large landowner explained his activity this way:

> When I gave Rafael some money because his wife had to go to the hospital that meant that later he would come and work for me. He has three sons, and he would bring them along too. If I did the same thing for Guillermo and Carlos and Teodor, then I would already have ten or twelve laborers who would come to me before they went anywhere else.

The overall result of these myriad instances of mutual help and support was an ecological community that more closely approximated the peasant ideal than one would ever have expected to find so close to mainstream political life in Somoza's Nicaragua.

Coffee and Ecological Interdependence

As in San Luis, the coffee economy in Pikin Guerrero played an important role in encouraging ecological interdependence. Although such cooperation might seem more natural in a social democracy such as Costa Rica, to find such patterns in Pikin Guerrero, where the national atmosphere was anything but conducive, is remarkable. It lends support to the generalized presence and effect of the peasants' political ecology in vastly different contexts. Nevertheless, despite the similarities with San Luis due to a coffee economy, it is important not to overestimate the extent of interdependence in Pikin Guerrero. Because Pikin Guerrero was located within a national political system notorious for greed and cruelty, ecological interdependence was much less robust than in San Luis. The peasants in Pikin Guerrero reported that interdependence had slowly and steadily declined over the last thirty years. Some wealthy members of the village refused to participate in any way in the support system. A number of landowners imposed cruel working conditions and exploitative wages, although others were kind, generous, and willing to fund community-development projects. A few villagers were left out of the mutual-support arrangements altogether. They relied entirely on local employment opportunities and on migration to provide work.

Yet the similarities to San Luis are still perceptible. Mutuality and the needs of the coffee industry in Pikin Guerrero functioned to restrain the most extreme differentiations in wealth and to cushion the position of the poorest villagers. Many villagers were essentially middle peasants, a kind of middle class that did not sympathize strongly with the revolution but that also lacked close ties to Somoza. This economic position had important political consequences in the 1960s and 1970s. It also left Pikin Guerrero better off than most peasant villages in prerevolutionary Nicaragua.

Ecological Community and Village Service

Pikin Guerrero's relatively good utilities and public services in the 1970s were further evidence of an intact ecological village system. It was not state policy to connect peasant villages to utility services during the Somoza regime, and Pikin Guerrero was not particularly favored by the state. Rather, utility services were installed by the community itself and subsidized by landed villagers. In addition to loans, medicine, and land, some wealthier villagers provided funds to build or improve roads or drainage systems, to pipe water into the community, or to bring electricity to the village. As one landless villager described it:

> Dr. Salomon [one of the larger landowners, but not, as far as I could learn, a physician] said he would pay for the electric wire and part of the money for the posts. He got the municipal government to pay for the rest of the posts. That was all the government did. That was everything they gave. Then we [villagers] had to dig the holes and plant those posts. They were really big, and it was difficult. It took many of us to put up those posts. We couldn't work on it all the time. We had to work during the day and then go on Sundays to erect posts. I didn't go every Sunday. I was just too tired. But someone went every Sunday, and there were always enough [people] to erect a few more posts. And that was the way we went, every Sunday, little by little, putting up that electricity. A lot of villages didn't have electricity until after the revolution. But we had ours from way back.

The contribution of village haves, such as Dr. Salomon above, made a crucial addition to ecological community in Pikin Guerrero. Such actions made a big impression on landless villagers. In their interviews, poorer villagers were careful to compare the social investment of village haves, and they could remember important contributions made more than one generation ago. These actions also had a positive impact on village haves. Quite apart from benefiting from electricity in their own homes (hardly a minor improvement), landed villagers such as Dr. Salomon found it easier to gather a working force at harvest time than it would otherwise have been. Dr. Salomon in particular was a favorite employer among the village landless. As one villager explained: "I always hurried over to Dr. Salomon's farm to see if he needed pickers. I knew I needed to pick, and he needed pickers, and I wanted to work for him if possible." In addition to electricity, Pikin Guerrero villagers had piped water into several central locations, built drainage ditch systems in some areas, and kept the road in a state of semirepair so that it was at least passable for auto traffic.

Individualist and communitarian explanations cannot fully explain this system of community service. From a short-term maximization perspective, it would have been easier for villagers to stay home on Sundays and for village landed to make no contribution to road repair and other improvements. The landed might, for example, have invested in private electric generators rather than helping install electricity for the entire village. Some villagers, landed and landless, did respond in this way. More often than not, however, villagers took turns with such projects. An explanation relying on community tradition would emphasize coercion and the existence of moral norms to exact participation. Coercion, of course, was a factor in the system. Landless villagers who sank no posts might also find their homes unsupplied by electricity. But it is too easy to attach one's own wire to the community supply for coercion to be fully effective. Furthermore, there were no traditional norms for supplying utilities to Pikin Guerrero, especially when electricity, for example, was arriving for the first time. Explanations based on tradition emphasize a village's desire to remain unchanged, whereas installing electricity is an example of voluntary community change and development. The willingness to install electricity illustrates dynamic community norms that exemplify interdependence but manifest themselves in modern ways. A sense of ecological community and of one's participating place in that community more fully captures what went on in Pikin Guerrero under the community service system.

The Village in the Wider Ecological Community of the Natural World

Most villagers in the communities studied so far entertained a vision of the village within a wider ecological community that included the natural world around them and affected mutuality within the community. For example, many villagers in Pedregal were aware of the condition of the ecosystem around the village. They used that awareness to discourage migration that would overtax the soil's carrying capacity. San Luis residents kept an awareness of their vulnerability to the Poás volcano present in their construction of a mutually supportive system and in their choice of political action. Their union, UPANacional is periodically called on to request disaster relief funds from the government.

Villagers in Pikin Guerrero also brought an awareness of the natural ecosystem to their village arrangements. Their principal worry with respect to the natural world was the declining productivity of their coffee trees. The gradual reduction in productivity had two causes: the slow spread of a fungus disease that attacked the tree leaves and the seepage of gas from the Santiago volcano. Both problems were essentially beyond the villagers' control. The fungus could be eliminated with extensive infusions of imported fungicides, but this was too expensive to be feasible even for large village landowners. The volcano was beyond human control entirely. Thus, the villagers were powerless to solve these larger problems encroaching on them from the natural world beyond the village. Their only option was to care for the trees as best they could and to try to retain as much productivity as possible for as long as possible. Peasant ecological awareness, of course, does not always necessarily entail action. It can simply be a part of general perceptions. At the same time, these natural threats increased their awareness of their own vulnerability and the fragility of their own existence. That understanding encouraged their maintenance of village mutuality and motivated both landed and landless alike to do their part to treat the trees as carefully as possible.

Contact with the Somoza Regime: The Social Community beyond the Village

Pikin Guerrero functioned with a remarkable degree of interdependence and mutuality given the national context. Despite conflict in the political atmosphere outside Pikin Guerrero and problems stemming from natural causes, villagers in Pikin did their best to sustain an ecological community, and they were fairly successful. That success had important political consequences in the form of quiescence. The political situation just beyond village borders in the urban areas of La Concepción and San Marcos was tense and oppressive. Villagers remembered feeling insecure and threatened when visiting local towns for errands. Yet there was no major national city close to the village and thus no principal source of either regime or revolutionary influence, as Managua and Masaya had been a source of such influence for Quebrada Honda. For most of the prerevolutionary period, the local area around Pikin Guerrero escaped the concentrated notice of both the regime and the revolutionaries. Even the presence of the National Guard was surprisingly low for western Nicaragua. The Guard's function was to repress revolutionary fervor and activism, which was more prevalent elsewhere than in the area right around Pikin Guerrero.

Pikin Guerrero was not, however, as isolated as Pedregal. The conflict, turmoil, and danger associated with a society in revolutionary turmoil were evident not far beyond village borders. In the course of a six-month period, most villagers would make at least one trip to Masaya and several to Managua. During these trips, they got a close look at the political situation just outside their village. During the tumultuous years of 1975 to 1978, when conflict slowly heated up in Nicaragua, villagers in Pikin Guerrero made every effort to keep their heads down and stay out of trouble. They knew what was going on outside the village. They also knew that, relatively speaking, they were more fortunate than many. Their reaction was to retreat as much as possible within village borders and to mind their own business.

Although the choice of quiescence and political inaction was clearly influenced by anxiety about the dangers of political action, it was not a result of direct repression. The geographic and social position of the village kept it somewhat isolated both from revolutionary influence and from regime repression for most of the prerevolutionary years. When repression did invade the village, its effect was ultimately to promote, not prevent, revolutionary action. Repression was what eventually drove these villagers into political action. In reality, quiescence in Pikin Guerrero arose out of the same kind of reasoning that had produced a similar choice in Pedregal. Villagers knew they were rela-

tively fortunate and hoped to safeguard that good fortune by a carefully selected political response which they hoped would allow them and their community to survive the turmoil intact.

Pikin Guerrero in the Revolutionary Struggle

For most of the prerevolutionary years, careful maintenance of interdependence and quiescence did preserve tranquillity in Pikin Guerrero. Eventually,
however, the violence and repression of the external world invaded village
boundaries, and villagers became victims of repression despite their quiescence and uninvolvement. Reluctantly they responded, unwilling to encourage the repression in any way and still hopeful that quiescence would protect
community. Eventually, however, they realized that only revolutionary involvement would preserve community, and as a group, they moved from quiescence to rebellion.

The revolutionary conflict that had taken over Nicaragua invaded Pikin
Guerrero only slowly. The National Guard, convinced that revolutionary con-
spiracy lay everywhere, sought out villagers and offered to pay them as informers. With tree productivity declining, the opportunity to increase personal income was tempting. Villagers reported, however, that there was so little
revolutionary activity taking place in Pikin Guerrero that informers had to in-
vent stories for the National Guard to earn their income. The position of informant thus became an opportunity to act on personal vendettas. One villager explained the situation as follows:

> The most dangerous people around here were not the Guard and not the mu-
> nicipal authorities either. The real problem around here was the ears [colloqui-
> alism for informers or spies]. They were always looking for trouble. They
> would just go and invent stories about people they were angry with, just tell
> the Guard that these people were revolutionaries, so that innocent people were
> arrested. The ears got to be very dangerous. You were afraid to cross them,
> afraid to get into an argument with them, afraid to defend yourself against
> them because they would report you to the Guard.

Because the system of spies interacted with normal personal tensions to bring
out the worst in a handful of opportunists who thought that through the National Guard they could maximize short-term gain, the situation exaggerated
village tensions so that they became political conflict. As personal vendettas
spilled over into politics, repression invaded the village. Villagers were arrested, tortured, and even killed for personal reasons rather than political action.
A few people were released from jail after paying high fines that stretched
family finances to the breaking point. In suffering repression, villagers became
more acutely aware of the nature of the regime that ruled Nicaragua.

As repression slowly increased, some villagers became discreetly involved
with the revolution. The poorest villagers, who had the most experience with

labor migration, were the first to join the revolution. Their travels in search of a livelihood made them more aware of the suffering beyond Pikin Guerrero, and migrant laborers suffered some of the worst exploitation in prerevolutionary Nicaragua. Their inclinations toward revolutionary participation were encouraged by the growing incidence of repression within the village.

> [The desire to fight] comes from the insanity and pain in which we lived, from the people's need. You didn't need glasses to see the suffering all around. There was no land. There was no liberty. There was no work. You fight so that there will come a time when there will be no exploitation.

> Things got so bad out there that we couldn't find any work even when we traveled a long way. Then things got worse and worse here [in the village] too. You got so you were afraid even here.

In September and October of 1978, when a handful of villagers began revolutionary activism, most still resisted revolutionary participation. They were afraid to act: "We thought that we could live in peace here, stay out of it. Maybe if we just stayed out of everything they would leave us alone. But we were wrong and things got really bad here. You were afraid to relax at home, thinking the Guard might come and arrest you."

Revolutionary participation by some increased repression still further. Although repression never approached the scale suffered in Quebrada Honda, where the Guard rolled tanks and truckloads of soldiers through the community, fear and the constant threat of arrest permeated Pikin Guerrero. Ultimately, the villagers reacted with anger and turned toward revolution. Villagers explained that the Guard and informers had created an impossible situation "where there was no peace of mind." The repression pushed them into action even though their economic circumstances were bearable. Their responses emphasize repression and disrespect from the outside world rather than poverty as the primary political motivators.

> I joined the revolution because of the injustices against the mothers [of those arrested] and against the boys [young people arrested]. And because of the way they treated the prisoners. They even had mothers in jail! The poor women went down to the jail to try to get their children out, and the Guard just arrested them too. It was horrible treatment. It makes you so angry you just have to do something. I also joined because of the injustice of the land [tenure system] and for the general inequality. I was sick and tired of Somoza always staying in power.

> It made no sense in that system how they treated you just because you were a peasant. They would make you wait for hours in an office building for any kind of service. They treated you just like a dog.

> I was tired of living like a slave, being treated like a slave in that society. I preferred to fight rather than live that way. I just got sick of it all.

If we didn't do something, they were going to destroy us all. We tried to live in peace but they wouldn't leave us alone. It got so bad, I just had to act.

At the height of the repression the village lost a native son and revolutionary, Pikin Guerrero. Pikin had been one of the primary revolutionary activists in the village, as well as a beloved and respected village member. His activism, which was general knowledge even before many villagers joined him in the revolutionary cause, was so widely known that the National Guard was searching specifically for him. They had searched in vain for several weeks because of village complicity in Pikin's activities. Villagers swore they had not seen Pikin and did not know where the young man was. The story as it was told to me was that Pikin had been betrayed by one or more informers when he was on his way to a meeting. As a result he was trapped by the National Guard and murdered.

Pikin's murder created bitter hatred and resentment in the community, and that animosity was still strong when I last visited in 1989. Several members of the family of informers who had betrayed Pikin were themselves murdered by FSLN supporters at the chaotic point of the revolutionary triumph in July 1979. Those still alive lived tense, acrimonious lives, ostracized by their neighbors. When I interviewed them they took the trouble to deny any part in Pikin's murder. Even today Pikin is a hero in the village. People talk about him and weep for him. After the revolution, in homage to their young martyr, the village, formerly known as "La Concha," changed its name to become thereafter the village of Pikin Guerrero.

Pikin's death motivated some villagers to take up his cause. Others simply became more committed to the revolution. Marela, a young married woman who had been a high school student in 1978, joined the revolution against the wishes of her husband and brothers. Later, after she had spent many months involved with revolutionary activity, she found out that her own father had also been a Sandinista. Both he and she had hidden their work from each other, she because she feared his disapproval, he because he wanted to protect her. Here is her story:

When I joined [the revolution] it was a dangerous decision. I don't know which was worse, hiding from my family or hiding from the National Guard. But the repression was incredible, and it was really bad at school. I could never study in peace. I was very angry at the Guard because they always came to the school to bother us. They always entered our classrooms and threw us all out and searched us. They went through our books and God save you if they found any subversive [revolutionary] literature on you.

Well, I hated that, and I hated them. Finally I felt I just had to do something. So I told José [her husband] I was going to a friend's house to study. Then I went to meet several other students and peasants at meetings. We met deep in the coffee groves at night. It's really scary in the groves. The trees are really thick and no one can hear or see you. But it's also pitch black in there, and sometimes I got scared. We would meet in a huddle and whisper. We planned distribution of literature, painting walls with FSLN signs, even transferring arms and messages. Once we were each supposed to bring a friend. We were trying to make more revolutionaries.

It was in a meeting like that where I met Pikin. I'll never forget him, the way he talked. He could explain things that I never understood before. And he had two eyes that were so dark and full, they just burned in his head. I admired Pikin very much. I cried for days when he was killed. But after that I just had to keep fighting. If you stopped, that was what they wanted you to do. They would have killed us all.

My father was a revolutionary, too. But I never knew until the day he died. I still don't know everything he was doing to help the FSLN. But he died in 1978. On the day he died he called me to his bed. He could hardly talk, but he took my hand and held it. Then with his last strength he raised himself on one elbow and with an incredible voice, I still don't know how he found that voice, he shouted "Long live the revolution! Long live the Sandinista Front!" And then he died. That shout was the last thing he did. And that was when I found out he was a Sandinista. I wish I had known before, but he always told me never to be a revolutionary. It was too dangerous.

By the final months of 1978, most of the village was supporting the revolution. Many of the younger generation joined the guerrilla military forces for temporary or extended periods of time. But as in Quebrada Honda, supportive actions did not necessarily involve combat. Entire families made and stored arms and bombs to be transferred to the guerrillas. One farmer whose land bordered on a forest dug a secret tunnel out of his property deep into the woods. His house was at a dead end in the road and positioned so that a lookout could see down the road from the doorway. His farm became a meeting place for guerrillas who could always disappear through the underground tunnel into the woods at the first sight of the Guard or an informer.

Villagers not directly involved in revolutionary activity of some kind made an equally essential contribution by joining and extending a generalized veil of complicity that concealed revolution from the eyes and ears of the Guard and informers. For example, one man, a foreman mildly crippled with polio, lived across the road from a large cleared space in the midst of a sugarcane field where guerrilla groups practiced military maneuvers. This foreman deliberately turned his head for several months while guerrilla groups practiced in that field. As he worked his employer's fields, he could watch a good distance down the road for informers and Guards. When he saw suspicious persons he would discreetly hang his hat on a nearby tree as a subtle signal of danger and then continue his farmwork. His signal allowed the guerrillas to melt into the cane long before they could be discovered. At one point, he was arrested and accused of revolutionary complicity, but he denounced the accusation vehemently, demanding to know how a cripple could possibly be a

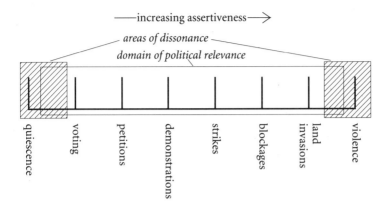

Figure 7.1. Pikin Guerrero: Spectrum of Political Activity

revolutionary. The Guard believed his protests and released him.

Another quiet, reclusive villager turned out to have operated a "safe house" that the Guard never discovered at all. Safe houses existed throughout prerevolutionary Nicaragua. They were houses owned by strong Sandinista sympathizers whose support for the revolution was unknown to the National Guard. Often safe house owners were considered by the Guard to be fine upstanding citizens whose relative affluence, business connections, or social position made them seem to be extremely unlikely Sandinistas. If they could do so undetected, revolutionaries fleeing from the Guard would disappear into these safe houses and escape. Often a secret exit allowed them to leave unnoticed.

The owner of this particular safe house was no more anxious to meet me than he had been to meet anyone else. He reminded me of Harper Lee's Boo Radley in *To Kill a Mockingbird*. I needed a special introduction from someone he trusted and an escort into his home by the same person before he would agree to see me. When I arrived he talked very little but just dutifully sat there, reluctantly willing to answer a few questions. "Yes," he assured me, "This had been a safe house. A lot of people hid here, and I got all of them out of here safely." He showed me a secret room behind the front door but he wouldn't let me go in the room. He just nodded toward it in an expressive fashion. At one point his eyes took on a far-away look. "I just wish that boy, Pikin, had made it here," he said softly.

In Pikin Guerrero, the preferred form of political action had been quiescence. In view of its failure to protect ecological community and given the national political context, villagers were forced to choose between quiescence and political violence. The national political scene barred all forms of collective nonviolence because they were ineffective and potentially suicidal. They would have had no protective impact on the community. The area of dissonance in Pikin Guerrero was thus the acceptability of violence (Figure 7.1).

Table 7.2. Pikin Guerrero: Acceptability of Violence as Form of Political Action, by Number of Sibling Deaths to Preventable Childhood Disease (N = 30, Missing = 0)

Number of Sibling Deaths	Acceptability of Violence (row percentages)		
	Low	Medium	High
0	50.0	6.3	43.8
	N = 8	N = 1	N = 7
1	50.0	0	50.0
	N = 1	N = 0	N = 1
2	50.0	50.0	0
	N = 2	N = 2	N = 0
3	100.0	0	0
	N = 3	N = 0	N = 0
4	100.0	0	0
	N = 1	N = 0	N = 0
5	100.0	0	0
	N = 2	N = 0	N = 0
6	0	0	100.0
	N = 0	N = 0	N = 1
7	0	0	0
	N = 0	N = 0	N = 0
8	100.0	0	0
	N = 1	N = 0	N = 0

Note: Chi-square = 16.66667. Tau C = .0506. Confidence level = 95 percent.

Statistical analysis of economic factors, socioeconomic factors, and the perception of injustice support the assertions about the multidimensional nature of political motivation made so far. Economic factors, specifically landownership and size of land plot, were not significant motivators in the decision to take political action. This confirms the ethnographic evidence that land access was not a serious problem for most villagers. Similarly, community interdependence had prevented extreme poverty in the village, so the only socioeconomic motivators that were statistically significant were those associated with poverty in past generations, sibling deaths to preventable childhood disease, and literacy. The experience of sibling deaths showed a significant relationship to attitudes toward the acceptability of violence. This significance even held with increasing numbers of sibling deaths. Those who lost siblings to preventable disease were significantly more inclined to support political violence than those who did not (Table 7.2). Illiteracy, reflecting the lack of a school available to villagers in Pikin Guerrero, was also statistically significant. Those who were literate were more inclined to support political violence than those

Table 7.3. Pikin Guerrero: Acceptability of Violence as Form of Political Action, by
Socioeconomic Experience of Illiteracy (N = 29, Missing = 1)

| Literacy | Acceptability of Violence (row percentages) | |
	Acceptable	Not Acceptable
Illiterate	33.3 N = 7	66.7 N = 14
Literate	62.5 N = 5	37.5 N = 3

Note: Chi-square = 1.00716. Tau B = .0807. Confidence level = 92 percent.

who were not. There was no significant difference in political attitudes between those who had one, two, or more than two years of primary school
(Table 7.3).

The ethnographic data indicate that the predominant concern of villagers
was for the preservation of community and individual survival within that
community. Their principal motivation toward political violence was in response to threats to the community that they perceived as unjust. The quantitative data support the ethnographic data. The perception of injustice was by
far the most significant indicator of the acceptability of political violence. The
perception of injustice in relation to the acceptability of violence was significant at the 0.0008 level, which means that there is less than a 1 in 1000 chance
that this relationship does not exist in the population (Table 7.4).

Conclusion

Pikin Guerrero is the only village in this study where peasants rapidly and
dramatically shifted their choice of political action. Yet with each choice, their
primary concern was the preservation of community and individual survival
within that community. Until late in 1978, the action most likely to meet those

Table 7.4. Pikin Guerrero: Acceptability of Violence as Form of Political Action, by
Perception of Injustice (N = 30, Missing = 0)

| Perception of Injustice | Acceptability of Violence (row percentages) | |
	Acceptable	Not Acceptable
Yes	75.0 N = 9	25.0 N = 3
No	16.7 N = 3	83.3 N = 15

Note: Chi-square = 7.92245. Tau B = .0008. Confidence level = 99.9 percent.

goals was quiescence. By the end of that year and during the last six months before the revolutionary triumph, villagers realized the futility of continued quiescence in maintaining individual and community survival. That realization led them as a group toward revolutionary activism as the only alternative in the struggle for survival. Thus by the end of this story revolution was the action most likely to preserve individual and community survival.

Pikin Guerrero is remarkable for the cohesion with which the village acted, both in quiescence and in revolution, and its story illustrates the versatility of the peasant political ecology. It explains more than one choice of political action by the same village as well as the decision to move from one extreme tactic to another. The story here also illustrates the adaptability that this perspective gives to peasants. Villagers were able to perceive which political strategy served their purposes best even as the outside world changed. A unidimensional approach that emphasizes either the constant supremacy of immediate self-interest or the predominance of group interest and tradition neither describes nor explains the Pikin Guerrero experience. During the quiescent years, short-term interest in the sense of a rational actor model can explain the choice of political quiescence but cannot account for generalized participation in activities such as village service. And for the precise reasons that short-term maximization can explain quiescence, it would predict continued quiescence in Pikin Guerrero, not a revolution. Throughout the brief period of revolutionary activism, short-term goals of rational action would have dictated that villagers become informers, not rebels, for the role of informant was certainly the more lucrative and less dangerous choice from an individual perspective. Some individuals operating from such a perspective did become informers, but most chose a strategy that addressed both group concerns and self-interest. Individuals such as the polio victim selected a path that was less rewarding than spying and more dangerous from a short-term perspective, but over the long term, such choices made a greater contribution to the community, to individual survival within the community, and even to society as a whole.

An emphasis on tradition and community norms such as that of the moral economy theory would also not describe or explain the Pikin Guerrero story. Although norms of reciprocity found in the moral economy theory partially describe economic and social relations between individuals in Pikin Guerrero, they do not define the full extent and complexity of ecological relationships between landed and landless and among landless villagers. They do not show why villagers joined village service, even when bringing innovations to the community. Norms and tradition do not explain villagers' awareness of interdependence with the natural world and the wider society. Finally, violations of subsistence norms cannot explain revolution in Pikin Guerrero. Thanks to the needs of coffee production and the presence of an intact ecological system, subsistence needs were not violated or even threatened in the village. This remained true right up to the time of the revolutionary triumph. Norms of reciprocity and rights to subsistence were observed by most landed villagers, and most poorer residents were economically protected by that adherence to tradition. Reciprocity and rights to subsistence were also not substantially undermined by Guard repression. Even the repression itself did not constitute the severe threat to general survival that it had in Quebrada Honda.

As in the other villages where peasants chose political action, the political ecological perspective that led to that action was itself reinforced by that action. The conviction of Pikin Guerrero villagers was reinforced by their experience as revolutionaries. As in Quebrada Honda, the village itself, threatened by increasing repression, needed the protection of revolutionary activists. Those activists in turn needed the protection of the village veil of complicity and the discreet cooperation of those like the safe house operator who quietly saved lives. Thus the belief in interdependence that brought on political action was confirmed and strengthened by experiences in the political arena.

The peasant view of interdependence within and beyond their village is best described by the ecological perspective. The actions that emerged from that perspective, both quiescence and rebellion, are explained by the theory of political ecology. It combines the multitude of peasant concerns and describes life and politics in Pikin Guerrero better than any unidimensional approach. The village was an interactive whole whose parts all contributed to and were dependent on the others. The theory of political ecology describes life within the village and actions such as village service. It explains villagers' political approach to the world beyond community borders and their concern for the natural environment as well as the wider society. As Nicaraguan politics changed so did village politics in interaction with it. A theory of interdependence that places peasants in interaction with society explains that change. As the nature of that interaction changed so also did the requirements of survival. In interaction with that wider world, Pikin Guerrero moved from quiescence to rebellion. The theory of political ecology explains that change and shows how each action protected individual and village existence at the same time. Finally, the description of village/society interdependence described in the theory of political ecology anticipates the way in which political action reinforced the peasants' ecological view of interdependence.

8 ▫ CONCLUSION

This book lays out an ecological theory of peasant political action that grows out of the peasants' political ecology. The study shows how and why the political ecology develops among peasants and describes its separate but intertwined elements. It explains how the peasants' political ecology has led to the development of a particular ecological mentality and how that mentality leads peasants to act politically. Finally, the peasants' political ecology helps illustrate why they choose certain political methods, why they must maintain a wide repertoire of political strategies, and how they move from one tactic to another.

In the stories of the six Central American villages studied here, individualist and community interests overlap and reinforce each other. The villagers' accounts of political action show how their desire to sustain individual and community as an interlocking, interdependent system led the peasants into political action and caused them to choose the political tactics they used. Their political ecology helps peasants determine the choice between quiescence and action and among different activist tactics. An application of the ecological perspective in each of the village cases shows how that view extends beyond village borders and affects choices of political action.

The peasant political ecology displays common characteristics that belong to the peasant class in a broad sense. In this study, these characteristics appear in diverse villages across different regions of a country and in the two very different countries of Costa Rica and Nicaragua. These common characteristics include a sense of overlap between individual and community needs and interests, a general commitment to mutual support, an understanding of interdependence beyond the village, and a willingness to draw boundaries that include the natural environment and society.

Although the characteristics of the political ecology are recognizable and similar in all of these villages, they are also shaped by the particular context and history of any given village. That context includes the nature of the state: political history and past experiences with political action: influences such as leadership, political organization, and religion; and the condition of the ecosystem in which the village is located. This context means that peasants in different villages see interdependence a little differently and draw boundaries of mutual support at different places. In Pedregal, for example, most villagers drew boundaries at the point of the local town and expected mutual support to extend that far but no further. In the other villages, on the other hand, villagers drew boundaries more widely and included the state within them. They expected interaction with the state of either a positive or negative kind. Costa Rican peasants expected mutual support between themselves and the state. Their political action reflected those expectations and demanded state support. In Quebrada Honda and Pikin Guerrero, interaction with the state was negative and destructive toward the villagers. Peasants responded by joining forces to destroy the Somoza government in hopes that a new government would be more willing to engage in mutual support and interdependence. Context, goals, and the nature of the state shape political tactics and cause peasants in each village to disagree about a different tactic or area of dissonance. Finally, the particular environmental concerns vary among villages, focusing on rainfall and erosion in one place, on volcanic ash or gas in another, and on hurricanes and hail in yet a third village. Thus the actual manifestation of the political ecology into particular political tactics will reflect context as well as the overall understanding of interdependence. This permeability of the political ecology is one of the factors that keeps peasant politics flexible, updated, and modern.

Some aspects of the peasants' political ecology can be measured. These include perceptions about land tenure and land usage that prioritize subsistence needs and the ability to work the land, a social context for the experience of poverty, and an underlying theory of justice that recognizes interdependence between individual and community and rejects the subordination of many to one. A numerical comparison of these factors also demonstrates the interactive importance of several different kinds of peasant concerns. In each of the preceding chapters, these factors have broken into three groups: economic factors reflected in the individual's land tenure position; socioeconomic factors and the social experience of poverty; and the perception of injustice and a violation of ecological community. The data on these three factors allow an examination of their impact on political attitudes in each of the six villages. Analysis of these data reveals that factors critical in one village are less important in another village.

A village-level examination of data allows a more precise understanding of political attitudes than would be possible without quantitative analysis but also has limitations. The economic and socioeconomic experience of each village is so unique that the statistical results are fascinating within the context of that village's particular story but may or may not be generalizable beyond the village. Furthermore, all analysis within the villages has been limited by the size of the pool of respondents for that community. In view of these limitations, it is useful to have a more complete view of the data used throughout the study. Fortunately the capacities of statistical packages allow this, despite the tremendous variation in village experiences and the need to compare different independent and dependent variables for each of the six villages.[1]

Throughout this book I have argued for a multidimensional theory for explaining peasant political action. The following tables present the results of regression analyses on all the data across all six villages and both countries. These equations offer empirical comparison of different political motives. The equations show that each kind of political motivation (each independent variable) achieves statistical significance or near significance and is an important indicator of the acceptability of the political tactic in the area of dissonance.[2]

The tables reveal that each of the three independent variables has an important impact on the acceptability of the relevant form of political action, even if that significance is not at a conventionally acceptable level of 95 percent or greater. Patterns in the direction of statistical significance are clear and indicate initial statistical support for the position I am arguing here. The patterns found here have less than a 10 percent chance of appearing randomly in the population. These results illustrate that only a multidimensional theory of motivation is appropriate for the peasantry. Any unidimensional approach leaves out a good deal of what is clearly politically important. Indeed, these results leave us with no alternative but to conclude that peasant political motives are both individual and group-oriented, individualistic and communitarian.

Readers accustomed to interpreting coefficients will see that in all three tables the level of significance and coefficient size of the perception of injustice is higher than that of the other independent variables. This variable includes peasant reactions to an action that violates ecological community and is perceived as unfair and dangerous. In each country, separately and in the combined data, the perception of injustice and of a violation of or threat to ecological community achieves the highest level of statistical significance of any of the three independent variables. This finding supports, both at the national and cross-national level, my assertions that concern for the survival of ecological community stands at the center of peasant political action.

Ecology in Historical Context

Although an ecological view of peasant society is unique within contemporary literature on the peasantry and certainly has not been proposed previously as a theory of peasant political action, there is a historical connection between ecology and farmers and between ecology and other groups who, like farmers, live close to the earth. In those settings, the term has also been used to describe interdependence. Native American Indians, for example, understood interdependence between people and nature. They often lived close to nature and through that proximity understood systemic interdependence.

Table 8.1. Tobit Estimation: One-tailed Test, Costa Rica, All Three Villages (N = 62, Missing = 8)

Variable	Coefficient	T-Statistic	Confidence Level (%)
Constant	.77290	3.4343	NA
Land ownership	.04847	1.2242	90
Socioeconomic experience	.16846	1.5570	90
Perception of injustice	.31929	1.6074	95

Table 8.2. Tobit Estimation: One-tailed Test, Nicaragua, All Three Villages (N = 88, Missing = 2)

Variable	Coefficient	T-Statistic	Confidence Level (%)
Constant	1.1727	11.971	NA
Land Ownership	.00824	.21522	90
Socioeconomic experience	.01764	.21609	90
Perception of injustice	.69706	8.6794	100

Table 8.3. Tobit Estimation: One-tailed Test, Costa Rica and Nicaragua, All Six Villages (N = 150, Missing = 10)

Variable	Coefficient	T-Statistic	Confidence Level (%)
Constant	.56031	3.1918	NA
Land Ownership	.03522	1.1981	90
Socioeconomic experience	.17902	2.4325	90
Perception of injustice	.38307	4.9477	100

They understood both their own dependence on nature and their obligation to sustain nature if they and future generations expected to survive.[3] Like many Native Americans, colonists who came to the North American continent from Europe to farm in a semisubsistence manner also had an understanding of human dependence on the community and the natural world. An awareness of such ecological interdependence is generally present in subsistence cultures whether indigenous or imported. In the early twentieth century, farmers were among the strongest supporters of what has since become the modern European movement for environmental protection. In fact, protection of the natural environment was seen as part of general policies in favor of farming. In Britain, Germany, and Romania political platforms that espoused environmental protection also supported protective policies toward the small farmer. Farmers associated with such policies supported steps designed to preserve the natural environment and were among Europe's first environmental ecologists.[4]

Ecology and farming thus share a historical connection that is a logical result of any trade that depends so heavily on nature for its success. It is therefore not surprising to find that a political ecology predominates among the peasants of this study and can help explain the nature of their social relations as well as their political actions. From this perspective, the disconnection from nature and the lack of awareness of interdependence between individual and society found in today's urban world is a new development and an important departure from the past. The size of contemporary urban societies and their relative affluence have deprived today's urban citizens of the political ecology that grows out of poverty and a village perspective.

It is much easier for peasants, as opposed to urban citizens, to conceive of middle-range consequences and of the blending of individual and group interests. They are advantaged by the small size of their immediate social world —the peasant village. The difference between the peasant perspective and the urban-society perspective is similar to the difference between a small pond and a large lake. The peasant village is like a small pond. Living in it is like sitting in a row boat in the middle of that small pond on a quiet summer day. If one drops a pebble from the boat into the pond one can see the effect of the action—a small splash and then a wave of ripples that move outward from the place where the pebble disappeared. If one waits long enough, sitting quietly and watching, eventually those ripples can be seen reaching all the way to the edge of the pond and touching the grassy bank.

From the row boat, one can see all over the pond from one bank to another. From within the peasant village, each peasant can see the full scope of the village from border to border. This is the small pond perspective that peasants have obtained by virtue of living where they live. They can see the effect of their actions within the village, just as the person in the boat can see the effect of dropping a pebble. The result is immediate, nearby, visible. By living in a small pond, peasants can also see the effect of their actions some time after the fact just as the person in the boat can see the ripple effect as it moves outward.

Living in a small pond where action and effect are visible, peasants can easily see the interdependence among villagers and between individual and community. They can see the immediate, middle-range, and long-term consequences of their actions and those of others. They can see as far as the ripple goes, either their ripple or that of their neighbors. The effect of that ripple may be either positive or negative, and peasants can assess which it will be. Peasants may choose to treat a wage-laborer well or to spend Sunday afternoon cleaning out the village irrigation ditch not only because it will yield positive individual results but also because such action contributes to community and to the supportive environment the individual needs to survive. As one landed peasant from Pedregal explained, "Well, I lend out my land because they [the village landless] live here too, and besides, if I lend out my small bit, others who have more will be more likely to do the same."

The small-pond perspective contrasts with that obtained by living in a large, complex, anonymous urban society. Urban living is like living in a huge lake, even like living in a Great Lake, for example Lake Michigan. From a boat in the middle of Lake Michigan water extends in every direction as far as the eye can see. Indeed, one can travel for hours in one direction before the shoreline even begins to become visible, emerging faintly in the distance. Out there on Lake Michigan, a boat seems insignificant as it is tossed by large waves. A pebble dropped leaves no visible effect as the ripple is rapidly swallowed up by the large waves everywhere. And yet the pebble does have an effect. In particular, many many thousands of pebbles dropped will have many small effects culminating in one large result. Yet it is difficult to see the ripple effect of dropping a pebble when so much else is happening out there in the middle of Lake Michigan. It is even more difficult to see the middle-range and long-term effect of action when one cannot even see the shore, much less the ripple as it arrives there.

An Ecological Perspective in the Modern World

Whereas an understanding of human interdependence describes a preindustrialized world and one from which urban society moved away, an ecological understanding of human dependence upon nature is beginning to return to industrialized society. Contemporary environmental ecology movements have begun to rediscover human interdependence with nature and the extent to which negative action at one point in the ecosystem adversely affects all of us somewhere down the line. This growing awareness springs from the perception of ecological disasters about to happen. The realization brings our world more into synchrony with that of the peasant. We are increasingly cognizant of human dependence on the good health of nature, and we see that destruction of our world will ultimately destroy us. We are concerned, for example, with the greenhouse effect, with smog over our major cities, with acid rain, and with deforestation. Our own self-interest leads us to concentrate on the foreseeable consequences of our actions and to redefine personal maximization as defense and protection of our world. In 1994 the word *ecology* is being heard more and more often in the context of contemporary politics. It has primarily surfaced as a political and environmental position of activist groups such as the Greens in West Germany and individual political candidates or planks in party platforms in other countries. Environmental concerns appear repeatedly in current events, political debates, and the creation of public policy. The common usage of the term *ecology* stresses the condition of the natural world and urges action that protects or re-creates it.

And yet, if the modern world is beginning to recognize interdependence with nature, that understanding of interdependence still falls far short of the peasants' political ecology. Although peasant concern for the natural environment is an important component in the political ecology, this book has offered a far broader usage of the term *ecology* than is commonly understood by environmental movements. The usage here extends the term beyond a concern for the natural environment alone.[5] The political ecology of the peasant brings to our understanding of the word *ecology* a social and political meaning that encompasses political relations and social and economic interactions among individuals and community, including the wider society beyond the peasant village and the natural world. Although this broad and inclusive usage of the term *ecology* may yet seem novel, a vision of interdependence among individual, village, ecosystem, and society has benefited the peasants in this study. A similarly broad understanding of interactive dependence may also benefit contemporary environmentalists and even industrialized society at large.

A political ecology that recognizes interdependence between individual and community interests has helped these peasants by leading them to choose the political strategy most likely to protect and preserve both individual and community survival. This is not to say that peasants arrive immediately at the best tactic, for there is a learning process that occurs, as evidenced in the unionization experience of El Hogar. Nor is it to argue that peasants everywhere always finally come down to a successful political strategy, for they have been known to fail and to be crushed and repressed as well. At the same time, these particular peasant groups have been surprisingly successful in choosing action that will protect community and self within community, and this was true both within democratic Costa Rica and authoritarian Nicaragua.[6]

The evidence from this study supports the advantages of assuming and acting on political ecology. As a result of such an outlook and of action that corresponds to it, the peasants in this study have been able to survive as villagers even as the modern world surrounds them and draws them increasingly into its fold. Peasants have often been portrayed as an anacronism, a fading, disappearing, and dying class over whom the wave of progress is about to roll. Oddly enough, the imminent disappearance of the peasantry has been predicted for three decades or more now while the class itself struggles onward, unconvinced (but perhaps not unaffected) by such pessimistic predictions.

I suspect that their political ecology is responsible for the continued survival of the peasantry because it has led peasants to consider and select among a wide range of political tactics and to allow themselves the possibilites of deliberate quiescence and collective nonviolence as well as of political violence. Theirs is a flexible strategy that provides a flexible response and allows peasant society to bend, adapt, and respond to an ever-changing world.

The ecological context can, of course, be defined too narrowly so that it becomes problematic and even dangerous. To the extent that a sense of community restricts itself to the village alone and becomes negative or even hostile to individuals who are not members of the group, it becomes exclusionary at the same time that it is protective of those who "belong" inside the community, and thus the community can slide into isolationism and separatism. Any student of the peasantry has also seen this exclusionary trait in peasant villages, which often manifests itself in the form of hostility to outsiders. Yet, when not narrowly defined, the peasants' political ecology is advantageous and has been such for the respondents in this study. In fact, as peasants become more and more involved in the world beyond their villages, they become less and less inclined to view outsiders with hostility and more inclined to expand the inclusive elements of their ecological perspective outward. The evidence from these cases is that the peasants here have begun to do precisely that.

A broad and inclusive political ecology that recognizes individual/community interdependence and allows for a flexible response to political and social circumstances might well benefit actors in the urban industrial world as much as it does the peasantry. The growing centrality of environmental concerns is our first evidence that such an approach may be slowly penetrating the consciousness of urban industrialized society. We have, for example, begun to recognize our dependence on nature and the extent to which our own health and even survival are contingent on living in a healthy, clean natural environment. Environmentalism recognizes that the individual is affected by and dependent on the wider natural world just as the latter is dependent on the individual and can be destroyed or saved by individual action. People who support clean air, recycling, conservation, and low levels of pollution recognize that single-minded pursuit of short-term maximization of benefits is neither rational nor responsible. Such irresponsibility may well preclude the future we aspire to and disallow any benefits at all. In the context of environmentalism, therefore, rationality has come to include responsible, foresightful behavior that looks to consequences beyond the immediate short term. In our own society, environmentalists are beginning to lead the way toward a recognition of individual/community interdependence that peasants have already achieved in their less complex world.

If the awareness of individual/community interdependence found in the environmental movement becomes more generalized and spreads into the political arena, a political ecology founded on environmentalism may build on itself and spread more widely. For example, the United States and other world powers may become willing to use military might to serve purposes other than the immediate, short-term interests of themselves alone. If this becomes true, then perhaps even the United States intervention in Somalia could be seen as an example of an embryonic political ecology at work. In Somalia United States action was both communitarian and self-interested, although the definition of self-interest is not immediate self-interest. Perhaps a new world order that follows upon the end of the cold war could be shaped by the heightened recognition of mutual interdependence that accompanies difficult economic times in the developed world. Cooperation between nations to protect the environment might create models of cooperation that shape action in other areas of global interest.

If we recognize a generalized interdependence between individual and community concerns, we may find areas of urban industrialized society where an ecological perspective has already proved useful, albeit by a different name. Church groups, for example, sometimes achieve an ecological interdependence in which individuals within the group are supported by the group and vice versa. Modern church communities have even been known to establish supportive systems in times of crisis that closely resemble Pedregal's medical support system. In businesses and service institutions, a mutually supportive atmosphere has often been associated with higher productivity and morale among members. For example, some experts have attributed superior competitiveness by Japanese automobile companies to a supportive atmosphere and the creation of community within the factory. Some Detroit automobile companies have found this explanation convincing to the point of carrying out some Japanese strategies within their own plants. We may find ourselves generally more successful and productive if we recognize interdependence around us and respond to it rather than denying or undermining it.

It is my suspicion that political, scholarly, and social debates outside the field of peasant studies might also benefit from a political ecology that allows for the possibility of mutual reinforcement between individual and community interests. An approach to understanding political action that does not require actors to be solely individualists or total communitarians may be a more fruitful approach to explaining activism.

Theories built by scholars who are products of our complex society reflect the either/or approach of our society. Such theories recognize immediate, short-term consequences of action or imagine long-term results that impact on future generations. The first of these, the short-term perspective of time underlies rational actor theories; the second, long-term perception of time underlies altruism and is implied in communitarian theories. Social science theories juxtapose these two views of time, just as they set group and individual interests and environmental protection and individual goals up against each other. Since we cannot imagine that people might subscribe to *both* visions of time and to *both* kinds of benefits, we set individual and group interests up against each other. Thus, the actors in our models are either selfish or altruistic but never both and never somewhere in between.[7] Theory has not yet fully recognized that actors can be both selfish and communitarian and that individual and group interests are one and the same. Yet, an image of human action that defines rationality more broadly as the peasants' political ecology does and admits of the overlap between individual and community goals may achieve a truer image of human nature and understanding of human action.

Just as a mutually exclusive attitude has dominated and handicapped scholarly discourse and theories of political action, inhibiting their explanatory capacity, an either/or perspective has also dominated political discourse and social choice among actors who are not peasants and who do not benefit from a small-pond perspective. The dichotomy has not maximized the gains for anyone. To the extent that a perspective of incompatibility between individual and community interests has determined action, and people have responded with extremism in one direction or the other, politics and political action have not always been successful and have sometimes even been destructive. One school of philosophy represented by laissez-faire capitalism and Keynesian economics has stressed individualist action to the detriment of the community. The "entrepreneurial spirit" of capitalism and other values cherished in Western society emphasize the merits of individual considerations. Such a position encourages people to strive toward the greatest profit, power, status, or prestige they can attain. The result has been extremes of individualism and self-orientation that are characterized by anomie, rootlessness, exploitation, and ecological destruction, all in the name of progress defined as maximized individual benefit and material gain. Another philosophy has countered this approach with the other extreme and has placed the importance of community above that of individuals. This approach has marginalized and delegitimized individual incentives and individualist goals. Such a position has led to authoritarian control over individuals by leaders who claim to be acting in the name of popular community interest because they cannot conceive of any legitimacy accruing to individual concerns. The result has been deteriorated morale across entire societies that has led to decreased productivity and inefficiency and has often survived only when buttressed by state tyranny in the name of the people. If, however, social science and politics can recognize and also admit the presence of both individualist and communitarian motives within human action, they can attain a more realistic view of human nature and political action. Such recognition may ultimately result in more humane, accommodating, and sustaining institutions and political systems within modern societies.

An ecological perspective and an awareness of interdependence, however, come with difficulty and only gradually in urbanized industrial society because we are disadvantaged by living in a large lake. We cannot immediately see the consequences of our actions and find it difficult to appreciate that our actions do have effects. Peasants, with the advantage of a small-pond perspective, have already achieved the view that our own society is only slowly approaching. By declaring that peasants are disappearing and awaiting their imminent demise, we purchase license to ignore them and perhaps even to injure them when in reality we might be better off by recognizing them and allowing ourselves to learn what we can from their vision of the world. Far from being an anachronism or a dying class in a modern world, as an adaptable class of survivors, peasants may have a good deal to teach urban society because they have achieved an ecological perspective that serves them better than the perspectives that dominate in the urban industrialized world.

APPENDIX   Methodology Combining
          Depth and Breadth

For the interested reader, this appendix provides a detailed discussion of the methods used in this study, both the methods used in the field for collecting data and the methods used for data analysis after field research. Data collection in this study utilized both anthropological data collection methods and the social science survey method. Data analysis was both qualitative and quantitative. Accordingly, this appendix may be of interest to a variety of students of the peasantry, as well as to anthropologists and statisticians alike.

Perspectives and Types of Data

One of the most thorny and controversial issues in the study of the peasantry is the choice and implementation of methodology. On the one hand the necessity of addressing complex or unexplored issues at the micro or individual level calls for sensitive, flexible interviewing along the lines of ethnography. This type of exploratory research can uncover facts, perspectives, and priorities unknown to the researcher prior to entering the field. It can lead him or her to ask essential questions that would not have been obvious beforehand, but without which the research would be incomplete and possibly irrelevant. In-depth interviewing also demands cultural sensitivity and a willingness to fit, insofar as is possible, into an alien world. It requires that questions be redefined to reflect the reality of a foreign culture, instead of the culture of the researcher. Anthropologists have traditionally been among the most skilled users of these kinds of methods, and they have a great deal to teach other social scientists about culturally sensitive ethnographic research.

On the other hand, a detailed microscopic view provides a great deal of depth without much breadth. Anthropological studies are frequently limited to one village, tribe, or kinship group. Comparative analysis, when used by anthropologists, normally relies on secondary sources. In addition, anthropology often addresses a static world, painting a picture of things as they are without asking how they might change or why. These limitations severely constrain the applicability of the findings and the amount of generalizable information that we can extract from most anthropological research. These constraints are of great concern to disciplines such as political science, sociology, and economics, which have recently begun to study the peasantry in relation to broader issues: the state and power, society at large, and the economy.

In search of breadth, these social sciences have neglected ethnographic research[1] in favor of techniques, such as the survey, that allow data to be collected from a wider base. Surveys permit the researcher to cover a large number of respondents and to include many different communities, regions, and even nations in the same study. Survey methods also provide a study size that lends itself to quantitative analysis. Unfortunately, in studying the peasantry an overemphasis on breadth can result in the sacrifice of depth.

Just as the perspectives of ethnographic and survey research have advantages and disadvantages, the types of data collected by both ethnographers and researchers also have strengths and limitations. Qualitative data gathered by ethnographers are more likely to be sensitive to cultural differences and to accurately reflect local realities. In exploring the subjective perspective of actors, ethnographers uncover issues that are perceived as essential by indigenous peoples and tell us how and why such concerns are important. At the same time, to present ethnographic data as they are collected is imprecise because, although it can reveal that a given issue is important (everyone mentions it, people become emphatic over it, people get angry or sad or suspicious when they speak of it), the exact importance cannot be measured. Furthermore, such data may be less than fully convincing because of their imprecision, limited perspective, and the biases of contemporary social science that tend to favor survey data.

Quantitative data gathered by survey researchers have all the strengths that ethnographic data lack. They are collected in a structured way and this may mean that, even in their raw form, they are more precise. The extent of coverage allows them to offer a broader perspective. Survey data access a large number of respondents, bring in two or more regions or countries, and produce a sample size that permits sophisticated statistical analysis. There is less scholarly prejudice against survey data, and they are generally viewed as "objective."

Nonetheless, survey data are not without their drawbacks. They may be difficult or impossible to generate, unreliable, incomplete, or manipulated. Data from developing countries are particularly susceptible to these problems. In reality, survey data may be as subjective as ethnographic data, depending on who collected it and its source. As with the electoral polls preceding the 1990 Nicaraguan elections, for example, surveys are vulnerable to the biases of the individuals, institutions, and political leaders responsible for asking the questions, conducting the census or survey, and presenting or publishing the data.[1] At each stage the data are subject to misuse or inaccurate presentation by those who have a position to defend. They may also be vulnerable to the biases or incomplete knowledge of an urban researcher, who may be insensitive to cultural differences. Most important to peasant studies, instruments designed to maximize breadth, reduce unexpected inputs, and standardize data collection circumstances often miss a great deal of local reality and thus generate data that are inaccurate and incomplete.

While no single study can address and compensate for all of these problems, I have taken an approach that acknowledges the limitations of both qualitative and quantitative methodologies and compensates for many of their weaknesses. I have combined the strengths of each method in the perspective used, the kinds of data collected, and in the analysis and presentation of those data. For example, the data were collected using several approaches. The ethnographic knowledge I obtained helped shape the questions that I asked in the field and directed the progress of the research. I combined ethnographic sensitivity to local culture with a large number of interviews and several surveys. I spent a great deal of time in peasant villages but unlike ethnographers and anthropologists did not limit myself to one community.

The data analysis for the study is both qualitative and quantitative. The methods for analyzing the data were sensitive to and reflective of the qualitative context understood through fieldwork. Quantitative choices were informed by a qualitative knowledge of local reality, and I selected statistical techniques and developed measurement indicators that would be faithful to an ethnographic understanding of the indigenous setting. This method allowed statistical analysis of ethnographically gathered data. Ethnographic knowledge also helped determine the extent to which statistical outcomes reflect local reality. The qualitative constraints on statistical methods caused me to utilize statistical techniques that help compensate for the inadequacies of ethnographic data and avoid imposing assumptions on such data that are, in reality, absurd. Thus the statistical results are valid on the basis of contextual and qualitative knowledge rather than on the basis of statistical confidence levels alone.

Qualitative Collection Methods

The principal raw data for this study come from 160 in-depth interviews with peasants in six villages, three in Costa Rica and three in Nicaragua. I arrived at each village with the intention of becoming a temporary member of the community, and stayed for approximately three months. Although naturally I could never shed the status of an outsider, I fit in to village life as much as possible. In each fieldsite, I lived with one village family and ate and slept in their home. Villagers acted as facilitators and were generally interested in and supportive of my research.

This method of study provided a more careful and deep understanding of personal and community perspectives than is normally obtained through traditional social science methods, but a less deep and detailed understanding than is normally achieved in anthropology. I spent enough time in each village to thoroughly explore the political history of the community and investigate individual and community political action and attitudes, but three months is insufficient time to conduct detailed household budget surveys or thoroughly explore kinship and ritual patterns that are important to anthropologists. Such anthropological detail, however, is not necessary for understanding the motivation to political action.

Within each village the interviews followed a standard format and covered the same set of questions. Given the complex and personal nature of the questions, however, respondents did not always answer them in the exact same order. I encouraged them to respond profusely and to talk as long as they liked, as this approach is preferable when dealing with peasant respondents who are often shy, reserved, intimidated, and possibly even frightened or unnerved by the presence of an Anglo English-speaking foreigner who is also "a professor." It takes a lot of careful effort to get such persons to open up and respond truthfully. One extremely important technique requires that the interviewer remain quiet and listen intently, indicating to the respondent that he or she is communicating something very important and encouraging the respondent to continue. To use a closed-ended question or to cut the respondent off just when one has begun to break the ice would be a grievous error.

The fieldwork required eighteen months during 1985, 1986, and 1987 in Costa Rica and Nicaragua. The six peasant villages constitute a purposeful sample, selected for the economic situations they exemplified and for the political actions villagers had chosen. They provide a broad view of a variety of peasant political actions taken in response to different levels of economic insecurity. The life style and poverty of these villagers are quite typical of the majority of the peasant population in these two nations, and the range of political activity is also typical of these countries. Normal economic problems range from inadequate credit and crop prices or landlessness, in Costa Rica, to potential starvation, in Nicaragua. The political actions undertaken include petitions, strikes, land invasions, and participation in the Sandinista revolution or violence against the Somoza regime. In Costa Rica all action had taken place under a democratic regime. In Nicaragua, the political activity studied was conducted under the Somoza dictatorship including participation in the Sandinista revolution.

In each country, I also selected villages with an eye to studying several of the principal crops grown by peasant farmers. In both nations this meant studying a coffee village as well as communities of staple-crop growers. In Costa Rica the choice of site was constrained only by these crop concerns and by patterns of land tenure that have eliminated the peasantry from some regions. The Costa Rican coffee village is San Luis; villagers in El Hogar and La Lucha grow staples. In Nicaragua, my choice of villages was further restricted by the Contra war. Contra attacks in rural areas of Nicaragua made solitary research dangerous in areas where the Sandinista army had not driven the

Contras out. This ruled out research in northern Nicaragua, which is also coffee country. Within the constraints imposed by the war, I sought out villages that grew crops typical of the Nicaraguan peasantry, including coffee and staples. In Nicaragua the coffee-growing village is Pikin Guerrero; in Pedregal and Quebrada Honda, villagers grow staple crops.

In each of the six villages, I conducted formal in-depth interviews with between 10 and 20 percent of male heads of household (except when there was no adult male living in the home). Just as the villages were chosen to provide diversity in the variables, interview respondents were specifically chosen to provide variation. Within each village, I interviewed both the very poor and the less poor, the energetic political activists and the less politically active. In Nicaragua this yielded a total of 90 interviews; in Costa Rica it produced seventy.

This qualitative methodology was crucial to understanding the peasant perspective, as it provides a full grasp of the experience of poverty among respondents and offers a full knowledge of the meaning and goals of resistance, political action, and loss or failure in the context of poverty. Also, this approach was essential to knowing peasant perceptions of community, social solidarity, village mutuality, and justice. My understanding of the peasant ecological perspective emerged as a result of this ethnographic approach. As I did not know that a political ecology existed in the villages before I did the fieldwork, I could not specifically search for it in the interviews. But, in trying to fully capture the peasant perspective, I became aware of the presence of an ecological view. Thus ethnography led to the construction of new theory.[2]

Qualitative research provided an intuitive guide for the quantitative analysis conducted. By the time I had finished research in a specific village, I could provide a nutshell sense of the community in the same way one might describe the "personality" of a university town after having lived there. I had a general feel for village majority opinion with respect to a specific political tactic or event. Similarly, I had listened long enough and closely enough to the respondents to have a sense of who they were as people, as village citizens, and as political actors. Just as we know our neighbors well enough to say with some assurance that "Mrs. X is not likely to buy a Cadillac," or "Mr. Y probably wouldn't like cats," I gained the same understanding of these villagers. I was able to use this knowledge as a guide by which to construct measures and select independent variables, and it also served as a series of checkpoints against which to compare the statistical results obtained.

Quantitative Collection Methods

In addition to the interviews described above, I surveyed all household heads in each of the three Costa Rican villages. This provided an additional 189 Costa Rican respondents. The reader should note that interviews and surveys were two different methods of collecting data. Interviews constituted long, in-depth encounters, which took two to three hours. With surveys, which consisted of a much shorter battery of questions, I attempted to blanket the village population by addressing all household heads. The surveys collected information that is typically required in a census and is neither controversial nor secret: educational level, number of children, etc. Also included in the surveys were questions asking about participation in legal political activities such as voting. The survey did not create a context in which to ask searching questions about deeply held values or about opinions of officially illegal political tactics. I was not able to duplicate the Costa Rican survey in Nicaragua, because surveys were officially illegal in Nicaragua during the years of my fieldwork there.[3] I partially compensated for the unavailability of survey data by interviewing a larger number of respondents (ninety interviews in Nicaragua as opposed to seventy in Costa Rica).

Construction of Measures: A Combined Perspective

The extensive ethnographic perspective was useful when choosing methods of data analysis and informed my selection of relevant variables. Field sites illustrated a variety of economic experiences and political activities. Qualitative understanding of each village revealed that separate indices of different types of economic experience had to be created for each village and thus tailored to reflect the historical experience of the community. Similarly, my analysis of political attitudes was more precise if I first learned which political tactics were most prevalent, most accepted, and most controversial in each village.

The Dependent Variable

As the purpose of my study was to understand and explain why peasants were motivated to engage in different kinds of political action, the dependent variable is political action, or, more specifically, attitudes toward different types of political action. The scope of the study, however, and the broad range of political tactics under scrutiny required that I construct political action into a dependent variable of quantitative utility in a variety of contexts. This was necessary because the different experiential contexts in six different villages caused the political-action variable to differ in form from one village to the next, as influenced by village culture and the national state. Political tactics that were appropriate, accepted, and considered necessary in one country were totally unacceptable in another country. Strategies that were common, constructive, and generally accepted under one form of government were extremely risky or even suicidal, and therefore senseless, under another government. Similarly, some actions were successful and popular in one village, but dangerous or useless in another community.

Political opinion in each village is thus partly the result of a process of political learning that each village goes through as it becomes more activist. Villagers may, for example, begin with one political tactic, such as petitions, and

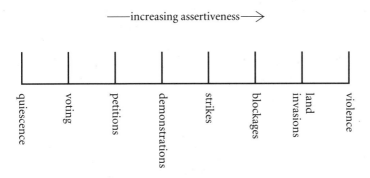

Figure A.1. Spectrum of Political Activity

abandon it because it proves useless. Joint experience with failure of petitions has led almost all villagers to ultimately reject that tactic because it is not fruitful. Evidence from the Costa Rican and Nicaraguan villages shows that peasants prefer milder political tactics and will only move to more assertive forms of action when those previously chosen prove unsuccessful. As villagers move from milder to more assertive forms of action, they come to a tactic about which they do not agree, reaching a point of internal disagreement or dissonance. The area of dissonance is the outcome of both village political learning and village difference of opinion, and represents the most assertive tactic that villagers might consider. Some find the assertive tactic acceptable because they are dissatisfied with milder tactics; others find it unacceptably assertive or risky. It is a tactic for which the outcome (success or repression and failure) is uncertain, and thus villagers disagree in weighing the risk of the tactic versus the likelihood of success. In San Luis, for example, peasants agreed that demonstrations, strikes, and blockages were acceptable; violence fell outside their range of experience and was generally unacceptable. Land invasion, however, fell within their range of conceivable experience but at the more assertive end of that experience. Villagers in San Luis disagreed over the acceptability of land invasions, and it thus became the "point of dissonance" for that village.

No village studied here ran the full gamut of political actions depicted in Figure A.1. Moreover, even within one country all the villages did not fully cover the spectrum. Thus violence was not part of political reality in Costa Rica, and voting was not relevant in Nicaragua prior to 1979. It was typical for the political experience of a given village to fall within a specific domain of tactics. I have called this the domain of political relevance. The typical range for San Luis is illustrated in Figure A.2. Within each village the area of dissonance fell at the more assertive (far right) end of each village's domain of political relevance. This is because the tactic at the area of dissonance walks the line between being ineffective and being unacceptably risky.

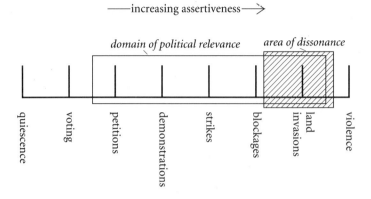

Figure A.2. San Luis: Spectrum of Political Activity

The area of dissonance has become the dependent variable of political action for each community, and its acceptability or unacceptability is explained by the independent variables. While there was variation in opinion about the acceptability of many different tactics across all the villages, taking each village separately, there was only variation in opinion about the tactic in the area of dissonance. When two or more communities are analyzed together, a composite of the areas of dissonance is created as a single dependent variable and the computer is instructed to read only the correct area of dissonance (dependent variable) for each community. This method allows for the creation of a dependent variable that is tailored or "custom made" to suit the political experience of each community.

The existence of a separate area of dissonance for each community would have remained hidden without ethnographic knowledge of each village and the in-depth perception acquired by living in the community. Without such insight, the correct dependent variable would never have been uncovered, and causal analysis would be meaningless. Villagers are not unthinking, mechanical political actors who blindly choose a political strategy without attention to the political context surrounding them, and they should not be treated as such in empirical analyses. In selecting political tactics, peasants carefully take into account the nature of the state, the political experiences of other popular groups, former community experiences, and the need to preserve community and act together. The perception of political reality is likely to be similar for members of the same village, but may very well be different among villages. Thus, it is not surprising to find that within one village there is general agreement about the acceptability or unacceptability of most tactics, but that this agreement doesn't occur between villages.

Independent Variables

Independent variables are factors that influence and explain a peasant's decision to participate in political action. My choice of independent variables reflects a theoretical orientation informed and molded by previous theories of political motivation that have emphasized either individual incentives or community-oriented motives which include concern over justice. More importantly, however, the variables I have chosen reflect an ecological understanding of peasant life, including the interactive, interdependent nature of life in the village. They take into account the peasant perception that a fair and just ordering of the world is one that respects ecological community and individual survival within that community.

The types of reward that motivate action and that are emphasized by different explanatory theories can be measured numerically and analyzed quantitatively, with differing levels of ease. While it is possible to measure economic incentives, rewards of status or power are much more difficult to quantify. A person's sense of justice or anger over violations of community—as well as motivations for injustice—are even more difficult to determine, particularly when set in the context of a community reward that distributes to a number of individuals. Given the difficulty of quantifying many of these types of motivation, it is not surprising that theories of peasant motivation frequently do not include quantitative data analysis.

Yet some such analysis, even of concepts that are hard to measure, serves several important purposes and can greatly increase our understanding of peasant political motivation. First, statistical analysis with empirical data rigorously tests theories of motivation. Second, quantitative analysis provides a more thorough comparison of motives, and gives an accurate indicator of the relative strength of each type of motivation. Finally, quantification allows a precise examination of an ecological explanation for political action.

In analyzing the data, I constructed three types of indices derived from peasant discussions of their motivations to political action. These measures reflect different ways that peasants perceive their system and community to be endangered and thus perceive themselves as threatened. The measures used here are (1) an economic measure that recognizes individualistic explanations of action; (2) a socioeconomic measure that captures the social meaning of economic poverty and incorporates a moral perception on poverty; and (3) a measure of perceptions of injustice that includes violations of peasant expectations.

Although quantitative analysis views each of these three measures separately and in comparison with each other, in the peasant world they are closely interrelated and interdependent. When peasants consider political action they do not consider economic, socioeconomic, and moral motives separately. Just as they perceive elements of their world as interdependent and interactive, so also is their motivation to political action. For example, economic crisis is also a violation of moral values and a threat to ecological community, and danger to the community is both an injustice and a threat to individual and group survival. Nonetheless, it is useful from the point of view of theory to separate out these motives and compare them statistically. The results offer empirical confirmation of my theoretical assertion that motives are multiple, interactive, and reinforcing. No single motive (economics, individual concerns, injustice) is shown to be always predominant. The prevalence of a mixture of motives illustrates empirically the need for a multidimensional theory of motivation that draws on both individual and community concerns.

The Economic Index

Arguments based on individual motivation posit that people are moved to political action by the promise of personal reward, including individual economic gain. Economic rewards can be called "pull factors," or potential future material incentives that pull peasants into political action. The emphasis on pull factors separates the individual from the group and ignores the extent to which economic expectations are part of community norms and create economic mutuality. Moreover, the uncertainty of political outcome for these respondents means that pull factors could never even be precisely described, much less counted on prior to the action taken. Given these problems with economic incentives in the form of pull factors, it is not surprising that future economic reward was not a significant indicator for political action. The outcome of political action was too uncertain, and any economic success that might derive from it was never guaranteed beforehand, much less known in measurable units. This uncertainty was even more true of revolutionary political action, which was more likely to result in arrest, torture, and death than in economic reward.

Nonetheless, immediate and past economic concerns were very important to respondents when they described their reasons for political action. They repeatedly mentioned economic problems as reasons for organization, participation, and choices among different political tactics. This is not surprising given the interdependence between individual economics and ecological community. Economic problems threaten community norms and disrupt the smooth functioning of human interdependence. Severe financial difficulties may, at worst, threaten subsistence needs that norms define as basic, and short of subsistence crises, economic problems undermine the ability of villagers to support each other and maintain community interdependence.

In the poverty of the peasant world, immediate economic problems are more powerful motivators than the lure of future economic gains. These immediate economic problems I have termed "push factors." They include poverty and economic crises that drive peasants into political action in hopes of solution and economic survival. Push factors can be more precisely perceived and understood and serve as more concrete reason for action than pull factors.

Based on my understanding of economic concerns among the respondents in this study, I make precisely this distinction and, in studying economic motivation to political action, address push factors. The study focuses on existing economic problems that were already undermining community, thus violating community norms and which peasants hoped to alleviate or solve through political action. The interviews revealed that economic problems and the community norms that surrounded them were of critical importance in pushing individuals to participate in political action. To help determine the economic status of villagers and to provide information on a range of variables, the interviews collected a wide assortment of economic data, including landownership and father's landownership,[4] frequency and location of employment (among those with little or no land) and ownership of consumer durables (radio, TV, motorcycle, automobile etc,).

Statistical comparison of individual economic indicators revealed that adult landownership bore the most consistently significant relationship to political attitudes and choices of political action across all villages and in both countries. ($p = .05$) Adult landownership was more significant as an indicator of political attitudes than either employment data or data on the ownership of consumer durables. It was also more significant than father's landownership during childhood. This last point suggests that political attitudes are formed during adulthood and in the process of earning one's own living in agriculture rather than during childhood. The first independent variable is therefore a measure of landownership.

Simple landownership, however (one manzana, two manzanas)[5] was not a linear indicator of political attitudes and, examined alone, did not show a strong relationship with the dependent variable of political attitudes. For example, attitudes toward political action and toward specific political tactics did not differ between owners of one manzana and owners of two manzanas. Peasants who owned two manzanas of land were not twice as likely to act and did not act twice as energetically as those who owned only one manzana. Ethnographic knowledge of the peasant perspective, however, solved this puzzle and allowed refinement of the economic measure of landownership to make it an accurate indicator. The peasants suggested a set of categories that indicate levels of living and economic security based on landownership rather than absolute size of landholding.

Thus respondents are divided into four groups: (1) the landless; (2) those owning one to four manzanas; (3) those owning five to nine manzanas; and (4) those owning more than nine manzanas. People within each group tend to act less differently than people in different groups. The peasantry experience a huge difference between being landless and owning a small amount of land (one to four manzanas). The landless are completely down-and-out and must rely entirely on the market and limited employment opportunities for survival. A small plot of land allows a peasant to grow just a bit of food to feed the family—enough to survive for a few months of unemployment. The difference is equivalent to having a small savings account and having no savings whatsoever while one is searching for a job. Peasants falling within the third group (five to nine manzanas) can rely entirely on their own land for survival. These people do not need outside employment and are thus more economically secure than those who have one to four manzanas. The difference is between having a small savings account that will soon run out and having a secure job. Those who own more than nine manzanas have more than enough to live on. They have the equivalent of a secure job and a large savings account. These group divisions are a faithful reflection of the peasant perspective on landownership as it determines economic security and therefore political action.

For one village I needed to weight the measure of acreage to maintain a consistent economic measure. In Pedregal, average land plot size was larger than in the other cases, but the quality of the land was so poor that the larger plots did not permit a better level of living. I asked peasants in Pedregal to compare the level of living they could make on their poor land with that made in more fertile areas of the country ("How many manzanas of land would you have to farm here in order to live as well as you could with one [or 2 or 5 or 10] manzanas in [a more fertile region]?"). I used their answers to construct a formula and weighted land plot sizes in this village to fit within the categories used for the other five villages.

The Socioeconomic Index

Beyond landownership, the data on economic level or poverty fall into four general categories: (1) the experience of hunger, (2) the experience of siblings' childhood deaths due to preventable diseases; (3) the experience of children's deaths in general due to preventable diseases; and (4) educational level (literacy, illiteracy, and education beyond simple literacy). Examined alone, none of these proved to be a significant indicator of political attitudes across all respondents ($p = .05$). This was because different villages had experienced poverty differently; poverty did not look identical everywhere.

Ethnographic knowledge of each village revealed that the failure of these variables to show up as significant indicators across the entire data set did not indicate that they were weakly tied to political action, but rather that the significance of any category of socioeconomic data varied among villages. Hunger, for example, might be statistically significant in two villages and not in the others. Thus the strength of correlation to different types of political action washed out when applied across all six villages at once. This discovery made intuitive sense, given the different contextual experiences of the villages. The experience of hunger was a significant indicator for political attitudes in those villages where many had experienced hunger, such as La Lucha, but not in more affluent villages, such as San Luis, where hunger was very rare. The difference in contextual socioeconomic experience is similar to the difference in contextual political experience. Just as land invasion was a part of political reality in some villages and not in others, the experience of hunger or children's deaths to preventable disease might be part of reality in one village but absent in another. Just as the point of dissonance or political disagreement was specific to each village, the significant politically motivating experiences of poverty were also specific to each community.

This realization enabled me to construct a socioeconomic index that would be a useful indicator of political attitudes by tailoring the index to the qualitative experience of each village. In some, the socioeconomic history was complex, and I needed to combine several kinds of socioeconomic data (for example, the experience of hunger or sibling deaths due to preventable childhood disease) to create an accurate indicator. Combining data was necessary because in a given village the experience of poverty took different forms. For example, poorer families might have lost a child to preventable disease or have experienced hunger, but were still able to send a child to school because of the continuous availability of education in the village.

The "custom-made" socioeconomic variable that emerged has a social and contextual element to it that makes it an important indicator of political action. The experience of hunger, illiteracy, or of one's children's dying from preventable disease takes place in a social context that shapes its social meaning. That social meaning includes a moral dimension and an assessment of relativity—what is and is not unusual in a given community context. Whether or not a socioeconomic loss becomes an indicator of political action depends on whether others in the same community are undergoing the same experience, that is, on whether or not the experience is widely shared or is an unusual experience of injustice or both.

The socioeconomic experience of individuals is also heavily influenced by the social and economic experiences of the community as a whole (when a road was constructed, when a school was completed, when land concentration among elites and land loss among villagers reached its peak). A new school services an entire community simultaneously, so that illiteracy may be common in one generation and almost eliminated by the next generation. The same is true of the availability of roads, health care, and other services. Village history thus partly determined which socioeconomic variables were relevant for each village and explained why no single socioeconomic variable was a significant indicator across the entire data set. In the poorest villages, the two Nicaraguan communities of Quebrada Honda and Pikin Guerrero, hunger was the most powerful socioeconomic indicator of political action. In La Lucha, Costa Rica, village sibling deaths to preventable disease were fairly common one generation ago when most respondents were children, but improved health services had largely eliminated such deaths among the current generation. In La Lucha, sibling deaths to preventable disease were a significant indicator, but children's deaths were not. In San Luis, a less poverty-stricken Costa Rican village, most of the indicators of socioeconomic deprivation were not significant. Most people had no experience of hunger, or of sibling or children's deaths due to preventable disease, and most were literate. In San Luis poverty levels were related to the number of years of grade school that respondents had completed, because poorer families had to pull children out of school earlier to put them to work. Less poor families kept children in school through grade six. In this village, educational level, or number of grades completed was the most powerful socioeconomic indicator of political action.

When analyzing two or more communities together, I used a composite of socioeconomic indicators, instructing the computer to read only the relevant socioeconomic index for each village. In Chapter 8, where all six villages are analyzed together, the composite includes the significant socioeconomic index for each village, and thus the empirical analysis includes an independent variable that is custom-made for each village just as the dependent variable (point of dissonance) is custom-made for each village. This made possible a general measure of the strength of socioeconomic experience across the entire data set, even though particular socioeconomic indicators are tailored to the qualitative historical and social experience of each community.

The Injustice Index

Perceptions of injustice are often important reasons for political action, and many studies of political action and motives have focused on this relationship. Central to this study of political motivation and action is the peasant perspective on the health of the surrounding ecological community. That community is defined more or less broadly depending upon the parochial or national perspective of villagers. Regardless of how ecological community is defined, however, a violation of it or threat to it constitutes a violation of peasant notions of how the world ought to function. Underlying such perceptions are peasant notions of justice and injustice, right and wrong. From the perspective of the theory proposed in this book, therefore, peasant perceptions of injustice—as determined by their view of the health of ecological community—are a key indicator of political attitudes and action and are central to understanding decisions about political action.

The data here indicate that injustice was a significant political indicator ($p \geq .05$) for many kinds of political action. Rural notions of justice play a critical role in the peasant political world. Decisions to take political action require attention to the individual perception of injustice, both injustice toward the respondent and injustice toward the community that the respondent needs for survival. Interviews probed peasant definitions of justice, fairness, and foul play. The data revealed both a fully developed consciousness of justice that reflected community norms and a clear sense of what was fair and what constituted a violation of moral norms protective of community.

My discussion of peasant notions of justice and the way in which violation of those ideals relates to political action is primarily qualitative and ethnographic. These approaches do the greatest justice to peasant reality and provide an excellent opportunity to understand political action in the context of violated ideals. Although there is no way to measure the strength of a sense of injustice, one can count how many people mention injustice in their interviews and the number of people who make that mention. Accordingly, the quantitative analysis of injustice here focuses on the number of people who mention perceptions of injustice, rights violated, or unfairness as reasons for taking political action. Within this category fall answers such as "because of the injustice around us"; "because of the injustice of the [tax system, payment system, banking system, repression]"; "because we are treated unfairly"; "for our rights;" "because we have a right to . . . "; and so on. Although this method of addressing injustice as a reason for political action provides only a rather rough measure, it taps an extremely significant motivator for political action. The resultant injustice index proves to be an exceedingly important variable in understanding the peasant political world.

Some respondents mentioned injustice or rights violated many times during an interview while others referred to such motivations only once or twice in the same time period. This difference did not prove to be one of emphasis, and those mentioning injustice multiple times did not necessarily have a greater sense of justice violated than those who mentioned it only once. Rather, the number of times injustice was mentioned related more to personality and to skill in articulating thoughts. Some respondents were profuse, wordy, self-confident, or more assertive than others and mentioned injustice repeatedly. Others were more reticent or more economical in their use of words and mentioned injustice only once without feeling any less strongly about it. The measure of injustice developed reflects one or more mentions of injustice during the interview.[6]

A Word about Empirical Results

In this study, the realities of peasant society combined with national and qualitative variables, constrained the sample size and limited the scope of quantitative analysis. The time required to conduct an interview that will uncover notions of justice, perceptions of justice violated, and attitudes about illegal as well as legal political action necessarily limits the number of interviews one can complete. In this study, the inclusion of six different villages in two countries provides variation in kinds of political tactics undertaken and in the nature of the state although limiting the number of interviews possible in each case. Furthermore, individual villages did not provide a sample size of more than a maximum of two hundred because peasant communities are relatively small. (In such villages 10 to 15 percent of the population is no more than twenty to thirty respondents.) Most villages in this study had about one hundred families; one had two hundred and one had only forty. The surveys, which expand the sample size, provide only limited data. They include economic and socioeconomic data but very little about attitudes toward complex and illegal political tactics and nothing about perceptions of justice. It is therefore appropriate that much of the analysis is qualitative and includes excerpts from the interviews themselves.

Despite these constraints, the empirical results achieved by comparing the measures developed above are fascinating. Analysis of political motivation comparing economic, socioeconomic, and injustice factors among the peasantry has not been attempted before. We have no explicit empirical test of the relative strength of these motives and no precise comparison of their relative explanatory power. Moreover, some statistical programs are specifically designed to handle data sets that are "small" by the standards of survey methodology. These programs compensate for sample size but do not impose on a small sample assumptions that are realistic only for larger samples. Thus, despite the limited sample size, the quantitative analysis moves knowledge of political action among the peasantry a substantial step forward. We emerge from the analysis knowing far more about actions, tactics, measures, and relative strength of motive than we knew beforehand.

The relationship between poverty and political action or between the independent variables and the dependent variable is not linear and precludes the use of simple multivariate regression. The dependent variable itself is also not linear. Although the spectrum of political activity moves from action that is less assertive to action that is more assertive, the relative assertiveness of each tactic is determined by the national political context within which the action takes place. For example, petitions to Somoza's government were far more risky and required far more assertive courage than did land invasions in democratic Costa Rica. Finally, even within one country, the conceptual jump between different political tactics is not uniform. The move from demonstrations to blockages may be smaller and easier than the move from blockages to land invasion. Notches on the political spectrum are not evenly spaced as are the notches on a ruler. They appear evenly spaced in Figure A.1 because of my graphics, not because of peasant perceptions. Peasants may perceive the jump from petitions to demonstrations as quite small but the jump from land invasions to violence as huge. Because the notches between tactics are of uneven size, the dependent variable does not increase in a linear fashion.

Cross tabulations provide one excellent way of comparing variables without assuming a linear relationship between them. All of the analysis of variables in this study includes a cross tabular examination of the relationship of each independent variable to attitudes about the political tactic that is at the point of dissonance (the dependent variable). This relationship is explored both within individual cases (villages) and across two or more. When cross tabulations include data from more than one village, both the nature of the socioeconomic variable and the political tactic being studied (point of dissonance) changes. When this occurs, a composite of variables is created so that the computer reads the correct socioeconomic index and the correct point of dissonance for each village.

Finally, an attempt to compare all three independent variables across all six cases with the separate point of dissonance for each village requires the use of tobit regression. Unlike cross tabulations, tobit includes more than one independent variable in a comparative analysis. The regression produces coefficients that allow precise comparison of the relative strength of each independent variable in relation to choices about and attitudes toward the most controversial political tactic within a given village context (the area of dissonance). This method provides some fascinating comparison of the relative importance of economic factors, socioeconomic factors, and injustice in motivating political action.

Tobit regression provides some latitude that standard multivariate regression precludes. It lends itself to the inclusion of dichotomous variables. In this study many of the variables are coded in a dichotomous rather than linear fashion: did X mention injustice as a motivation (yes/no)?; did Y experience sibling deaths to preventable disease (yes/no)?; is tactic Z acceptable or not (yes/no)?. Tobit permits regression analysis without requiring linear coding.

This limited quantitative analysis constitutes an initial step beyond interpretivism and toward a more formal model for understanding peasant politics. As such it moves the field beyond the standard interpretive theory of peasant political action. While neither the data nor the results presented in the book fully meet all of the rigorous statistical standards applied to larger data sets, such standards are not appropriate to these data. These ethnographic data offer evidence and knowledge of peasant reality that a larger data set never could provide. At the same time, using more inclusive statistical standards (including, for example, the examination of confidence levels between 85 and 90 percent) for analyzing these unique data allows us to use statistics to learn more from the ethnographic data than we could from interpretivism alone.

It is my hope that this study will provide students and colleagues with a method of research and analysis that can be duplicated. Among other things, I have attempted to operationalize and compare two general kinds of political motivation that appear elsewhere in the literature about peasant political action. The struggle to interpret my findings in comparing and evaluating these motives has led me to develop a new theory of political action that is multidimensional and that combines motives. Other studies that follow could conduct even more extensive comparisons of the motives addressed here. With a sufficient investment of resources, subsequent studies could increase the sample size, allowing more sophisticated quantitative analysis of political motivation among the peasantry and more certainty of the direction of relationships among variables.

NOTES

Chapter 1. The Peasant Political Ecology: Politics and Community

1. An argument in favor of the mutually compatible interests of individual and society is also found in the work of well-known anthropologist Ruth Benedict. Although Benedict does not offer a theory of political action, she does write that there is no antagonism between the role of society and the role of the individual. A conviction of such antagonism is one of the most misleading misconceptions of the nineteenth century. Benedict notes the presence of an awareness of interdependence among "primitive" peoples but an absence thereof in modern society. *Patterns of Culture* (New York: Penguin Books, 1934), 232–35.

2. The same distinction can be made for other theories of decision making. Take, for instance, the rational actor model. The rational actor theory does not maintain that actors consciously think "I am a rational actor. What decision will be most likely to serve my interests from a rational point of view?" Rather, individuals simply think in terms of self-interest and this can be described as the calculation of a rational actor.

3. The word *ecology* has taken on a variety of connotations associated with the world of nature, only some of which apply here. Yet if we begin with a dictionary definition, the word need not necessarily be confined to the environment or nature. *Ecological* simply describes the interaction among components within a system.

4. Anna Bramwell defines contemporary ecology similarly. She addresses both the biological aspects of energy flows within a closed system and the normative attentiveness to nonhuman, natural concerns inherent in modern usage of the term. Nonetheless, Bramwell's definition is still less broad than my own since it does not include interdependence between individuals or the community and the wider society, relationships where interdependence and interactive energy flows are also evident. See Anna Bramwell, *Ecology in the Twentieth Century: A History* (New Haven: Yale University Press, 1989), 4–6.

5. The question of whether people are self-interested individualists or community participants capable of safeguarding the common good is quite old and has not been limited to the field of peasant studies. For example, it surrounded the framing of the United States government and is expressed in the opposing positions of Madison and Hamilton. Opposing positions in this debate over human nature and human action also affected politics in Europe. Protest against the perceived individualist orientation of the British government, such as that launched by the Levellers and Diggers, stressed the human place in society and undertook action that emphasized or supported hu-

man community. Reactions to the French Revolution, both in Britain and on the Continent, fell into camps that roughly correspond to this individualist/communitarian debate. One can even find the individualist/communitarian debate in the tension between church and state in the Middle Ages. In the fifteenth and sixteenth centuries the church stressed the individual place in the community and sought to include social concerns in economic and political decisions. Thus the church denounced individual choices that exploited others, such as usury and extortion, and even established courts to enforce its values, appealing to Bible texts as the source of guidance. Heads of state, on the other hand, argued for individual interests, particularly their own, and the individual right to rule according to personal decisions and preferences. With the rise of commercial capitalism in the eighteenth century, the hand of individual interest was greatly strengthened, and the influence of the church was gradually eliminated from the sphere of politics and governance altogether.

6. Amartya Sen also advances an argument that a strictly traditional rational actor placed in a social context would be perceived as foolish. "Purely economic man," he writes, "is a social moron." See "Rational Fools: A Critique of the Behavior Foundations of Economic Theory," in *Beyond Self Interest*, ed. Jane Mansbridge (Chicago: 1990 University of Chicago Press, 37.

7. Michael Taylor has also done work that considers ways in which individual interest overlaps with community interest instead of being entirely at odds. See, for example, *Anarchy and Cooperation* (London: John Wiley and Sons, 1976) and Michael Taylor, ed., *Rationality and Revolution* (Cambridge: Cambridge University Press, 1988).

8. In an impressive cross-national, historical study Victor Magagna also argues that defense of community—and the protection community provides to popular interests—explains peasant political action better than any other theoretical construct, including class. Although Magagna's study focuses only on rebellion and does not examine the political result of peasant interaction with society and nature, he sees community preservation as central in peasant political motives in each of his historical case studies (Britain, France, Spain, Russia, and Japan). *Communities of Grain: Rural Rebellion in Comparative Perspective* (Ithaca: Cornell University Press, 1991).

9. Barrington Moore, *Injustice: The Social Bases of Obedience and Revolt* (White Plains, N.Y.: M. E. Sharp, 1978), 37–38.

10. E. P. Thompson, *The Making of the English Working Class* (New York: Pantheon, Books, 1963), 60, 62 and 63, and "The Moral Economy of the English Crowd," *Past and Present* 50 (Feb. 1971): 79.

11. Thompson, "The Moral Economy," 131.

12. Moore, *Injustice*, 25.

13. Jeffery Gould finds that Nicaraguan peasants specifically eschew farming techniques and specific cash crops if they are known to harm other individuals and the community in general. This approach contrasts sharply with that of capitalist farmers who are not peasants and not participants in a peasant community. *To Lead As Equals: Rural Protest and Political Consciousness in Chinandega, Nicaragua, 1912-1979* (Chapel Hill: University of North Carolina Press, 1990).

14. Individual needs and survival may be threatened by a natural disaster. Because such an event is not caused by human agency, however, it does not violate norms of relative equality. Natural disasters may strike rich and poor alike. Disaster evokes political action only when it is triggered by a human agent (landlord, tax collector, state representative) and thus violates norms of relative egalitarianism and resistance to subordination.

15. Jean Jacques Rousseau writes that "it is against the law of nature . . . that a hand-

ful should gorge themselves with superfluities, while the starving masses lack the barest necessities of life." While his terminology is perhaps unnecessarily inflammatory, his argument is essentially that of the peasants, . . . and visa versa. See *Discourse on the Origin and Foundation of Inequality among Mankind*, 1754 (New York: Washington Square Press, 1967), 246. Tolstoy recognized the rule of custom and shared social values with respect to human needs and the unnatural possession of more than is needed. "Things really produced by a man's own labour, and that he needs, are always defended by custom, by public opinion, by feelings of justice and reciprocity, and they do not need to be protected by violence." But vast holdings of land or productive goods that are needed by the people are so contrary to the people's natural sense of justice that they must be defended by laws, police, courts, prisons, and other instruments of governmental violence. Leo Tolstoy, *The Slavery of Our Times* (New York: N.p., 1900), 124, quoted in T. Anderson *Russian Political Thought* (Ithaca: Cornell University Press, 1967), 241.

16. Moore, *Injustice*, 38; Moore's emphasis.

17. Scott, *Moral Economy*, 1976. In a quite unrelated context reciprocity such as that which Scott describes is also called "reciprocal altruism." There also the implication is that of a bilateral relationship, whereas political ecology describes a more complex, multilateral system of exchange. See Christopher Jenks, "Varieties of Altruism" in Jane Mansbridge, ed., *Beyond Self Interest* (Chicago: University of Chicago Press, 1990), 61.

18. Reciprocity, as described by Scott in *Weapons of the Weak*, overemphasizes the role of coercion in village exchange. While coercion is certainly one tool that landed and landless both employ, coercion is most effective in two-way exchange relationships. Any exchange patterns that are more diffuse and complex than two-way relationships must also rely upon a sense of how each individual depends upon the community as a whole. As Figure 1.1 suggests, without a sense of ecological community free ridership is too easy and too tempting.

19. In the Amazon jungle of Brazil the Kayapó Indians have organized to protect nature not only against their own trespasses but also against developmental interests from the main cities. This effort has brought the Indians into contact with environmentalist movements abroad as well as domestically. Studies of Kayapó cultivation have found that these Indians have developed a diversified system of agriculture and other land use which is well suited to the tropical ecosystem and minimizes the potential for environment degradation. See Marianne Schmink and Charles H. Wood, "The Political Ecology of Amazonia," in Peter D. Little, Michael M. Horowitz, and A. Endre Nyerges, eds., *Lands at Risk in the Third World: Local Level Perspectives* (Boulder: Westview Press, 1987).

20. Even where external groups and factors do not play a role, peasants may organize for conservation and just distribution of natural resources. Such organization may, in fact, be easier when peasants are left to their own devices, free of external factors. For example, in harsh Andean areas where the water supply is critical, peasants have organized for wise use of that supply and for overseeing its equitable distribution. Similar mechanisms of control are used for scarce land supplies. In these systems, while individuals clearly depend upon the community, the latter also depends upon individual maintenance and involvement in order to keep going. For details on these systems see César Fonseca, "El Control Comunal del Agua en la cuenca del rio Canete" and Enrique Mayer, "Tenencia y control comunal de la tierra: caso de Laraos," both essays in Comunidad y Producción en la Agricultura Andina," ed. César Fonseca and Enrique Mayer (Lima: Fomciencias, 1988).

21. Joan Martinex Alier also argues that social movements of the poor always include an environmental component because of the extent to which the poor perceive their

dependence upon nature. "Ecology and the Poor," *Journal of Latin American Studies* 23, no. 3 (October 1991).

22. Any informed student of developing countries can think of examples where peasants are destroying some part of their environment. Critics of the position I am offering here have been eager to point out these examples to me. However, the investigator who finds such examples and points a finger of blame solely at the peasantry is in serious danger of drawing fast conclusions based on limited knowledge. In cases where peasants are degrading their environment, that degradation is usually part of a long process in which many factors (development, capitalist farming, new methods of cultivation, political decisions, mechanization) have preceded such peasant action and have pushed peasants to a point where they have no choice. In such cases a minimal historical investigation will reveal that prior to the intervention of such factors the peasants who are now degrading their environment did once live in a more ecological and sustaining relationship with the ecosystem.

Examples of such ecological relationships with nature abound. For discussions of external pressures forcing peasants to degrade their environments in Brazil, the Sudan, and the Philippines, respectively, see Schmink and Wood, "The Political Ecology of Amazonia," 45, Michael Horowitz and Muneera Salem-Murdock, "The Political Economy of Desertification in White Nile Province, Sudan," and James N. Anderson, "Lands at Risk: Perspectives on Tropical Forest Transformations in the Philippines," in Little, Horowitz, and Nyerges, *Lands at Risk*.

Sometimes even the best of intentions, including efforts to decrease peasant poverty, have evolved into situations where some peasants are trapped and have no option but to degrade their environment. Cognizant of peasant abilities to develop practices that are not environmentally destructive, some developers have advocated creating development strategies that incorporate the advice and knowledge of the local peasants. See, for example, Donald Messerschmidt, "Conservation and Society in Nepal: Traditional Forest Management and Innovative Development," in Little, et al., *Lands at Risk*.

23. My thinking with regard to peasants and their relationship to nature has been clarified as the result of several discussions of the peasant political ecology during a conference on "the dimensions of peasant power" at the University of Colorado in April 1992. In particular I am grateful for the input and constructive criticism of several participants in that conference, most notably Ronald Herring, Teodor Shanin, James Scott, and William Kelly.

24. The Kayapó Indian struggle is one well-known example of the latter.

25. Eric Wolf, *Peasant Wars of the Twentieth Century* (New York: Harper and Row, 1969).

Chapter 2. The Broader Context: Contrasting Political Traditions

1. Most of Latin America shares a similar culture, ethnicity, religion, and geopolitical position. Another study or an extension of this study that sought to include these characteristics as independent variables rather than constants, as I do here, would have to include cases from outside Latin America.

2. For an extensive exploration of colonial Costa Rica see Elizabeth Fonseca, *Costa Rica Colonial: La Tierra y el Hombre* (San José: EDUCA, 1984). See specifically 40–42, 54, 290, 321.

3. Samuel Stone, *La dinastía de los conquistadores: La crisis del poder en la Costa Rica contemporánea* (San José: EDUCA, 1975), 107.

4. Fonseca, *Costa Rica*, 68.

5. Ibid., 119.

6. Mitchell Seligson, *The Peasants of Costa Rica and the Development of Agrarian Capitalism*, (Madison: University of Wisconsin Press, 1980), 156–61.

7. See, for example, the history of Costa Rican labor in Vladimir de la Cruz, *Las Luchas Sociales en Costa Rica* (San José: Editorial Universidad de Costa Rica, 1983), particularly chapters 1–3.

8. One debate in the literature on Costa Rica revolves around the prevalence or lack thereof of smallholders in rural areas. These peasants have suffered financial crisis in recent decades and their numbers are increasing beyond the land base available to support them. Nonetheless, their numbers and their political power are substantial relative to their counterparts elsewhere in Central America, and they have had an important influence on the course of political development in Costa Rica.

9. Ibid., 33–35, 47–48.

10. Ibid., 31–32.

11. Jeffrey Casey Gasper, *Limón, 1880–1940* (San José: Editorial Costa Rica, 1979), 21.

12. Seligson, 67–70. For a famous fictional account of the hardships of life on the banana plantations see Carlos Luis Fallas, *Mamita Yunai* (San José: Editorial Costa Rica, 1966).

13. Gasper, *Limón*, 123–24.

14. Ibid., 48.

15. The word *precarismo* is Costa Rican Spanish for the phenomenon of land invasion while *precarista* means land invader. The terms derive from the word *precario*, "precarious" in English, which indicates the insecurity of land tenure under which these peasants operated.

16. One hectare = 2.471 acres. The earliest dollar/colón exchange rate available is for 1922, when one dollar equalled four colónes. The charge imposed by United Fruit was probably higher than the equivalent of 50 cents, since Costa Rica went off the gold standard in 1914. See Franz Pick, and René Sedillot, *All the Monies of the World: A Chronicle of Currency Values* (New York: Pick Publishing Corp., 1971), 71.

17. Francisco Rojas Aravaria has argued that in the present crisis in Central America Costa Rica is reaping the rewards for greater independence from foreign interests. The country has more control over its own fate than, for example, Honduras, which was never able to exercise as much control over the foreign banana industry as was Costa Rica. See Rojas, "Costa Rica y Honduras: A Similares Problemas Soluciones Distinctas," *Estudios Sociales Centroamericanos*, 43 (1987).

18. Ibid., 21.

19. Seligson, *The Peasants of Costa Rica*, 64.

20. Oscar Arias, *Quien Gobierna en Costa Rica?* (San José: Editorial Universitaria Centroamericana, 1984), 52, 60, 250.

21. Ibid., 94–95.

22. Seligson argues that land invasion may be the most important strategy peasants have for surviving the future. He offers some other interesting examples of land invasion as a common political tactic among the Costa Rican peasantry. *The Peasants of Costa Rica*, ch. 5.

23. Whereas displacement from the land frequently results in migration to cities in search of factory employment, this trend is less prevalent in Costa Rica because of the extremely small industrial base and the relatively few industrial jobs.

24. Jaime Wheelock Roman, *Raices Indigenas de la Lucha Anticolonialista en Nicaragua*, (Managua: Editorial Nueva Nicaragua, 1981), 32.

25. Ibid., 43.

26. Ibid., 53–54.

27. Ibid., 75–79.

28. The William Walker affair was symptomatic of unbridled party rivalry and a feeble state. In the hopes of attaining military supremacy over the Conservatives, the Liberal party invited in a U.S. citizen named William Walker. Walker agreed to come but retained an independent agenda and purpose. Caught up in the pre–Civil War struggle for control of the United States legislature, Walker intended to annex Central America onto the southern United States, thus greatly extending southern slave territory. In the 1850s he attempted to take personal control of Central America. He failed only because the political and military resistance he encountered extended far beyond the borders of Nicaragua.

29. J. Booth, *The End and the Beginning* (Boulder: Westview Press, 1982), 67–69. Booth writes that exact estimates of Somoza García's fortune are not available.

30. In Spanish, "Nicaragua es mi finca."

31. *New York Times*, July 20, 1979, quoted in Booth, *The End and the Beginning*, 34.

32. López Pérez was executed for the assasination and assumed a place in Nicaraguan heroic folklore as a result.

33. Nicaraguans frequently refer to Sandino's army as "El Pequeño Ejercito Loco de Sandino."

34. See also Thomas Walker, *Nicaragua: The Land of Sandino* (Boulder, Colo.: Westview Press, 1986) pp 100–101 Unlike the peasants and other Nicaraguans, the United States government continued to believe that Somoza held popular support which was confirmed by electoral victories. Walker argues that Somoza deliberately maintained an elaborate democratic facade for the purpose of winning United States support. The use of an electoral front to conceal a nondemocratic hold upon political power was certainly a tradition that enjoyed a long history in Nicaragua.

35. For a thorough study and discussion of the development of agrarian capitalism and the agro-export sector in Nicaragua prior to 1979, see also Laura Enríquez, *Social Transformation in Latin America: Tensions between Agro-Export Production and Agrarian Reform in Revolutionary Nicaragua* (Ph.D. diss. University of California, Santa Cruz, 1985). For a summary of laws affecting peasant labor, see particularly 74 and 82. For a discussion of the impact of agro-export development on landlessness and poverty, see 83 and 101–5.

36. See also Booth, *The End and the Beginning*, 93–95, for a description of human rights violations, torture, and the growing resolve of the population in response to the repression. The Nicaraguan revolution is estimated to have cost approximately 50,000 lives. In a country of three million this represents 1.6 percent of the population. Walker points out that in the United States this would have been equivalent to the loss of roughly 4.5 million people, more than seventy-five times the U.S. death toll in Vietnam. See Walker, T., *Nicaraguan in Revolution*, (New York: Praeger, 1982) 20.

37. The FSLN divided its military struggle into four separate fronts converging on Managua from the four directions, north, south, east, and west. Of the four fronts the eastern front was the weakest.

Chapter 3. Ecological Harmony and Quiescence: Pedregal, Boaco, Nicaragua

1. One manzana = 1.75 acres.

2. This figure is derived by asking respondents how much land they thought a villager needed to own in order to support a family without having to work other than on his own land.

3. James Scott, *Weapons of the Weak: Everyday Forms of Peasant Resistance* (New Haven: Yale University Press, 1985).

4. James Scott, *The Moral Economy of the Peasant: Subsistence and Rebellion in Southeast Asia* (New Haven: Yale University Press, 1976). The term *moral economy* and the norms associated with it were first studied by British historial E. P. Thompson. See "The Moral Economy of the English Crowd," *Past and Present* 50 (February 1971).

5. The ability of Pedregal peasants to protect the soil in their area and to keep it relatively productive thus far stands in marked constrast to the extreme soil deterioration found in other parts of Nicaragua where the peasant economy was driven out by agroexport interests. This is most noticably true in northern Nicaragua where the cotton industry run by large landlords has nearly destroyed soil productivity in a region that was once much more agriculturally productive than Pedregal's region of Boaco. Jeffrey Gould, *To Lead as Equals: Rural Protest and Political Consciousness in Chinandega, Nicaragua, 1912–1979* (Chapel Hill: University of North Carolina Press, 1990).

6. While Pedregal did not have electric service, the next village out toward the main highway did. Carlos lived at the edge of Pedregal and had illegally run a bare wire between his house and the most outlying electric line in the next village. This long stretch (500 or more yards) of unprotected electric wire posed a danger for both villagers and the surrounding forests, but Carlos was more concerned with the convenience for his own home.

7. For a fuller discussion of the moneylenders, see also Laura Enríquez, *Social Transformation in Latin America: Tensions between Agro-Export Production and Agrarian Reform in Revolutionary Nicaragua* (Ph.D. diss., University of California, Santa Cruz, 1985). The effect of moneylenders on a peasant community and on individual political attitudes will be discussed in Chapter 6.

8. Although all villagers were nominally Catholic, there was no church nearby that they could attend regularly, and no priest visited the village. Active involvement required leaving the village and traveling to Teustepe or to a peasant home between the village and the town.

Chapter 4. Integration and Accommodation: San Luis, Alajuela, Costa Rica

1. In recent years the prevalence of yeoman farming in Costa Rica has been a subject of debate. Scholars have argued that land tenure was never as egalitarian as had been imagined. Lowell Gudmunson, *Costa Rica Before Coffee: Society and Economy on the Eve of the Export Boom* (Baton Rouge: Louisiana State University Press, 1986). Others have pointed out the growing level of landlessness in recent decades, Seligson, Mitchell, *Peasants of Costa Rica and the Development of Agrarian Capitalism*, Madison, University of Wisconsin Press, 1980.

2. Women in San Luis knew very little about the subjects of this study: agriculture, political action, unionization. This was unfortunate, since as a result it was unproductive to interview most peasant women. The two women who were exceptions to this rule are interviewed here.

3. One manzana = 1.75 acres. Respondents have an incentive to understate landholdings since taxes are assessed on land. The local municipality, however, keeps records of land ownership that showed the average landholding among all San Luis residents to be 11.5 manzanas.

4. Respondents were asked how much village land an individual needed to support a family. The figure 5.75 is an average of the responses given.

5. The peasant capacity to work longer and longer hours, to pare back living expens-

es more and more, and to tighten the belt one notch and then another is also the capacity that allows peasant family farming to weather economic crisis longer after a large capitalist farm, which must make a profit in order to pay wages, would go under. Chayanov used this argument to assert that, far from being inefficient, the peasant family farm was more efficient and productive than either the capitalist farm or the state-run collective. See A. V. Chayanov, "On the Theory of Non-Capitalist Economic Systems" and "Peasant Farm Organization," reproduced and translated in Daniel Thorner, Basile Kerblay, and R. E. F. Smith, *The Theory of Peasant Economy* (Madison: University of Wisconsin Press, 1986).

6. For a more detailed, historical analysis of the experience of UPA and other Costa Rican peasant unions see Leslie Anderson, "Mixed Blessings: Disruption and Organization among Costa Rican Peasant Unions," *Latin American Research Review* 26, no. 1, (1991).

7. In fact, the Costa Rican communist parties do not advocate violence and never have. Yet UPA members know that communism elsewhere has been associated with violence, and they do not want that in Costa Rica.

Chapter 5. Ecological Community: El Hagar and La Lucha, Costa Rica

1. Subsequent to the events described in this chapter Rolf was persecuted by Costa Rican government authorities. He was arrested on false charges and was forced to hire a lawyer before he could clear his name. In the end he was never convicted of any crime, and he was released. However, the experience made him nervous about publicity, and he requested that I change his first name and omit his last name in telling his story.

2. IDA's guidelines for the redistribution of land specify that land recipients must be peasants who have some knowledge of the agricultural trade and not ex-proletarians. They must also be landless and should never have received land from IDA previously. The problem is that IDA very rarely uses the guidelines because it so seldom redistributes land. The application of these guidelines to peasant land invaders amounts to a contradiction of the official state position that maintains that land invasion is illegal. Nevertheless, this is the practice frequently followed when land invaders have succeeded in forcing IDA to redistribute invaded land.

3. The written media have been the most energetic participants in this campaign, particularly the newspapers, *La Nación* and *La República*. The years 1981 and 1982, during the height of the land invasion, are the most fruitful dates to look for examples of this campaign. See *La Nación,* 7/7/81, 7/8/81, 6/17/82, 6/18/82, 6/23/82, and *La República,* 7/7/81, 6/22/82, 7/25/82. See also the newspapers' coverage of the peasant demonstration in San José, September 15, 1986. In early 1989 UPAGRA initiated a suit for slander against the newspaper, *La Prensa Libre,* and against Sergio Fernández, the director of Costa Rica's intelligence agency. Fernández and the newspaper alleged that UPAGRA's leaders received military training in Cuba, were importing arms from abroad, and were training members for a violent overthrow of the state. UPAGRA drew the line, found itself a lawyer, and sued Fernández for fourteen million colones and the newspaper for thirty-five million colones. Over a six-month period the state tried every conceivable tactic to have the suit thrown out of court. It failed and court proceedings began in August, 1989. It remains to be seen what will actually come of the suit. If it is successful, perhaps future contributors to the discrediting campaign will be more prudent about their accusations.

4. This example illustrates one of the ironies of statistical examination of relationships among variables. The methods demand variation in the independent variable if

we are to be able to observe whether or not the relationship is significant. This remains true even if there is no true variation in that variable in the real world. Thus if almost everyone mentions injustice as a reason for political action, the statistical tables present that variable (injustice) as having no significant relationship to variation in the dependent variable. I did, in fact, examine the statistical relationship between the mention of injustice and perceptions about the area of dissonance for each village (land invasion in El Hogar and violence in La Lucha). The relationship was in the expected direction: those who perceived injustice were more likely to find acceptable the tactic located in the area of dissonance. Due to lack of variation in the independent variable, however, the relationship was not statistically significant.

Chapter 6. Peasant Revolution: Quebrada Honda, Nicaragua

1. I have chosen to call these Nicaraguans "peasants" because that is what they call themselves, even though some worked periodically as laborers in local cottage industries or as domestic workers. The fact that they call themselves "peasants," implying that they work the land, cannot be considered merely force of habit. It also represents an underlying culture of resistance to Somoza's regime, which prevented them from working the land. Stoler refers briefly to a similar form of cultural resistance among farmers on Sumatra's east coast. See Laura Ann Stoler, "Plantation Politics and Protest on Sumatra's East Coast," *Journal of Peasant Studies* 13, no. 2 (January 1986):139.

2. The Somoza family itself was the most flagrant example of elite land concentration. At the time of the revolution in 1979 Anastasio Somoza himself owned 20 percent of Nicaragua's prime farmland. David Kaimowitz, "Nicaraguan Debates on Agrarian Structure and Their Implications for Agricultural Policy and the Rural Poor," *Journal of Peasant Studies* 14, no. 1 (October, 1986):106.

3. Figures here draw upon the official exchange rate during the time in question. According to the International Monetary Fund *International Financial Statistics* the Nicaraguan economy was very stable during the 1960s and 1970s. The exchange rate went from ¢7.05/$1 in 1958 to ¢7.03/$1 in 1978. Dollar conversions of these figures are done at the 1968 exchange rate of ¢7.05/$1.

4. Diseases most often mentioned included gastrointestinal disorders, malaria, pertussis, polio, and malnutrition.

5. Among the Nicaraguan peasants, people who collaborated with the Guard and were paid to spy upon the revolutionary activities of their neighbors were known as "ears" ("orejas").

6. Laura Enríquez has argued that the system deliberately imposed these conditions on the peasantry. Elites who deprived peasants of support in a land base knew they would thereby be able to count on peasant labor at harvest time.

7. One quintal = 100 kilograms or 200 pounds of cotton.

8. Unfortunately, Ramón's grandfather had died long before I undertook this study so I was unable to talk with him.

9. This dynamic is not peculiar to Nicaraguans. When operating as a guerrilla in the mountains of Guatemala, Mario Payeras also found the peasant population increased its participation with the guerrillas in response to repression by the Guatemalan army: "Pointing their guns at the women and children, the soldiers would make the adult males come out of the huts. They were never seen again. Terror began to spread. . . . In less than a week we tripled our membership, augmented by the peasants who sought our protection." Mario Payeras, *The Days of the Jungle* (New York: Monthly Review Press, 1983), 79.

10. Universities and high schools were the scene of numerous guerrilla activities and many revolutionaries were also students. Students in Nicaragua usually wear a uniform but many had stopped wearing it for reasons of safety.

11. The reader familiar with the difficulties of fieldwork among peasants will ask whether the respondents actually did what they said they did or whether they were lying about their revolutionary participation. This concern is particularly relevant since I was interviewing at a time when the Sandinista revolution held great social prestige, and those who had fought the Somoza regime had much to be proud of. Even respondents who did actually participate in the revolutionary struggle might be inclined to embellish and exaggerate the importance of their own contribution and the danger they encountered in the process.

Exaggeration and lying, of course, are always a potential problem when dealing with subjective material and when one needs the perception of the respondents themselves. In this case I was able to counteract respondent misrepresentation by cross-checking respondents' stories with other interviewees. After the revolutionary victory secrecy was no longer necessary, and by the time I got to the community residents had a reliable sense of who had actually done what. Furthermore, I spent enough time with these villagers to myself gain an excellent sense of who was or was not a reliable respondent. If anything, I found that many of the most courageous revolutionaries were quite modest about their own contributions to the struggle. As a result of this in-depth knowledge I am certain that the stories given above are an accurate representation of reality.

12. Jenny Pearce finds that Salvadoran peasants also exhausted nonviolent means of political participation before turning to violence. One Salvadoran peasant told her that "the idea of armed struggle emerged when all peaceful means had been exhausted. One could see that the enemy didn't care at all for legal and peaceful means." Jenny Pearce, *The Promised Land* (London: Latin America Bureau, 1986), 183.

13. As a variable related to political action, sibling deaths was particularly interesting in Quebrada Honda; the acceptability rose with the number of such deaths experienced. (see Table 6.5)

14. In a study of the average revolutionary participant, Vilas also finds that the certainty of repression and the ineffectiveness of remaining uninvolved as a form of self-protection drove individuals to action. "When becoming a victim of repression ceases being what happens to someone else—because that someone else is a *Sandinista*, or an *agitator*, or a *subversive*, or is *sought out* for a role in a situation far from one's own—and starts being what happens to *anyone*, even when that anyone remains passively at home, then remaining passively at home no longer serves as a defense. Fear of repression as something outside of daily life is transformed into a daily certainty of repression and opens the way for the necessity of an active defense." C. Vilas, *The Sandinista Revolution, National Liberation, and Social Transformation in Central America* (New York: Monthly Review Press, 1986), 121 (author's italics). In her study of Nicaraguan women, L. Maier finds the same results. As one of her respondents put it, "I told my aunt, 'If they'll let me fight in this condition [pregnant], I'll fight,' because even if I stay home a bullet or a rocket or a bomb'll get me. So either way I die." L. Maier, *Nicaragua: La Mujer en la Revólucion* (Mexico: Ediciones de Cultura Popular, 1980), 12.

Chapter 7. From Quiescence to Rebellion: Pikin Guerrero, Masaya, Nicaragua

1. In the early 1980s coffee became less and less financially viable. The productivity of coffee trees in the area gradually declined due to the combined effects of gas seeping

from a nearby volcano and a disease that affected the coffee leaves. Although the disease could be reduced with large inputs of technology, the financial gain from such inputs would not cover their cost. Coffee profitability in the area would remain low, in part due to the low overall quality of coffee from the area and in part due to the volcano gas. The balance of these factors led the Sandinista government to phase out coffee production in this region by slowly decreasing credit availability for coffee production and gradually increasing credit availability for peasant producers willing to grow fruit trees or vegetables. By the late eighties coffee production had decreased considerably in the area. Today villagers in Pikin Guerrero are producing fruit and vegetables along with coffee or in its stead.

2. For a more extensive comparison of social patterns and political outcomes in San Luis and Pikin Guerrero, see Leslie Anderson, "Agrarian Politics and Revolution: Micro and State Perspective on Structural Determinism," *Journal of Theoretical Politics* 5, no. 4 (October 1993).

3. For a discussion of similar patterns in Colombia in the 1800s see Catherine LeGrand, *Frontier Expansion and Peasant Protest in Colombia, 1830–1936* (Albuquerque: University of New Mexico Press, 1986).

4. A morbid tale reached me through several villagers. One particularly cruel landlord was making his way home alone along an isolated mountain trail in the wee hours of a Sunday morning. He never arrived but his body was found hacked to pieces with machetes, a grim reminder of the price that might be paid for flagrant violations of the rules of village mutuality.

Chapter 8. Conclusion

1. The statistical packages for these analyses were SPSS and TSP.

2. For the purpose of these statistical results I am using a confidence level of 90 percent (.90) as the cut-off point for achieving statistical significance. This is below the conventionally acceptable level of 95% (.95) but is quite acceptable given the small size of the data set. (N = 70 in Costa Rica; N = 90 in Nicaragua; N = 160 total)

3. Ann Bramwell, *Ecology in the Twentieth Century: A History* (New Haven: Yale University Press, 1989).

4. Ibid.

5. The official written philosophy of the Green party in West Germany also includes some attention to social concerns other than the environment.

6. Lawrence Dodd argues that there is a learning process that can occur in national societies. When societies learn, they can, like the peasants, respond differently and more appropriately to new circumstances and thereby weather severe crises. Alternatively, societies may fail to learn and may be destroyed by such crises. See "Political Learning and Political Change: Understanding Development Across Time," in Lawrence Dodd and Calvin Jillson, *The Dynamics of American Politics: Approaches and Interpretations* (Boulder: Westview Press, 1994).

7. A more recent and sophisticated version of the rational actor theory still argues that individuals are primarily selfish and that, by accident, selfishness leads to collective action with inadvertent collective results. Mark Lichbach, "What Makes Rational Peasants Revolutionary? Dilemma, Paradox, and Irony in Peasant Collective Action," paper presented at a "symposium on the dimensions of peasant power," University of Colorado, April 28, 1992. To be published in *World Politics* 46, April 1994.

Appendix: Methodology Combining Depth and Breadth

1. For a discussion of biases in surveys of Nicaraguan electoral opinion see Peter Miller, "Which Side Are You On?," *Public Opinion Quarterly* 55 (1991):281–302.

2. The well-known social scientist Alfred Schutz specifically advocates this approach in studying social phenomena. He writes that all reality is viewed through human perspectives that are subjective in some ways. Yet it is precisely because of this truth that we need to study the subjective human experience. Moreover, in doing so we will find that human perspectives on the same phenomenon differ somewhat. At the same time, we will find that there is an underlying similarity in all the subjective views that people hold of a given phenomenon. Helmut R. Wagner, ed., *Alfred Schutz on Phenomenology and Other Social Relations* (Chicago: University of Chicago Press, 1970).

3. Fortunately, as the Contra war has tapered off since 1985, it has become easier to conduct surveys in Nicaragua, although the government continues to maintain that such research is illegal. Surveys were quite common surrounding the 1990 elections.

4. Land is usually owned by males and passed from father to son. If a woman inherits land it usually passes into the control of her husband upon her marriage.

5. One manzana = 1.75 acres.

6. A search for multicollinearity revealed no statistical correlation among the three independent variables. Although peasants see economic problems and injustice as connected to each other and the latter as a manifestation of the former, the method of data collection itself eliminated correlation among variables. The correlation matrices were as follows:

In Costa Rica

	Economic index	Socioeconomic index	Injustice index
Economic index	1.00000		
Socioeconomic index	0.02365	1.00000	
Injustice index	−0.01121	−0.05923	1.00000

In Nicaragua

	Economic index	Socioeconomic index	Injustice index
Economic index	1.00000		
Socioeconomic index	−0.06209	1.00000	
Injustice index	−0.015431	0.30878	1.00000

INDEX

Moncada, Jose Maria, and Sandino, 33
Monimbó: and National Guard, 133; revolutionary battle, 133
moral economy, 6

National Guard: Anastasio Somoza García, 34; in battle of Monimbó, 133; contact with Pedregal, 54; with labor migrants, 130; in Masaya, 133; origins, 34; personal stories, 130–31, 135–37; in Pikin Guerrero, 154; use of spies, 154–55
National Production Council (Consejo Nacionál de Producción [CNP]): corruption, 97, 101–3; under Figueres, 27; as state policy, 28, 97; struggle with UPAGRA, 102–3; tension with peasants, 101–2
natural disaster: in context of interdependence, 12; and peasants as environmentalists, 12
non-violence: collective action, 76–79; protest, 76–79, 80–81

Panchito, 2, 4, 5, 6, 14
participant perspective, 3; and crop management, 109–10; and revolutionary participation, 129
Party: FSLN, 36–37; National Liberation, 27–28; Nicaraguan Conservative, 33, 35, 36; Nicaraguan Liberal, 33
Pedregal: area of dissonance, 60; contact with guerrillas, 55; contact with National Guard, 54; description, 41–42; under dictatorship, 22–23, 52–54; domain of political relevance, 60; ecological equilibrium, 51; ecological interdependence, 44, 47–49, 50–51, 58; land management, 45–46, 50; land quality, 43; location, 38; medical support system, 48–49; natural ecosystem, 49–50; part of ecological equilibrium, 50–51; public services, 42; in revolution, 55–56; theory of political ecology, 59–60
Pedro, 4, 5; story of, 1
Perez, Rigoberto Lopez. See Lopez Perez, Rigoberto
Pikin Guerrero: access to, 145; area of dissonance, 159; coffee farming, 147; under dictatorship, 154–55; domain of political relevance, 159; interdependence, 148–49, 150, 153; interdependence with nature, 153; landlessness, 147, 150; land ownership, 146; land rental, 150; loca-

tion, 37, 145; and National Guard, 154; public services, 146; in relation to La Concepción, 145; repression, 156–57; in revolution, 155–59; revolutionary martyr, 157, 159; safe house, 159; socioeconomic indicator of poverty, 148; spies, 155
pluralism, development of, in Costa Rica, 26
political ecology, 5; elements in, 7, 165–67; examples of, 171–72; as exclusion, 171; historical context, 166–67; measurement of, 165; mentality, 7, 163; in the modern world, 169, 171; and the natural environment, 168; in Quebrada Honda, 119, 127; in revolution, 119; peasant boundaries, 165; peasant perspective, 6, 14, 156, 162–63, 165; and political choices, 170; statistical tests, 167; theory of, 8, 119, 165
political tolerance, 23
Popkin, S., 6

Quebrada Honda: access to, 121; area of dissonance, 139; domain of political relevance, 139; ecological interdependence, 126; introduced, 119; labor migration, 124–26; land concentration, 122; landlessness, 123; land rental, 124–25; location, 37, 120–21; political ecology in, 119, 136; poverty, 121–22, 124, 130; public services, 121; revolutionary participation, 133–35, 136–38; socioeconomic indicators of poverty, 139; and Somocistas, 122; usury, 122
quiescence, 5, 6, 7; in Nicaraguan Revolution, 55; in Pedregal, 39, 55; as political strategy, 39

Rama, 42
Ramón: in Nicaraguan Revolution, 130–31; and Sandino, 130
rational: action, 6, 7; actor, 15; responsible, 8
rebellion: battle of Monimbó, 133; against Spanish colonization, 31–32
reciprocity: compared with ecological community, 48; diagram, 48; and political ecology, 10; and San Luis, 70
repression: with labor migrants, 122; by National Guard, 125–27; in Nicaragua, 31; personal memories, 122–25, 125–27; in Pikin Guerrero, 154–58